END OF STORY?

End of Story?

Same-Sex Relationships
and the Narratives of Evangelical Mission

ANDREW PERRIMAN

 CASCADE *Books* · Eugene, Oregon

END OF STORY?
Same-Sex Relationships and the Narratives of Evangelical Mission

Cascade Books
An Imprint of Wipf and Stock Publishers
199 W. 8th Ave., Suite 3
Eugene, OR 97401

www.wipfandstock.com

PAPERBACK ISBN: 978-1-5326-7017-6
HARDCOVER ISBN: 978-1-5326-7018-3
EBOOK ISBN: 978-1-5326-7019-0

Cataloguing-in-Publication data:

Names: Perriman, Andrew.
Title: End of story? : same-sex relationships and the narratives of evangelical mission. / Andrew Perriman.
Description: Eugene, OR: Cascade Books, 2019. | Includes bibliographical references and index.
Identifiers: ISBN 978-1-5326-7017-6 (paperback) | ISBN 978-1-5326-7018-3 (hardcover) | ISBN 978-1-5326-7019-0 (ebook)
Subjects: LCSH: Homosexuality—Religious aspects—Christianity. | Homosexuality—Moral and ethical aspects. | Bible and homosexuality. | Evangelicalism.
Classification: BR115.H6 P47 2019 (print) | BR115.H6 (ebook)

Manufactured in the U.S.A.   NOVEMBER 1, 2019

For my friends Duncan, Gabriel, and Joyce

Contents

Contents

Acknowledgments

THIS BOOK HAD ITS origins in discussions held by a church planting mission about how to respond to the legalization of same-sex marriage in Europe and America. A lot of people in and around the organization contributed to the debate, and I am grateful for their input. They know who they are. But I especially want to thank my friend Wesley, who worked closely with me on the early stages of this project, sometimes disagreeing with me quite forcefully, but always perceptive, grounded, and supportive. The book has evolved a long way beyond its original purpose; it presents my own point of view, and not that of the mission; but I hope it still reflects and speaks to the very practical and pastoral concerns with which we began.

Abbreviations

Achilles Tatius *Leuc. Clit.*	*Leucippe and Clitophon*
Apoc. Ab.	*Apocalypse of Abraham*
Aristotle *Pol.*	*Politics*
Aristotle *[Probl.]*	*Problems*
BDB	Francis Brown, S. R. Driver, and Charles A. Briggs. *Hebrew and English Lexicon of the Old Testament.* Electronic text corrected, hypertexted, and prepared by OakTree Software, Inc. Version 4.4.
Cicero *Dom.*	*De domo suo*
Cicero *Phil.*	*Orationes philippicae*
Cicero *Red. sen.*	*Post reditum in senatu*
Dio Chrysostom, *Ven.*	*Venator (Or. 7)*
Dionysius of Halicarnassus *Ant. rom.*	*Antiquitates romanae*
Epictetus *Diatr.*	*Diatribai (Dissertationes)*
Hippocrates *Off.*	*De officina medici*
Josephus *Ag. Ap.*	*Against Apion*
Josephus *Ant.*	*Jewish Antiquities*
Josephus *J.W.*	*Jewish War*
Juvenal *Sat.*	*Satirae*
Let. Aris.	*Letter of Aristeas*

Longus *Daphn.*	*Daphnis and Chloe*
LSJ	Henry George Liddell, Robert Scott, Henry Stuart Jones. *A Greek-English Lexicon.* Thesaurus Linguae Graecae online edition.
Lucian *[Am.]*	*Amores (Affairs of the Heart)*
Martial *Ep.*	*Epigrams*
NICNT	The New International Commentary on the New Testament
NICOT	The New International Commentary on the Old Testament
Ovid *Metam.*	*Metamorphoses*
Philo *Abraham*	*On the Life of Abraham*
Philo *Contempl.*	*On the Contemplative Life*
Philo *Spec. Laws 3*	*On the Special Laws 3*
Philo *Spec. Laws 4*	*On the Special Laws 4*
Plato *Charm.*	*Charmides*
Plato *Euthyd.*	*Euthydemus*
Plato *Leg.*	*Leges*
Plato *Symp.*	*Symposium*
Plutarch *Amat.*	*Amatorius (Dialogue on Love)*
Plutarch *Lyc.*	*Lycurgus*
Plutarch *Pel.*	*Pelopidas*
Ps. Phoc.	Pseudo-Phocylides
Seneca *Ep.*	*Epistulae morales*
Sib. Or.	*Sibylline Oracles*
Suetonius *Cal.*	*Caligula*
Suetonius *Tib.*	*Tiberius*
T. Naph.	*Testament of Naphtali*
TDNT	*Theological Dictionary of the New Testament.* 10 vols. Edited by Gerhard Kittel and Gerhard

Friedrich. Translated by Geoffrey W. Bromiley. Grand Rapids: Eerdmans, 1964–76. Accordance edition hypertexted and formatted by OakTree Software, Inc. Version 2.9.

Theocritus *Id.*	*Idyll*
WBC	Word Biblical Commentary
Xenophon *Anab.*	*Anabasis*
Xenophon *Mem.*	Memorabilia
Xenophon *Symp.*	*Symposium*

CHAPTER 1

The Story So Far

THIS BOOK HAS BEEN written primarily, and perhaps optimistically, with the *evangelical missional church* in mind, as it is confronted with the challenges of rampant secular modernity in Western societies. In an ideal world, "evangelical" would simply designate the church as it seeks faithfully to bear witness in all respects to the hopeful, transformative, and God-given power of the biblical narrative. It is unfortunate that, at a time of significant renewal in the field of New Testament studies, the word is barely serviceable in a work such as this because of its association, on the one hand, with a thin but heady salvationism distilled from the pulped mash of Scripture and, on the other, with controversial modes of social and political conservatism. I speak of the "power of the biblical narrative" rather than of the "gospel" (*euangelion*) because I think that the good news, as it was proclaimed first to Israel, then to the nations, and is now proclaimed today, always gains its relevance and force from the historical narrative that frames it. But we also have to call "evangelical" that self-conscious populist movement within the modern church that holds to the truthfulness of the Bible and the centrality of the cross in defiance of theological liberalism and progressivism.

By "missional" I mean the church as it endeavors to recover some *forward* momentum in its engagement with society following the broad collapse of the Western Christian worldview—or Christendom—over the last two hundred years. Again, this is not the standard definition, but it is in keeping, I think, with the dynamics of the biblical argument. On the one hand, I have *restricted* the scope of mission to the Western context—a civilization that used to be Christian but that is now mostly secular in its fundamental ethical and metaphysical commitments. On the other, I have *extended* the definition along a temporal axis to include both the narrative that accounts for the current state of affairs and *plausible future projections.* The *story* of the missional people of God did not stop when it got to Jesus, and it is still unfolding today. The "problem" of same-sex relationships was and is part of that story, and I will attempt to address it on that assumption, with two overarching questions in mind. First, how do we determine the "ends" of the story? I say "ends" because, however we imagine the final dénouement, there are multiple crises, climaxes, and cliffhangers along the way. Secondly, and conversely, how do the "ends" of the story determine the response of the church to the normalization of same-sex relationships in the modern era?

Naming the particular topic is also difficult. The history of the word "homosexual" has left it, too, with some unsavory associations (disease, perversion, criminality, "homophobia").[1] But it remains the obvious and probably necessary counterpart to "heterosexual." The more or less neutral language of "same-sex" sexual relations, relationships, and marriage may be preferable, but the phrasing can be unwieldy, and some stylistic variation is required. In that case, Wesley Hill's policy of not using "homosexual" as a noun in order to "send a subtle linguistic signal that being gay isn't the most important thing about my or any other gay person's identity" seems a good one.[2] Our real subject is gay (male same-sex) and lesbian (female same-sex) relationships, not the wider spectrum of sexual identities referenced by the LGBT+ nomenclature. Bisexuality, no doubt, may be expressed in different ways but would appear to be by definition promiscuous, and the debate over transgenderism, though of enormous interest currently, is of a different kind and beyond the scope of this study. But the simple LGBT tag will serve as a convenient way of identifying the general social phenomenon.

A good part of the book is taken up with an examination of the biblical material relating to same-sex sexual relations along with the first-century cultural background. This will not be merely a remapping of a well-trodden and very muddy exegetical field. The intention is to tell a credible *story* about this aspect of human sexuality—a story that begins with creation, then runs through Israel's possession of the land and the clash of kingdoms anticipated in the New Testament, to the profound and unfinished

---

1. Vasey warns that the term "homosexuality" carries "the conceptual background of its nineteenth-century inventors and . . . the possible implication that there is a single transcultural phenomenon called homosexuality" (Vasey, *Strangers*, 73).

2. Hill, *Washed and Waiting*, 31; cf. Williams, *Roman Homosexuality*, 6.

reorientation of the world that we know as modernity, and on toward a final repair of the eternal rupture between God and his creation.

There is no "mission" in Scripture without some awareness of the controlling narrative context. For example, if the "mission" of the Jews in Babylon was to "seek the welfare of the city" (Jer 29:7) as we are sometimes told, the instruction presupposes the long narrative of exile, survival, flourishing, and return from exile. It is not a bare injunction to pursue social transformation. When Jesus sent out his disciples to proclaim the imminence of the kingdom of God, to heal the sick, raise the dead, and cast out demons, their "mission" belonged to a Jewish story ("Go nowhere among the Gentiles and enter no town of the Samaritans, but go rather to the lost sheep of the house of Israel") that reached back to the ancient precedent of the destruction of Sodom and Gomorrah and forwards to the appearance of the Son of Man before they had gone through all the towns of Israel (Matt 10:5–23).[3] I will suggest that missional engagement with the Western world today, whether we mean by that social action, or gospel proclamation, or constructive engagement with the LGBT community, is hampered greatly by the fact that we have very little sense of a guiding "prophetic" narrative. Evangelicals are adrift on the sea of history, somewhere between Pentecost and the second coming, with only an empty, flat, hazy horizon ahead of us. We need to get some historical bearings. So this is not, in the first place, an argument either for or against same-sex relationships as a matter of Christian ethics; it is an attempt to reframe the controversy narratively.

Before we start on the task, however, I want to attempt a brief overview of the background and context of the debate. In this chapter, I will outline the social developments that have culminated in the legalization of same-sex marriage in North America, much of South America, most of Western Europe, South Africa, New Zealand, and Australia. In chapter 2, we will look at how the evangelical world has been dealing with the issue, and ask what is at stake for churches, missions, and other organizations, for leaders and laypeople, as we pick our way nervously through the minefield of the LGBT controversy. The initial impetus for this book came from the deliberations of a church-planting mission trying to think these matters through in the secular Western context, and I think it may be helpful to register and foreground that perspective, albeit in a patchy and limited fashion, before we get to the biblical, historical, theological, and hermeneutical questions.

3. See Perriman, *Coming of the Son of Man*, 26–28.

Part of the reason for doing so is that I hope this book will be read by people who are more interested in the "narratives of evangelical mission" and have not been paying too much attention to the debate about same-sex relationships.

THE MODERN UNDERSTANDING OF HOMOSEXUALITY

Nothing happens in a vacuum. There is a historical and social setting for the biblical texts that responsible interpreters must take into account, whatever the topic under investigation. But a missional hermeneutic must also reckon with the various contexts *in which the Bible is read today*: we read with an awareness of a long history of interpretation and application; we read under diverse and changing social, cultural, and intellectual conditions; and our reading is formed—for better or for worse—by personal experience and by the experience and circumstances of the communities of which we are part. The modern biblical-theological debate about same-sex relationships has come about because characteristically Western commitments—in essence, to scientific description, on the one hand, and to personal freedoms and rights, on the other—have brought about a fundamental change in social attitudes, driving a wedge between the present and the past.[4] This is the given *narrative setting* for our engagement with the biblical texts.

As long as the church controlled the moral debate in the West, same-sex sexual activity was regarded as willful sin or moral perversion.[5] The terms "heterosexual" and "homosexual" were introduced toward the end of the nineteenth century as the phenomenon came to be understood as a distinct psychological condition. Now it was possible to *be* a "homosexual" and not just happen on occasion to engage in sexual activity with a person of the

4. "Relentless conscience and relentless reason," Peter Berger says, have become "the major agents of autonomization" in the modern world (Berger, "Western Individuality," 330). The Report of the House of Bishops Working Group on Human Sexuality says that the civil rights movement "has been extraordinarily powerful in shaping public discourse and a rights-based approach to equality is now so well embedded in much Western thinking as to be almost taken for granted by many" (Pilling, *Report of the House of Bishops*, 13).

5. For an overview of developments in the homosexuality debate in the American church in the second half of the twentieth century see Toulouse, "Muddling Through," 21–28; Via, "Bible," 3–4. The shift in the perception of homosexuals from being degenerates to being diseased to being disordered to being affirmed, at least by some, belatedly tracks developments in Western society at large. For a useful account of the emergence of "gay identity" since the late seventeenth century see Vasey, *Strangers*, 92–112.

same sex. It was something of a watershed. David Halperin quotes George Chauncey: "The differentiation of homosexual desire from 'deviant' gender behavior at the turn of the century reflects a major reconceptualization of the nature of human sexuality, its relation to gender, and its role in one's social definition."[6] Craig Williams quotes Eve Kosofsky Sedgwick to similar effect:

> What was new from the turn of the century was the world-mapping by which every given person, just as he or she was necessarily assignable to a male or a female gender, was now considered necessarily assignable as well to a homo- or a hetero-sexuality, a binarized identity that was full of implications, however confusing, for even the ostensibly least sexual aspects of personal experience.[7]

The last few decades have seen the decriminalization and demedicalization of homosexuality and the growing consensus that there is nothing unnatural, disordered, or morally objectionable about same-sex sexual behavior, whether it is understood to be innate, conditioned, or chosen. In the United Kingdom the 1957 Wolfenden Report on Homosexuality and Prostitution recommended that "homosexual behaviour between consenting adults in private should no longer be a criminal offence," a recommendation that was enshrined in law ten years later in the Sexual Offences Act.[8] Why it took so long, I do not know. In 1973 the American Psychiatric Association decided to remove homosexuality from its list of "disorders treatable by psychiatry." The American Christian psychologist Mark Yarhouse writes: "There was a definite shift thirty to forty years ago in which mental health professional organizations declared that homosexuality was no longer a mental disorder, and we've seen more recent attempts to portray it as a healthy expression of sexual diversity."[9] Andrew Davison makes the point categorically: "The medical opinion on this is rock solid. Homosexuality is not damaging to people; it is the assumption that it is 'unhealthy' that damages them."[10]

---

6. Halperin, *One Hundred Years*, 15.

7. Williams, *Roman Homosexuality*, 7.

8. The Bishop of Durham, Michael Ramsay, later Archbishop of Canterbury, played a major role in setting up the Wolfenden Committee (Pilling, *Report of the House of Bishops*, para. 46).

9. Yarhouse, *Homosexuality*, 30.

10. Davison, *Amazing Love*, 17.

Homosexuality has become simply another way of being normal, even bourgeois: "The flagrant sexual display celebrated by 1970s gay liberation, complete with the bump-and-grind floats in pride parades and S and M whips and chains, appear to have gradually given way to conventional domestic routines."[11] In the words of another Christian psychologist, David Myers: "sexual orientation in some ways is like handedness: Most people are one way, some the other. A very few are truly ambidextrous. Regardless, the way one is endures."[12] Broadly speaking, in the popular mind the "essentialist" view of same-sex behavior has prevailed over the "social constructionist" view, even if it remains very difficult to discover, in any particular case, what combination of biological and psychosocial factors has determined the orientation.[13] This has strongly weighted the argument in favor of *affirming* the legitimacy of same-sex relations: if the behavior is "a manifestation of some inner essence, is relatively stable over time, and is characteristic of a distinct segment of the population, then the appropriateness of moral judgment is called into question."[14] If it is *who you are*, in the deepest sense, it cannot be wrong. That said, most supporters of LGBT rights would insist that a *socially constructed* same-sex orientation should also not be subject to moral censure. In a libertarian age people are free to choose whom they have sex with, whatever the reasons for the choice, provided no harm is done. These developments are sustained *both* by scientific description *and* by the presumption of the individual's right to choose. So Bernadette Brooten observes that many lesbians argue that lesbian existence is "a choice and a political act within the current

11. Browning, *Fate of Gender*, 38. Paul asks: "Why has a conservative view of LGBT persons as 'normal' rather than a liberationist 'queer' image triumphed?" (Paul, *From Tolerance*, 11).

12. Quoted in Gushee, *Changing Our Mind*, 28; see also Marin, *Love Is an Orientation*, 39–43, on the issue of whether same-sex attraction is innate or attributable to environmental factors such as childhood abuse.

13. The Australian evangelical sexologist Patricia Weerakoon concludes, on the basis of a limited survey of the literature, that a "biological predisposition" toward same-sex desire "subsequently is experienced and understood by individuals, as influenced by their sociocultural positioning." But a predisposition falls between predetermination, on the one hand, and childhood trauma or personal choice, on the other. Nature and nurture are "intertwined in potentially mutually reinforcing manners" (Weerakoon and Weerakoon, "Biology," 327; cf. Pilling, Report of the House of Bishops, para. 202). For a useful summary of the current view of the biology of same-sex attraction see Davison, *Amazing Love*, 24–26.

14. Jones and Yarhouse, "Use, Misuse, and Abuse," 79.

conditions of patriarchy."[15] The church is more likely to be persuaded by arguments from modern science than from modern conscience, but the two strands, both of which are always subject to revision, probably cannot be disentangled.[16]

The libertarian argument may become increasingly important if recent attacks on the new consensus, from very different directions, gain traction. The neutrality and objectivity of a lengthy study published in *The New Atlantis*, in which the psychologists L. S. Mayer and P. R. McHugh argue that the "understanding of sexual orientation as an innate, biologically fixed property of human beings . . . is not supported by scientific evidence," have been called into question.[17] More significant, perhaps, is the work of Lisa Diamond, herself a lesbian, on sexual fluidity. In a *New Scientist* interview she states that sexual fluidity "means that people are born with a sexual orientation and also with a degree of sexual flexibility, and they appear to work together. So there are gay people who are very fixedly gay and there are gay people who are more fluid, meaning they can experience attractions that run outside of their orientation."[18] In 2014 the Royal College of Psychiatrists in the United Kingdom issued a position statement asserting that "sexual orientation is determined by a combination of biological and postnatal environmental factors," and allowing that sexual orientation is not immutable and may "vary to some extent in a person's life."[19] Some evangelical commentators drew attention to the fact that this is a step back from the earlier view taken by the college that "sexual orientation

15. Brooten, *Love Between Women*, 243.

16. Cf. Davison, *Amazing Love*, 32: biology does not remove the moral responsibility of the individual; but equally, we cannot simply "dismiss what we know about the human constitution, as if that were irrelevant to our ethical thinking."

17. Mayer and McHugh, "Sexuality and Gender"; the quotation is from the executive summary: https://www.thenewatlantis.com/publications/executive-summary-sexuality-and-gender. It has been welcomed by conservatives but dismissed as "bogus" by others (e.g., Shermer, "Beware Bogus Theories").

18. Grossman, "Sexuality Is Fluid"; and Diamond, *Sexual Fluidity*. Also Pilling, *Report of the House of Bishops*, para. 200: "Rather than thinking about the human population in terms of a fixed binary division between two sets of people, those who are straight and those who are gay, it seems that we need to accept that while there is a large majority of people who only ever experience heterosexual attraction and a smaller number who only experience homosexual attraction, there is also a significant minority of people who either experience some form of bisexual attraction or who move between heterosexual and homosexual attraction at some point or points in their life."

19. Royal College of Psychiatrists, "Statement on Sexual Orientation," 2.

is biological in nature, determined by genetic factors . . . and/or the early uterine environment."[20] But the college still insists that there is "no evidence to go beyond this and impute any kind of choice into the origins of sexual orientation" and deprecates therapeutic attempts to change it.

Social, medical, and technological developments in the modern era have at the same time dramatically changed the dynamics between partners in *heterosexual* relationships. Marriage today is very different from the unequal patriarchal arrangement for the purpose of procreation known in the ancient world and, for that matter, presupposed in the "household codes" of the New Testament.[21] Marriage is now seen primarily as a socially and legally supported framework for a long-term relationship between two equal members of society, and only secondarily as a context for child-rearing. In light of this it has seemed unfair to exclude people in long-term same-sex relationships from the institution of marriage.[22] The logic of same-sex marriage has been questioned by religious conservatives on the grounds that only the biological complementarity of the man and the woman keeps marriage from being opened up to more than two people. Kevin DeYoung, for example, asserts that it is "mere sentiment and lingering tradition which leads many progressives to insist that same-sex unions ought to involve the commitment of two persons and only two persons."[23] He may be right. The further extension of "marriage" at some point to include polyamorous relationships, which are only the modern egalitarian equivalent of Old Testament polygamy, certainly cannot be ruled out. But it would appear that the model of a formalized long-term, more or less exclusive, relationship between two people, which we call marriage (or perhaps something like "civil partnership"), will remain central to how Western societies do

20. See, for example, Horrocks, "Changing Views." The 2007 Royal College of Psychiatrists statement is no longer available online.

21. See DeFranza, "Journeying," 88; Brownson, *Bible*, 264; and Song, *Covenant and Calling*, chap. 3, Kindle loc. 820 of 1831: "in general throughout both Testaments texts come readily to hand that appear to take for granted and actively to teach that men and women are to be placed in an unequal, hierarchical relationship both in marriage and in social relationships more generally."

22. Browning sets out the US Supreme Court's reasons for endorsing same-sex marriage (Browning, *Fate of Gender*, 30–31). Justice Kennedy, who wrote the majority opinion, argued in essence that "because American society—and most of European societies as well—no longer regards the traditional gender roles as the only basis for marriage, then simple fairness, simple justice . . . cannot any longer allow the states to discriminate against and penalize same-sex couples."

23. DeYoung, *What Does the Bible*, 31.

"family" for the foreseeable future. What threatens the institution most seriously is not same-sex marriage or polyamory but the failure of personal commitment. Under the conditions of modernity it has become extremely difficult to keep a marriage going throughout a lifetime. What we often mean now by "long-term" is something more like "seasonal." In any case, the secondary function of child-rearing is being made available to same-sex couples by way of adoption and surrogacy. So if even heterosexual marriage today is a very different social arrangement from biblical marriage, Megan DeFranza asks whether it can be "revised yet again to better honor the humanity of gay, lesbian, and bisexual people and the biblical truth that they too are made in the image of God and equally capable of ordering their relationships and sexual lives in ways that honor God, benefit the common good, and promote their own growth in health and holiness."[24]

THE SHOE IS ON THE OTHER FOOT

That is the question that the church is wrestling with at multiple levels, and it is not going to get any easier. We should expect same-sex relationships and behavior to be increasingly depicted, promoted, and normalized in popular culture and in the media. This will be partly a matter of ideological and political pressure, no doubt. Darel E. Paul lays the blame firmly at the door of America's legal and corporate elites, while "the wider public remains divided on the issue."[25] But it also reflects real and seemingly irreversible changes that have been taking place in Western secular culture. For future generations, LGBT people will simply constitute another set of unremarkable minorities in the kaleidoscope of modern pluralism, fully entitled to the same respect and support as other differentiated communities. The widespread legalization of same-sex marriage in the West over the last decade is probably to be regarded as a game-changer for the church's relationship to wider society. Setting out the background to his proposal for a disciplined, separationist, quasi-monastic "Benedict Option" for the church, Rod Dreher says that the US Supreme Court's decision to

---

24. DeFranza, "Journeying," 90.

25. See Paul, *From Tolerance*, 3; and Yenor, "How the New Corporate Elite": "Only when America's corporate managerial elite embraced homosexuality and same-sex marriage as an essential expression of diversity did America cross the 'cultural Rubicon.' Normalization of homosexuality and acceptance of same-sex marriage became class values for our new class of corporate managers . . ."

affirm the constitutional right to same-sex marriage was "the moment that the Sexual Revolution triumphed decisively, and the culture war, as we have known it since the 1960s, came to an end."[26] For single gay and lesbian people who come to faith, celibacy remains a challenging but religiously compelling option. But will churches be willing or able to require people in well-established same-sex marriages, quite possibly with dependent children, either to refrain from sexual activity within the marriage or to divorce in order to maintain an acceptable standard of discipleship? Not conforming will only get more difficult.

Finally, we should keep in mind the fact that the promotion of LGBT rights is not an isolated social or ethical issue. It is part of a much broader shift away from the traditional Judeo-Christian paradigm and a redefinition of what it means to be human according to an emerging, technologically advanced, globally conscious, humanistic worldview. The drive toward same-sex marriage is a "class(ification) struggle"—in the words of Alastair Roberts, a struggle "for the control of the symbolic reality of society and whose categorizations of the social order are dominant."[27] It is one of many visible signs that Western society is going through the painful and exhilarating process of reinventing itself. Summarizing Philip Rieff's 1966 study *The Triumph of the Therapeutic: Uses of Faith After Freud*, Dreher says: "What made our condition so revolutionary . . . was that for the first time in history, the West was attempting to build a culture on the *absence* of belief in a higher order that commanded our obedience."[28] The revolution is continuing apace. The intense public interest in *transgenderism* currently— now that same-sex marriage has been put to bed—is clear evidence that Western society has not yet finished its reevaluation of the fundamental givens of human identity and moral life, even if in practice only a small number of people are participating in the experiment.[29] For some it is a

26. Dreher, *Benedict Option*, 9.

27. Roberts, "Why American Elites," commenting on Paul, *From Tolerance*. The phrase "class(ification) struggle" is Paul's.

28. Dreher, *Benedict Option*, 42–43.

29. Cf. Paul, *From Tolerance*, 152: "Once a moment of stability is seemingly reached, the ground shifts and the battle is rejoined at a new revolutionary frontier"; and Dreher, *Benedict Option*, 43: "The Romantic ideal of the self-created man finds its fulfillment in the newest vanguards of the Sexual Revolution, transgendered people." Dreher quotes Justice Anthony Kennedy's quintessentially humanist—Dreher calls it "nihilistic"— explanation of the Supreme Court's reaffirmation of abortion rights in 1992 (*Planned Parenthood vs. Casey*): "At the heart of liberty is the right to define one's own concept of existence, of meaning, of the universe, and of the mystery of human life" (Dreher,

simple matter of having the freedom, given the medical resources available, to be the person they feel themselves to be. But in the wider debate, transgenderism is being swung as a battering-ram against some of our deepest cultural assumptions about what it means to be a girl or a boy, a man or a woman. With each advance, as the dust of controversy settles, the moral logic is consolidated, and the world moves on. To the traditionalist these developments may have the appearance of moral decline, but to the secular mind they are being pursued as a significant moral gain. It is beginning to feel as though the shoe is on the other foot. Glynn Harrison writes:

> The ideas that have so effectively torpedoed traditional Christian morality are remarkable, however, in not only offering new and radical perspectives on what it means to be human, but in laying claim to the moral high ground as well. This observation is important because the sexual revolution is often portrayed as a descent into moral anarchy when what is actually being offered is a new moral vision about the nature of human flourishing.[30]

The simple fact is that over the last two hundred years a new post-Christian land mass has emerged with slow tectonic inevitability; and unsurprisingly it is post-Christian people who are multiplying and filling and subduing this "new creation," this "age to come"—exploring it, mapping it, dividing it up, settling on it, fighting over it, and importantly, trying to work out where the outer limits are, how far we can push the scientific-humanist-libertarian paradigm before things begin to break down again. The pressure to move on is immense. There are those who argue that the trend toward the full affirmation of same-sex equality can be reversed. Sean McDowell and John Stonestreet, for example, advocate using the same techniques that LGBT campaigners used to overhaul American culture. They point to the success of the strategy promoted in Kirk and Madsen's

---

Benedict Option, 43–44). The journalist Frank Browning suggests that we have to understand "trans-identity, trans-promotion, trans-discussion as signaling an ongoing state of transition that has no fixed endpoint but that reveals a near universal state of fluidity that we all—either as individuals or as societies at large—may or could inhabit from time to time" (Browning, *Fate of Gender*, 29).

30. Harrison, "Better Story." According to Davison, when the church is perceived to be weak on equality and human rights, it becomes not merely inconsequential but a "toxic brand": "The Church needs to take seriously the fact that people's commitment to these standards is a moral and ethical imperative, not some secularist whimsy" (Davison, *Amazing Love*, 82).

book *After the Ball: How America Will Conquer Its Fear and Hatred of Gays in the '90s* and argue that the church can learn from it "how cultures can be influenced and changed." The progress made by the pro-life movement since *Roe v. Wade* is cited as an example of what can be done to cancel the effects of such milestone legal decisions.[31] But the present book has been written on the assumption that Christianity no longer has a claim on the future of Western society. Like the exiles in Babylon the church has to get used to living in someone else's world. Only this time there is no realistic prospect of return.

31. McDowell and Stonestreet, *Same-Sex Marriage*, 78–79.

CHAPTER 2

Recent Developments
in the Evangelical-Missional World

EVANGELICAL CHURCHES, MISSION ORGANIZATIONS, and individuals have
been confronted with these developments and have had to respond, though
not always publicly, and no doubt sometimes by burying their heads in the
sand. Any attempt to outline the scope and course of these responses is
going to be inadequate. The field is too large and changing too quickly. But
we can at least give an impression of the state of play by noting some of the
main events and trends that have defined the recent progress of the debate
as societies in the West and beyond have moved toward the legalization
of same-sex marriage. My experience and perspective are largely confined
to the North American and British contexts, which no doubt introduces
certain biases and blind spots; but given the current dominance of
anglophone evangelicalism and the forces of globalization, it seems likely
that the account will have a more general relevance.

A SLOW CHANGE OF MIND

To begin with, there has been a marked shift toward the acceptance of
homosexuality *as a fact of Western life* by the evangelical community in
recent decades. According to British Social Attitudes survey data published
in 2017, approval of same-sex relationships among all religious groups grew
markedly over the previous five years; "notably now well over half (55%)
of Anglicans say same-sex relationships are 'not wrong at all,' an increase

of 24 percentage points since 2012."[1] This coincides with an increase in the influence of evangelicals in the Church of England.[2] The 2013 Pilling Report on Human Sexuality concluded its review of survey data with the admission that "we seem to be witnessing, over the last three decades, very rapid changes toward the inclusion and acceptance of homosexuality and homosexual people. The Churches are not immune from this trend."[3] In June 2017 the Scottish Episcopal Church became the first major denomination in the United Kingdom formally to approve same-sex marriage. In the same year the Anglican archbishops of Canterbury and York published a pastoral letter in response to the decision of General Synod to reject a House of Bishops report urging a "culture of welcome and support" for gay Christians. The letter called for a "radical new Christian inclusion in the Church" which not only is grounded in Scripture, reason, and tradition but also takes account of a "proper 21st century understanding of being human and of being sexual."[4]

There has been a similar drift toward the acceptance of same-sex marriage in the mainline churches in the rest of Europe. For example, Reidar Hvalvik has noted a recent shift in opinion in the Lutheran Church of Norway. In 1995 eight out of eleven bishops believed that sexual activity should be confined to heterosexual marriage. In 2014 the situation was reversed: only three bishops still maintained the traditional position.[5] In 2015 the Church of Norway voted to allow ministers to perform same-sex marriages in its churches. On the other hand, in a rare display of public opposition to the legalization of gay marriage in France, the *Manif pour Tous* ("Protest for All") movement organized protests among Catholics, Protestants, Muslims, and Jewish organizations. The law was passed in 2013. The strength of support may have been attributable at least in part to anti-government sentiment and a general feeling among the French that gender theory is an Anglo-Saxon import.[6] The principle objection was that same-sex marriage

1. British Social Attitudes 34, Moral Issues, 9 (http://www.bsa.natcen.ac.uk/media /39147/bsa34_moral_issues_final.pdf); and Sharmon and Jones, "Half of Anglicans."

2. See Hailes, "How Evangelicals."

3. Pilling, *Report of the House of Bishops*, para. 173.

4. "Letter from the Archbishops of Canterbury and York following General Synod," February 16, 2017, https://www.churchofengland.org/more/media-centre/news/ letter-archbishops-canterbury-and-york-following-general-synod.

5. Hvalvik, "Present Context," 147.

6. Gaffney, "Anti-Hollande Sentiments."

undermines the fundamental idea that children are the product of a father and a mother and are entitled to be raised by a father and a mother.[7]

In the United States evangelical disapproval of homosexuality is much stronger. A 2017–18 Public Religion Research Institute survey showed that only 34 percent of white evangelicals expressed support for same-sex marriage. But this was a major gain from the 14 percent recorded ten years earlier, and the report found evidence of a trend "toward majority support," notably because younger evangelicals are generally less hostile toward homosexuality than their parents.[8] According to a 2017 Pew Research Center study 47 percent of evangelicals born after 1964 favor same-sex marriage compared to only 26 percent of those born between 1928 and 1964.[9]

In an appendix to the 2013 Church of England *Report of the House of Bishops Working Group on Human Sexuality*, David Runcorn highlights the tendency of evangelicals to give way eventually on issues of social change: "A reading of Evangelical history reveals a tradition that, though often fiercely reactive at first, will move to revise, reverse or adopt 'including' positions on important social and ethical issues it previously opposed on the grounds of Scripture. The list would include slavery, apartheid, usury, divorce and remarriage, contraception and women in society and the Church."[10] It is a narrative of incremental adaptation to modernity, and one of the questions we are having to ask is: how does this process of adaptive change relate to the narrative that we find in the Bible?

Leading the Way

The debate among evangelicals has largely been driven by prominent individuals, churches, and organizations taking an explicitly pro-LGBT stance. Steve Chalke, founder of the Oasis Trust, has probably been the most high-profile British evangelical leader to speak publicly in favor of monogamous same-sex relationships. In 2014 the Oasis Trust was expelled from the Evangelical Alliance over its unwillingness to modify material published online and on social media regarding its understanding of human sexuality.[11] The

7. See http://www.lamanifpourtous.fr/qui-sommes-nous/notre-message/.

8. Riess, "Same-Sex Marriage."

9. Bailey, "Poll shows a generational divide."

10. Runcorn, "Evangelicals."

11. Zylstra, "Major Ministry"; Trimmer, "Steve Chalke's Oasis Trust."

Oasis Foundation promotes an Open Church Charter to encourage and support churches that want to develop a more inclusive attitude toward the LGBT community. It states: "We guarantee that any person, regardless of sexuality or gender identity will find our local church to be a place of welcome, embrace, inclusion, affirmation and sanctuary."[12]

Protest has taken a similar course in the United States. For example, in 2014 Ken Wilson, founding pastor of Ann Arbor Vineyard Church and a Vineyard national board member for seven years, wrote "A Letter to My Congregation" explaining why he could no longer support the traditional conservative exclusion of LGBT people. The document was later published as *A Letter to My Congregation: An Evangelical Pastor's Path to Embracing People Who Are Gay, Lesbian and Transgender in the Company of Jesus.* Threatened with disaffiliation from Vineyard, Wilson resigned from the Ann Arbor church and joined the Blue Ocean network of churches. Also in 2014 the influential evangelical ethicist David Gushee announced a change of mind on the issue in a series of blog posts in the Baptist News Global online news service. The posts were quickly published in book form as *Changing Our Mind*, the third and "definitive" edition of which appeared in 2017.[13] Gushee asks whether as evangelicals we should not "change our mind and our practices in relation to Christian LGBTQ people and their relationships—not because we are under pressure from a hostile culture to do so, but because within the terms of our own faith we might now conclude that this is one of those cases in 2,000 years of Christian history where we have gotten some things wrong."[14] Rob Bell, who should probably be classified as "post-evangelical," told Oprah Winfrey in 2015 that the church only confirms its irrelevance "when it quotes letters from 2,000 years ago as their best defense, when you have in front of you flesh-and-blood people who are your brothers and sisters, and aunts and uncles, and co-workers and neighbors, and they love each other and just want to go through life."[15] In the turbulent air left by these pioneers it appears that a small but growing number of evangelical churches are taking a cautiously pro-LGBT stance.

A quite sophisticated "evangelical" defense of the affirming position on ethical, theological, and biblical grounds has been put forward by writers and scholars such as Matthew Vines, who is gay, and James

12. https://openchurch.network/content/sign-open-church-charter.

13. Gushee, *Changing Our Mind*, xi–xvi.

14. Gushee, *Changing Our Mind*, 16–17 (italics removed).

15. Kuruvilla, "Former Megachurch Pastor."

Brownson, whose change of mind was catalyzed by personal factors.[16] The main arguments have been, first, that the modern ideal of egalitarian, monogamous same-sex relationships is not intrinsically "sinful" (they do no harm and, indeed, may be "characterized by positive motives and traits instead, like faithfulness, commitment, mutual love, and self-sacrifice"[17]); and secondly, that such relationships are quite different from the cultic or blatantly exploitative practices presupposed by the biblical prohibitions.

While established evangelical bodies have generally defended the traditional view of marriage, wider social acceptance has encouraged the emergence of new networks and organizations that take an explicitly gay-affirming evangelical position. Accepting Evangelicals, for example, in the United Kingdom describes itself as "an open network of Evangelical Christians who believe the time has come to move towards the acceptance of faithful, loving same-sex partnerships at every level of church life, and the development of a positive Christian ethic for lesbian, gay, bisexual and transgender people."[18] In the United States the Gay Christian Network aims to "transform attitudes toward LGBTQ . . . people and bring about a day when the church is the biggest ally and defender of LGBTQ people rather than a chief opponent."[19] The European Forum of Lesbian, Gay, Bisexual, and Transgender Christians has been campaigning since 1982 for equality for LGBT people "within and through the Christian churches of Europe."[20]

Autobiographies by two prominent homosexual British women with strong evangelical credentials were published in 2018. In *Just Love: A Journey of Self-Acceptance* Jayne Ozanne documents the path she took from high-profile member of the Archbishops' Council, through the traumatic process of accepting her sexuality, to her current role as director of the Ozanne Foundation, which "works with religious organisations around the world to eliminate discrimination based on sexuality or gender in order to embrace

---

16. Brownson, *Bible*, 11–13.

17. Vines, *God and the Gay Christian*, 12. Cf. Via, "Bible," 25: "If it cannot be demonstrated that homosexual practice is harmful in itself—in mutual, consensual, committed relationships—then it cannot be shown . . . that it is sinful."

18. http://www.acceptingevangelicals.org.

19. https://www.gaychristian.net/what-is-gcn/. On the Roman Catholic side, the unofficial group DignityUSA, founded in 1969, "works for respect and justice for people of all sexual orientations, genders, and gender identities—especially gay, lesbian, bisexual, and transgender persons—in the Catholic Church and the world through education, advocacy, and support" (https://www.dignityusa.org).

20. https://www.euroforumlgbtchristians.eu.

and celebrate the equality and diversity of all."[21] Vicky Beeching was a well-known worship leader on the United States evangelical circuit until she "came out" as gay in 2014. Her book *Undivided: Coming Out, Becoming Whole, and Living Free From Shame* follows a parallel trajectory to Ozanne's. Both bear witness to the severe strain that the suppression of homosexual identity can put on the mind and body. Both make a compelling appeal for evangelical acceptance of LGBT Christians. Neither addresses the biblical and ethical "issues" in any depth, but in the United Kingdom at least, these testimonies may do more to represent and gain acceptance for a version of evangelical homosexuality than the conventional theological apologia. That said, there have also been numerous comparable autobiographies written by gay and lesbian people who have rejected same-sex relations and have pursued either celibacy or heterosexual marriage. Wesley Hill's *Washed and Waiting: Reflections on Christian Faithfulness and Homosexuality*, for example, is a deeply personal attempt to "put into words some of the confusion and sorrow and triumph and grief and joy of the struggle to live faithfully before God, in Christ, with others, as a gay person."[22]

Retractions and Reactions

The dilemma faced by prominent evangelical bodies and individuals is illustrated by a couple of high-profile retractions, one corporate, the other by an individual. In 2015 World Vision, a major evangelical aid, development, and advocacy organization, announced that it would employ people in same-sex marriages, only to reverse the decision two days later, presumably in response to objections from conservative supporters and funders. Ed Stetzer has since identified a move among even quite progressive evangelical organizations—such as World Vision—to repudiate same-sex sexual behavior as a departure from the will of God and to reaffirm the traditional view that marriage is between a man and a woman.[23] InterVarsity, *Christianity Today*, and Fuller Seminary are among a number of US organizations that have reiterated their commitment to the traditional

21. Ozanne, *Just Love*. For the Foundation see https://ozanne.foundation.

22. Hill, *Washed and Waiting*, 22. Also Bergner, *Setting Love in Order*; Hallett, *Still Learning to Love*; Butterfield, *Secret Thoughts*; Selmys, *Sexual Authenticity: An Intimate Reflection*; Selmys, *Sexual Authenticity: More Reflections*; and Tushnet, *Gay and Catholic*; Perry, *Gay Girl, Good God*.

23. Stetzer, "Evangelicals."

model of marriage and opposition to same-sex relationships.[24] Then, in an interview with Religion News Service in July 2017 Eugene Peterson, author of the massively popular Message Bible, appeared to express the view that he welcomed the current "transition" toward the acceptance of gay and lesbian Christians.[25] The disclosure kicked open a hornet's nest of criticism, and LifeWay Christian Stores, America's largest Christian retailer, threatened to drop his books. The next day Peterson withdrew the comments.[26]

In August 2017, as an act of further entrenchment, the Council on Biblical Manhood and Womanhood published the Nashville Statement, affirming marriage exclusively as "a covenantal, sexual, procreative, lifelong union of one man and one woman, as husband and wife."[27] The Statement insists that same-sex desires and behaviors have no biblical legitimacy, that it is "sinful to approve of homosexual immorality or transgenderism," and that this is not "a matter of moral indifference about which otherwise faithful Christians should agree to disagree." Several counter-statements were offered in response.

In the very different world of Anglicanism, the 2013 Pilling Report notes that new structures such as the Global Anglican Future Conference (GAFCON) and the Fellowship of Confessing Anglicans have been created to "focus opposition to what they see as the growing threat to Christian teaching posed by secularization and especially by liberal attitudes to sexual morality."

Some campaigners and activists have endeavored to position themselves impartially between the conservative evangelical church and the LGBT community. Andrew Marin is a good example. The Marin Foundation says that its approach is to partner strategically "with conservative and progressive religious entities and the LGBTQ community; as well as with churches, NGOs, higher educational institutions and government agencies to make a sustainable difference in today's religious and secular cultures."[28]

24. See Wax, "What's Really Going On."

25. Peterson is quoted as having said: "I wouldn't have said this 20 years ago, but now I know a lot of people who are gay and lesbian and they seem to have as good a spiritual life as I do. I think that kind of debate about lesbians and gays might be over. People who disapprove of it, they'll probably just go to another church. So we're in a transition and I think it's a transition for the best, for the good. I don't think it's something that you can parade, but it's not a right or wrong thing as far as I'm concerned" (Shellnutt, "LifeWay").

26. Shellnutt, "Actually, Eugene Peterson."

27. https://cbmw.org/nashville-statement.

28. http://www.themarinfoundation.org/about-us/mission/.

Conversion Therapies

Conversion or reparative therapies aimed at "curing" people of their homosexuality remain controversial. Exodus International, an umbrella organization for a number of conversion ministries, was shut down in 2013 on the grounds that such therapies are at best ineffectual and at worst positively harmful. In 2017 the General Synod of the Church of England backed a motion saying that conversion therapy has "no place in the modern world."[29] Mental health professionals in the West mostly advise against attempts to change sexual orientation. The American Psychological Association is of the view that "there is insufficient evidence to support the use of psychological interventions to change sexual orientation."[30] The Royal College of Psychiatrists in the United Kingdom says that it would not "support a therapy for converting people from homosexuality any more than we would do so from heterosexuality."[31]

Nevertheless, some Christian researchers claim that there is evidence of at least limited success, and a number of religious organizations still offer treatment for unwanted same-sex attraction. Joe Dallas draws attention to the dilemma faced by people who are genuinely not comfortable with their innate same-sex orientation but whose desire for change is dismissed as "internalized homophobia" by the psychiatric profession. The only course presented to them is to come to terms with their homosexuality. Dallas recognizes, however, that the scope for change is mostly confined to managing

---

29. https://www.churchofengland.org/media-centre/news/2017/07/general-synod-backs-ban-on-conversion-therapy.aspx. See also Peter Ould's critique of the proposal (Ould, "It's Easy to Talk"); and Davison, *Amazing Love*, 30–31. The Executive Report on a 2018 Faith and Sexuality Survey (https://ozanne.foundation/faith-sexuality-survey-2018/) carried out by the Ozanne Foundation in the United Kingdom concludes: "The well-being of the LGBQ+ community is said to be significantly impacted by the experience of attempting to change sexual orientation, and that their spiritual well-being and religious faith is said to be negatively affected by the inner conflicts they have experienced because of their sexual orientation."

30. "Resolution on Appropriate Affirmative Responses to Sexual Orientation Distress and Change Efforts" (http://www.apa.org/about/policy/sexual-orientation.aspx).

31. Psychiatrists, "Statement on Sexual Orientation," 2. See also "Memorandum of Understanding on Conversion Therapy in the UK" (https://www.psychotherapy.org.uk/wp-content/uploads/2016/09/Memorandum-of-understanding-on-conversion-therapy.pdf): "All the major psychological professional bodies in the UK have concluded that conversion therapy is unethical and potentially harmful."

same-sex erotic desires, particularly in the case of people who have never felt opposite-sex attraction.[32] Yarhouse writes:

> For those who report a change, it tends to come in the form of a reduction in homosexual attractions, but these reductions are typically not complete. A smaller number of people also report an increase in heterosexual attraction. In some instances this may be attraction to the opposite sex in general; in other cases it may reflect attraction to only one individual of the opposite sex, such as a person's spouse. I think it may be helpful to everyone involved to recognize that 180-degree change or categorical change is less likely.[33]

In the end, it seems that the same uncertainty must attach to sexual orientation change as to the scientific explanation of same-sex attraction: if all we can say with any confidence currently is that homosexuality is a complex amalgam of innate and psychosocial variables, we must allow that the success of efforts to modify a person's *experienced* sexual orientation will be correspondingly unpredictable and constrained.

WHAT IS AT STAKE?

The question of how evangelical churches and mission organizations should respond to the pressure to conform their views and practices to changing social norms in the area of same-sex lifestyle and behavior is serious and urgent. This book will not attempt to provide practical pastoral and missional solutions. The prior *hermeneutical* task in dealing with this and other symptoms of cultural marginalization, I suggest, is to tell a comprehensive story that is both in honest continuity with Scripture and transparent about the place of the church in the modern world. We too often isolate theory from practice, theology from church, dogma from experience, narrative from history, and as an act of resistance to this tendency, I want to try to keep the full extent of the challenge in mind. If we ask what is at stake as we

---

32. Dallas, "Another Option."

33. Yarhouse, *Homosexuality*, 90; see also Jones and Workman, "Homosexuality," 103–4; Jones and Yarhouse, "Use, Misuse, and Abuse," 112–16. Pilling, *Report of the House of Bishops*, para. 216, notes that because of the controversy surrounding sexual orientation change therapies "there have been no randomized, controlled trials of such therapy in recent years." Gushee's reference to the "total failure of the 'ex-gay' movement" seems an overstatement (Gushee, *Changing Our Mind*, 27).

seek to understand the controversy and make practical pastoral and missional decisions, a number of issues stand out.

1. The core biblical idea that humanity was created as male and female.

The social validation of same-sex relationships and the affirmation of the rights associated with this, whatever the immediate ethical justification, can be seen as part of a much larger and more complex reappraisal of what it means to be gendered humanity. In the long run, it may be more important—and it may have more positive social impact—to affirm the simple *original blessing* of the creation of humanity as male and female, when culture is blurring the binary distinction and multiplying gender options, than to oppose the particular move toward same-sex relationships.[34]

2. The availability of an adequate view of marriage to serve as the basis for speaking about the relationship between God and his people, between Christ and the church.

In both the Old Testament and the New Testament the covenant relationship between the "Lord" and his people is frequently compared to the marital relationship between a man and his wife. There is naturally concern that the extension of marriage to include same-sex couples will weaken or obscure the theological point. DeYoung asserts, for example, that "the redemptive-historical significance of marriage as a divine symbol in the Bible only works if the marital couple is a complementary pair."[35] Arguably, though, it is difference in *social status* rather than difference in gender that is principally at issue in the biblical paradigm. The metaphor works in a patriarchal context because it says something about the higher status of the Lord and his condescension toward his people—a dimension that is barely tolerable in the modern world.[36] In this regard, the effect of the legalization of same-sex marriage has been to underline the essentially *egalitarian* nature of modern marriage. Of course, those who hold to a complementarian

---

34. Roberts, "Bill Nye."

35. DeYoung, *What Does the Bible*, 32 (italics removed).

36. Gudorf makes the point that metaphors are one-directional: the use of heterosexual marriage as a metaphor for the covenant relationship does not make heterosexuality normative. Moreover, it would be "nonsensical to use this heterosexual metaphor to condemn intimacy between same-sex persons, since the metaphor's original use was to assert the intimacy between a masculine God and a collection of Israelite males" (Gudorf, "Bible and Science," 131–32).

view of the relation of the man to the woman will have less difficulty affirming the function of marriage as a sign of the covenant.

3. The promotion of a healthy sexuality in the church and the witness of the church in this regard at a time when sexual identities and boundaries in secular Western society are in a state of flux.

The church has been put on the back foot in a number of respects over this controversy, but at the same time it has been presented with an opportunity to restate and reaffirm what it understands by good, God-honoring sexual behavior, and why. If nothing else, the heterosexual Christian community has come under pressure to put its own house in order if it is not to be accused of hypocrisy.

4. The identity, dignity, and well-being of LGBT people.

The conservative Christian view is that same-sex behavior—and possibly also same-sex attraction—is sinful. Gay and lesbian people, however, are likely to regard same-sex attraction as a good and constitutive part of their identity. It is who they are. Marin writes: "when gay and lesbian sexual behavior is challenged or questioned, they perceive their entire being as a person—their whole identity—as being under attack. When this occurs they feel as though their distinct individuality as a GLBT person has been effectively negated."[37] At stake, therefore, in this controversy is not just the rightness or wrongness of their behavior but how gays and lesbians are seen—and see themselves—as people. Marin notes the contempt of gays and lesbians for the formula "love the sinner, hate the sin": "If behavior equals identity, then hating gay sexual behavior is the same thing as hating the gay person."[38] A significant part of Chalke's argument for the full inclusion of LGBT people in the church is that exclusion can be severely damaging to mental health. "Why am I so passionate about this issue? Because people's health and safety as well as their lives are at stake. Numerous studies show that suicide rates among gay people, especially young people, are comparatively high."[39] In the background there is the broader question of the extent to which any perceived psychological and moral problems (depression, alcoholism, drug abuse, promiscuity, etc.) in the LGBT

37. Marin, *Love Is an Orientation*, 38.

38. Marin, *Love Is an Orientation*, 46.

39. See his *Premier Christianity* article calling for a "new Christian understanding of homosexual relationships" (Chalke, "Bible").

community have been the consequence of discrimination and of the absence of the range of support structures available to the heterosexual majority.[40]

5. The integrity of existing same-sex relationships.

Davison argues that the church has to come to terms with the fact that same-sex relationships cannot now be dismissed arbitrarily as reprobate. A significant number of gay and lesbian relationships demonstrate exactly the personal qualities that we look for in a heterosexual relationship: "We encounter in gay and lesbian relationships the same sort of virtues that we pray for in the marriage service: love, trust, joy, commitment, unity, loyalty, growth, and mutual support."[41] The church puts itself in a very difficult position—perhaps in a very damaging position—if it refuses to acknowledge and support the intrinsic *goodness* of such relationships.

6. Personal relationships with LGBT people.

Many people wrestling with the theological problem already have close relationships with people of same-sex orientation, whether friends or family members. As Todd Wilson says, "Unlike their parents, most younger evangelicals know gays and lesbians as classmates and teammates, as colleagues and friends. . . . They're hard to dismiss as sinful and wrong—regardless of what the Bible says or the church teaches."[42] It is important to recognize now that the matter cannot be addressed in the abstract; we also have to reckon with the force of sometimes quite distressing personal stories. It is this tension, perhaps more than anything else, that gives urgency to the dilemma for evangelicals.

7. The loving and respectful inclusion of LGBT people in and around missional communities.

Missionaries and church-planters are especially motivated to reach marginal, disregarded, and disadvantaged sections of Western society with the love of God. We would not want to be saddled with a theology, policy,

---

40. See the balanced but somewhat dated discussion of whether homosexuality is a psychopathology in Jones and Yarhouse, "Use, Misuse, and Abuse," 106–12; also Gudorf, "Bible and Science," 122–24; Pilling, *Report of the House of Bishops*, paras. 205–8.

41. Davison, *Amazing Love*, 20.

42. Wilson, *Mere Sexuality*, 31.

or mindset that gets in the way of serious, honest, loving, and transparent engagement with the LGBT community. Marin registers the intense pain of sincere gay and lesbian people in the US context who find themselves condemned by conservative evangelical churches, often churches in which they grew up, and effectively alienated from the God worshiped there. He states that "at a baseline level all the GLBT community wants from God is (a) to have the same intimate relationship with God that evangelicals claim to have; and (b) to safely enter into a journey toward an inner reconciliation of who they are sexually, spiritually and socially."[43]

8. The faith and well-being of same-sex Christians.

The evangelical church is being challenged not only by the gap that has opened up between traditional church teaching and the ethical stance of secular culture but also by the fact that a significant number of LGBT people are professing a sincere "evangelical" faith. Phyllis Bird has noted, however, that many LGBT Christians, "faced with a perceived conflict between biblical norms and their own sexual needs, have been driven to the tragic options of divided lives, divided consciences, denial of sexual expression, contorted rationalizations, rejection of biblical authority and the Bible itself, self-hate, and even self-destruction."[44] The church as a whole, whether it affirms same-sex sexual relations or not, is presented with the stubborn reality of LGBT believers and has to work out how to relate to such people and their families pastorally, over lifetimes. This includes providing a meaningful place and pastoral support for Christians who admit to same-sex attraction but choose celibacy. Emily Hallock suggests that prominent celibate same-sex attracted Christians such as Rosaria Butterfield, Wesley Hill, Sam Allberry, and Ed Shaw "may be among the most important witnesses of our time."[45]

9. The freedom of churches and Christian organizations to act in accordance with explicit religious convictions.

The clash between the right of LGBT people not to be subjected to discrimination and the right of religious communities to act in accordance with faith and tradition is not going to be resolved any time soon and may

43. Marin, *Love Is an Orientation*, 30.
44. Bird, "Bible," 143.
45. Hallock, "Man of Honor."

prove unresolvable. If churches and Christian organizations take a conservative position on the issue, they will have to find good ways of accommodating, skirting, or resisting unsympathetic legal requirements and social pressures.

10. The reputation of churches and Christian organizations in the eyes of their denominations, networks, supporters, and local communities.

On the one hand, as things stand, evangelical bodies that take an affirming stance may find themselves censured and ostracized by the wider evangelical community, no matter how hard they try to mitigate and defend their action. On the other, if evangelical churches and organizations take an explicit position against the inclusion of LGBT people, they are likely to find themselves increasingly alienated from and distrusted by the secular world around them. Speaking of the situation in the United States, Gushee warns that "conservative Christian universities with discriminatory policies related to gays and lesbians may one day lose the right to educate students who receive federal financial aid."[46] Churches and Christian organizations that receive state funding for social and humanitarian work would similarly be at risk.

11. The credibility of the church's witness in secular Western societies.

The Anglican theologian Robert Song warns that it is "a position of considerable peril for the mission of the churches . . . when one of the first things people associate with them is hatred of gays and other sexual minorities."[47] It has frequently been observed that the church's stance on same-sex relations and marriage has been a major reason for the alienation of young secular people in particular.[48] Davison thinks that it has

46. Gushee, *Changing Our Mind*, 12.

47. Song, *Covenant and Calling*, Preface, Kindle loc. 133 of 1831. Cf. Wilson, *Letter*, chap. 2, Kindle loc. 905–7 of 3155: "People here view any exclusionary policies toward gay people as unjust, a moral wrong. They want nothing to do with organizations that do such things. They see the church making accommodations for the divorced and remarried . . . while enforcing exclusionary policies against gay people." Gushee quotes Public Religion Research data (Gushee, *Changing Our Mind*, 3); see also Fetsch, "Millennials."

48. Cf. Pilling, *Report of the House of Bishops*, para. 346: "Missiologically, it is clear that the shifts in popular opinion on sexuality constitute a challenge which the Church cannot ignore. We have been told by numerous respondents that younger people in particular find the Church's teaching on homosexuality a major stumbling block in the way of receiving the gospel message."

become "well-nigh impossible to articulate a theological conviction that loving and faithful gay relationships are wrong without seeming extreme and fundamentalist."[49] We do not hold to beliefs on the basis of whether or not they are publicly acceptable, but we have to recognize that this is, in important respects, a debate about the future of the church, which makes the mission to younger generations a matter of central concern.

12. The witness of the church to culturally conservative communities which are likely to oppose same-sex relations.

Missional churches and projects are increasingly finding themselves in a difficult buffer zone between Western secular liberals and traditional religious conservatives, especially immigrant communities. Peter Riddell has noted, for example, the sharp division in Australia in the run-up to the November 2017 poll between the largely Caucasian "fashionable electorate of inner Melbourne," which was firmly in support of same-sex marriage, and the "non-English speaking migrant populations" in western Sydney, which were mostly opposed.[50] He concludes that the divisions "reflect not merely ideological perspectives but issues of ethnic, cultural, and religious identity. Australian society is likely to become much more polarised in coming decades." As I finish preparing this manuscript, I read in *Christianity Today*: "After days of passionate debate, deliberation, and prayer—and years of tension—the United Methodist Church (UMC) voted Tuesday to maintain its traditional stance against same-sex marriage and non-celibate gay clergy, *bolstered by a growing conservative contingent from Africa.*"[51] We need an approach to same-sex relations and relationships that will keep us in this politically uncomfortable buffer zone and allow us to mediate with respect both to religious values and social practice.

13. The integrity of the global witness of the church.

The global "mission field" is also likely to become more polarized. On the one hand, we are having to reckon with the growing presence—through globalization and migration—of social and religious conservatism from outside the secular West, perhaps aggravated by conservative American

---

49. Davison, *Amazing Love*, 88.

50. Riddell, "Australia."

51. Steele, "United Methodists" (emphasis added).

missionary activity.[52] On the other, we can expect secular Western societies to reinforce the defense of civil liberties in the face of cultural intrusion.

14. *The unity of the church.*

There are few indications as yet that the church in the West is finding ways to repair the deep divisions that have opened up between traditionalists and progressives over this issue. The thesis presented in this book introduces a narrative dynamic into the debate, which cuts across many of the standard fault lines. In some ways, that just makes matters worse, but I am firmly of the view that a serious historical perspective, with regard both to the interpretation of Scripture and to the re-formation of the church in the post-Christian West, will prove itself invaluable in the long run.

15. *The authority of Scripture and the integrity of interpretation.*

The biblical texts have inevitably been put under considerable stress in the disputes. We have a responsibility to read the Bible well, but also to demonstrate its continuing credibility as the narrative, theological, and formational basis for the life and mission of the church in the modern world. Luke Timothy Johnson, writing from a Catholic perspective, argued in a Commonweal article some years back that the church's current preoccupation with homosexuality and relative complacency regarding far more widespread heterosexual disorder (the commodification of sex, sex trafficking, pornography, clerical pedophilia) suggests that this crisis "has less to do with sex than with perceived threats to the authority of Scripture and the teaching authority of the church."[53] The direct contradiction between the biblical statements and modern sexual ideology makes this an especially acute test of the church's loyalty to Scripture. Is this the point down the slippery slope when we finally go over the edge of the precipice and into free fall? This book will not address all the questions asked, all the objections raised, all the alternative readings proposed, but a major thrust of the approach will be to think through the nature of the engagement of Scripture with its historical context and its perspective on the role of the people of God in an unfolding and not always predictable future.

---

52. See Kaoma, "U.S. Christian Right."
53. Johnson, "Homosexuality and the Church."

TESTING TIMES

The family of Abraham—that people which believes itself to have been "chosen," qualified, and equipped to serve and bear witness to the one, true, living creator God—passed the test of maintaining that witness under the political-religious conditions of the Ancient Near East, though hardly with flying colors. It took conquest and exile finally to establish the conviction that Israel was the servant of a righteous God and Savior beside whom there is no other (cf. Isa 45:21). This "missional community" then passed the test of faithfully maintaining that witness under the political-religious conditions of the Hellenistic period, though again at considerable cost—the persecution of the Jews by Greece, Roman occupation and the destruction of Jerusalem and the temple, and of course, the suffering of the Son of Man and his disciples. Now the priestly community which serves the living God in the name of the exalted Jesus and in the power of the Holy Spirit is facing another test—to maintain a credible witness to the dynamic reality of a good, just, living, and knowable creator God under the radically different conditions of secular modernity. Tellingly, as we will see, the "problem" of homosexuality has proved to be a crux in each of these existential crises. I think we can assume that the church will scrape through, will pass the test, will maintain its witness, because God is faithful. But we cannot assume that it will be easy. In fact, if history is anything to go by, we can assume that it will be very difficult.

CHAPTER 3

Humanity, Homosexuality, and the Land

THE DISCUSSION OF THE relevant biblical material here reflects a solid commitment to understanding the texts *according to the circumstances and perspectives of the communities for which they were written.* If we are to be true to the calling to establish, develop, and maintain churches that bear witness to the central truth that Jesus Christ is Lord, we have to take very seriously the large-scale biblical narratives that frame and make sense of that confession. But I also think that if we are to do mission well, interpretation must be undertaken not as a purely *historical* exercise but as part of a lively two-way conversation with the church as it constantly reimagines and reconstructs a place for itself in the world. The story of the witness of the people of the living God does not end with the New Testament. It is still being told today as we endeavor to serve him as a priestly and prophetic people, in the power of the Holy Spirit, confessing that the crucified Jesus now sits at the right hand of the Father, in a rapidly changing post-Christian environment.

In this chapter we look first at the creation accounts, which must give us some sort of template for how God intended humanity to be, and then at the story about the land of Israel that frames the explicit condemnation of same-sex relations in Leviticus. Chapter 4 will provide an overview of the Greek-Roman cultural background to the New Testament. Chapters 5 and 6 will then locate the few brief New Testament texts in their own story about the kingdom of God. In chapters 7 to 9 we will look at how the situation that confronts the church today may be understood both as a disruption and as a continuation of the biblical stories. I will suggest, in particular, that a new narrative frame for the witness of the church in the secular Western context is coming into focus, which is forcing a radical reappraisal of how the church embodies an ideal created or recreated reality.

IN THE BEGINNING . . .

Man and Woman in the Image of God

Humanity was created in the image and after the likeness of God as male and female (Gen 1:26–27). Stanley Grenz states that "in the image of God he created him" and "male and female he created them" are to be understood as parallel statements, so that the one interprets the other: to be created in the image of God is specifically to be created as male and female.[1] But the reasoning is not strong: "The narrator does not appear to view sexuality as simply a biological phenomenon limited to procreation, which humans share with the animals"; and in the end Grenz seems to be left in two minds. Two considerations suggest that being "male and female" is not an interpretation of being in the image and likeness of God. First, it is difficult to see how, in an Old Testament theology, the image of God or of the divine council ("let us make") would be gendered, either internally or externally—are we to suppose that a male God has a female consort?[2] Secondly, in the context of the creation account, being in the image of God *sets humanity apart from the living creatures*, which were created not in the image of God but "according to their kinds" or species (Gen 1:20–25). This difference is expressed concretely in the progressive exercise of dominion over all living creatures: "Let us make man (in Hebrew *'ādâm*) in our image, after our likeness, and let them rule over the fish of the sea," etc. (my translation). Gordon Wenham says that "the divine image makes man God's vice-regent on earth."[3] The blessing of humanity (Gen 1:28) is for that purpose. Human sexuality is not an expression of what it means to be in the image of God; it has to do with how the mandate to exercise dominion will be worked out in practice.

There is certainly no basis for making the Trinity, in which three differentiated persons are nevertheless one, a normative model for human sexual relationships, as is suggested in InterVarsity's 2012 theological statement in

---

1. Grenz, *Social God*, 273; cf. Wilson, *Mere Sexuality*, 69: "It means that being male and female is essential to being created in God's own image."

2. See on this point Grenz, *Social God*, 288–93.

3. Wenham, *Genesis*, 31–32.

response to the LGBT movement: "This combination of differentiation and oneness of women and men enable them especially to reflect God's image in their relationships with each other."[4] Humanity as a whole reflects the image of God not in its *internal* relationships, whether sexual or social, but in *its relationship to the rest of creation*. The attempt to ground sexuality in the doctrine of God, whether by complementarians or by egalitarians such as Grenz, whether in order to proscribe or to accommodate same-sex relationships, is a dubious theological ploy that overloads exegesis and interferes with the empirical description of human behavior.

So how are we to understand the existence of humanity (*'ādâm*) as male (*zākâr*) and female (*nĕqêbâ*)? According to the narrative, the binary simply constitutes the basis on which humanity will be fruitful and multiply and thus extend the sphere of its dominion (Gen 1:28). It is not that the "*mode* of human existence in the divine image is that of male and female together," as Richard Davidson argues from the parallelism in verse 27.[5] It is that the *manner* of human propagation in order to fulfill the divine mandate is given in the fact of being male and female. Song explains the logic of the passage with precision: "being created in a relationship of male and female is what enables humankind to procreate; being able to procreate enables it to fill the earth and subdue it; being able to rule the earth enables it to fulfill its role as bearing the image of God."[6] There is nothing in this narrative that directly precludes same-sex relations as a marginal feature of human society. A same-sex minority would not prevent humanity from fulfilling the creation mandates. Perhaps, as Megan DeFranza suggests, "Adam and Eve, male and female, could be interpreted as the majority, the broad categories, rather than the exclusive model for all humankind."[7] Or in David Runcorn's words: "What is 'typical' does not exclude what is atypical."[8] But the exceptions are not expressly considered in the text, and there is nothing elsewhere in the Old Testament that points to the toleration of people in same-sex relationships on such grounds. Quite the opposite.

4. InterVarsity, "Responding to the LGBT Movement," section II. See also Song, *Covenant and Calling*, chap. 3, Kindle loc. 885–95 of 1831.

5. Davidson, *Flame*, 39–40.

6. Song, *Covenant and Calling*, chap. 1, Kindle loc. 451–53 of 1831. Cf. Paul, *Same-Sex Unions*, 7: "the idea appears to be that humanity (*'adam*), male and female (*zaqar* and *neqevah*), reproduce, populate the earth and govern it as the offspring of the creator, ruling as his vice-regents and with his delegated authority."

7. Cf. DeFranza, "Journeying," 71, cf. 90, 97.

8. Runcorn, "Evangelicals."

Man and Woman as "One Flesh"

In the Eden story woman is created from the "side" of man because no "helper fit for him (*kĕnegdô*)" was found among the animals (Gen 2:18). She is, therefore, of the *same bone and flesh* as Adam (Gen 2:23), not another creature from the earth. She is of the same "species," so to speak. What is indicated here is not the biological complementarity of the man and the woman but their social and cultural compatibility: they are capable of *companionship* (the man is no longer "alone") and *collaboration* (Eve works with him in the garden). The "helper" (*ʿēzêr*) is typically an equal or stronger person who comes to the aid of someone in time of need; more often than not in the Old Testament the *ʿēzêr* is God (e.g., Exod 18:4; Deut 33:7; Ps 70:5; Hos 13:9). The woman *delivers* the man from his aloneness;[9] the word can hardly be made to mean "a sexually differentiated partner for procreation."

The unusual prepositional expression *kĕnegdô* means something like "corresponding to him."[10] Interpreters who wish to find in this text an argument for the traditional definition of marriage will often maintain that the word carries the idea that the man and the woman were *biologically* differentiated from each other.[11] But the purpose of *kĕnegdô* is clear and limited: it serves to distinguish Eve from the animals, not from the man. Adam gave names to the animals, but "there was not found a helper fit for him (*kĕnegdô*)" (Gen 2:20). We would hardly expect God to have brought the animals to Adam to see if he would mate with any of them.[12] This curious incident is central to the definition of the expression. The *ʾādâm* needed another creature to rescue him from his singularity or aloneness *as keeper of the garden*. What he failed to find among the animals was not sexual complementarity—procreativity does not enter the second creation account until after the expulsion from the garden, and then in rather negative terms (Gen 3:16). What he failed to find was *likeness of kind*. Hence the woman was produced *from his side, of the same flesh*. As Matthew Vines

---

9. See Wenham, *Genesis*, 68; Hamilton, *Book of Genesis*, 176.

10. See Speiser, *Genesis*, 17.

11. See, for example, DeYoung, *What Does the Bible*, 27.

12. Davidson thinks that the lesson is that "human sexual activity is to take place not with animals as sexual partners (bestiality) but only between human partners" (Davidson, *Flame*, 21). But this is entirely outside the scope of the narrative.

says, "Adam and Eve were right for each other, not because they were different, but because they were alike."[13]

To read sexual difference or complementarity into an expression that at heart carries only the idea of being "in front of" or "in the presence of" is warranted neither by lexicology nor by context.[14] Something of the contextual significance of the term, arguably, is suggested by the use of the preposition *neged* elsewhere in Genesis: Hagar sat down "opposite" (*mineged*) her son, "a good way off, about the distance of a bowshot" (Gen 21:16); and in a story to which we will return in a moment Jacob says to Laban, "In the presence of (*neged*) our kinsmen point out what I have that is yours, and take it," and then instructs him to set the stolen item "before (*neged*) my kinsmen and your kinsmen, that they may decide between us two" (Gen 31:32, 37). The connotations of kinship that surface here are entirely appropriate for the story of the creation of the woman: *neged* defines the sphere in which members of the same kinship group relate to each other. Biological difference and complementarity may be presumed in other respects, but it is not what is signified.

If it is not about procreation, however, then surely another male could in principle have solved the problem of Adam's aloneness? If the fundamental concern addressed in Genesis 2:18–25 is not the need to reproduce but the existential isolation of the first human creature, the need for a companion and co-laborer of the same species or kind, have we not opened up some sort of theological space for same-sex relationships? Up to a point I think that the answer to this question has to be yes. We are actually closer here to a modern "companionate" model of marriage, as Todd Wilson calls it, than a procreative model.[15] But there are limits to this line of reasoning. First, if the passage is not about the origins of procreation, then it is also not about sex. So the most that might be said is that if two men or two women live and work together, that is consistent with the creation vision; we are not meant to be alone; but the vision would not include sexual relations. Secondly, there is no getting around the fact that the quandary of the singular human is resolved *by means of the created binary of male and female*. The primal *'ādâm* is the "man" (*'iš*) out of whom the material for building (*yiben*) the "woman" (*'iššâ*) was taken (Gen 2:23). In the earlier

---

13. Vines, *God and the Gay Christian*, 46.

14. According to *BDB* s.v. דגנ the substantive *neged* means "what is conspicuous or in front, always as adv. or prep. in front of, in sight of, opposite to."

15. Wilson, *Mere Sexuality*, 78.

account God created ʾādâm as "male and female" (Gen 1:26–27); and in the opening of the "book of the generations of Adam" it is said that God made ʾādâm in the likeness of God as male and female, "and he blessed *them* and named *them* ʾādâm when *they* were created" (Gen 5:2).[16] Thirdly, the story culminates in the assertion that a man and a woman become "one flesh." I do not think that "one flesh" is a figure for sexual union as such, but the passage, nevertheless, clearly has in view the relationship between husband and wife as the generative basis for family and community.

The language of being of the same bone and flesh, as James Brownson points out, is used in the Old Testament to signify shared kinship bonds.[17] For example, Laban says to his nephew Jacob, "Surely you are my bone and my flesh!"; Abimelech reminds his mother's family, "I am your bone and flesh" (Gen 29:14; Judg 9:2; cf. 2 Sam 5:1; 19:12–13; 1 Chron 11:1). That a man and a woman become "one flesh," therefore, should probably be understood not in terms of sexual union but as the basis for "family" as a broader network of social relations.[18] The phrase "one flesh" looks back to the *creation* of the woman from the body of the man: God made the "rib"—that is, presumably, the bone and flesh—that he had taken from the man into a woman (Gen 2:22). The woman is "bone of my bones and flesh of my flesh," which is Old Testament kinship language (2:23). Therefore, when a man leaves his father and his mother—that is, leaves one family or kinship group—he becomes "one flesh," a new bone and flesh, with his wife. Again, it is a way of saying that a woman is of the same kind or species as a man.[19] It is not Adam and Eve who "become one flesh," notice. They *start out* as "one flesh"; they are already a kinship group. Rather, it explains what

16. Gagnon argues that Adam was originally a "binary or sexually undifferentiated human" who was split in two with the creation of the woman and reunited in the sexual union of "one flesh" (Gagnon, "Bible and Homosexual Practice," 61; for a critique see Brownson, *Bible*, 26–29; and Davidson, *Flame*, 19–20).

17. Brownson, *Bible*, 86–90; cf. Vasey, *Strangers*, 116; and Wenham, *Genesis*, 71: "This does not denote merely the sexual union that follows marriage. . . . Rather it affirms that just as blood relations are one's flesh and bone . . . so marriage creates a similar kinship relation between man and wife. They become related to each other as brother and sister are."

18. Against Davidson, *Flame*, 46–47, who says that the "physical act of coitus is the primary means of establishing the 'innermost mystery' of oneness."

19. There is no basis here for the claim that sexual intercourse, being "one flesh," is the God-given "sign" of the covenant of marriage (against InterVarsity, "Responding to the LGBT Movement," 2–3). It is incorrect to say that "joining together in one flesh is a profound and unique way of reflecting the image of God."

is *subsequently* known to happen in societies: a man and a woman come from different families, the man cleaves to the woman, and they form a new kinship group.

Ian Paul argues against this correction of the traditional view that Brownson has misunderstood how language works: "Brownson is suggesting that because 'flesh' is used metaphorically in reference to family ties, it no longer has a literal sense. This is a bit like noting that in certain subcultures 'brother' means 'friend,' and concluding from this that 'brother' therefore no longer actually means 'male sibling.'"[20] I think this is back to front. If the kinship meaning has linguistic priority in the Old Testament, then we should probably conclude that the no less figurative description of the man and the woman as "one flesh" in Gen 2:24 has been derived from the broader kinship idea, rather than the other way round. There is no established or ordinary usage of "one flesh" as a way of speaking about marriage or sexual union in the Old Testament. I am inclined to agree with Brownson: "there is nothing in the language of 'one flesh' anywhere in Scripture that even remotely suggests that this unitive meaning of marriage is subordinated to the purpose of procreation."[21] We have been misled by the fact that the derived or secondary linguistic usage in the creation story happens to have such a prominent position at the beginning of the Bible.

Some other passages have been thought to point to a sexual union interpretation of "one flesh" but can be discounted. First, we are told in the next verse that "the man and his wife were both naked (*'arûmmim*) and were not ashamed" (Gen 2:25). But this should not be taken to mean that sexual union is in view. In the Old Testament the act of *uncovering* a person's "nakedness" (*'erĕwāh*) connotes sexual intercourse or abuse, but the language is quite different: *'erĕwāh*, in effect, is a reference to the genitalia (cf. Exod 20:26; 28:42; Lev 18:6–19; 20:11, 17–21). What we have in Genesis 2:25 is an association of nakedness—either literally or metaphorically—with a broader social and ethical disgrace.[22] Hosea is told to plead with Israel to put an end to her whoring and adultery, "lest I strip her naked (*'arûmmāh*) and make her as in the day she was born" (Hos 2:3). The point is that this association belongs to the fallen state of humanity; it was not so in the garden. Secondly, when Jesus quotes this verse in commenting on divorce, he adds, "So they are no longer two but

---

20. Paul, *Same-Sex Unions*, 10.

21. Brownson, *Bible*, 89.

22. Against DeYoung, *What Does the Bible*, 27.

one flesh"—so what God has joined together, man should not separate (Matt 19:5–6; cf. Mark 10:7–9). He is thinking of the man and the woman as a *social* unit.[23] There is no reason to suppose that he had in mind the man and woman in *sexual* union: this is rather something that happens within the frame of the social-legal arrangement (Matt 19:7–9). Thirdly, Paul, no doubt playing rhetorically on the idiom, changes the phrase to "one body" when he wants to express the seriousness of sexual union with a prostitute (1 Cor 6:15–17).

It has been argued from this, however, that if "one flesh" does not refer to sexual union but to the shared biological identity of the wider family, the language may be stretched to include same-sex relationships. Brownson thinks that there is nothing in the biblical idea that would necessarily "exclude committed gay or lesbian unions from consideration as one-flesh unions, when the essential characteristics of one-flesh unions as kinship bonds are held clearly in view."[24] Likewise, Michael Vasey has argued that the "one flesh" metaphor does not provide a blueprint for monogamous marriage as we understand it today. "It does not of itself preclude the possibility that certain individuals in a society may not fit the general pattern and may respond in a different way to the mysterious duality of gender."[25] But because a kinship group of one *bone and flesh* has its origins in the creation of the woman from the body of Adam and exists and is extended only through heterosexual union and procreation, it does not seem possible to classify same-sex unions as "one flesh" in biblical terms. One man cannot say to another, "You are flesh of my flesh," unless they happen to be *biologically related* as members of a kinship group that is the result of men and women having sex with each other.[26] It could be argued that stable, egalitarian same-sex relationships may find a place within, and may contribute positively to, the modern equivalent of extended kinship groups—local communities, societies—not least by reducing the *destabilizing* impact that a more promiscuous and dissolute LGBT culture may have. But it cannot be

23. Cf. Vasey, *Strangers*, 116–17.

24. Brownson, *Bible*, 109.

25. Vasey, *Strangers*, 118.

26. In Lev 18:6 the phrase "inner flesh of his flesh" (*šĕʾēr bĕśār*) serves to differentiate between close relatives and the wider kinship group (Hartley, *Leviticus*, 293), where modern same-sex relationships could perhaps be located.

claimed that same-sex marriage is included in or validated by the specific affirmation in Genesis 2:24 that husband and wife are "one flesh."[27]

HOMOSEXUALITY AND THE LAND

Stories of Homosexual Rape

Three early and rather difficult Old Testament stories are sometimes thought to have a bearing on the debate.

After the flood, Noah plants a vineyard, gets drunk, and sprawls in a state of undress in his tent (Gen 9:20–21). His son Ham, who is father of Canaan, sees Noah's "nakedness" and informs his brothers outside. Shem and Japheth walk backwards into the tent and cover their father without looking on his nakedness. When Noah wakes up and discovers what his son has done, he curses Canaan and by extension the Canaanites. Because uncovering a person's nakedness is often a euphemism for illicit sexual activity in the Old Testament, it has sometimes been inferred that Ham committed an incestuous same-sex act with his father. Robert Gagnon, for example, holds that this is a "kitchen sink" drama whose purpose is to show "how truly bad the ancestor of the Canaanites was by multiplying heinous offenses: not just rape but also a case of incest and of male-male intercourse, and the worst combination of these possible, namely, penetration of one's own father."[28]

There are two problems with this rather prurient argument. First, if Ham has committed an illicit sexual act, it is more likely to have been with his mother than with Noah. Deuteronomy 22:30 states: "A man shall not take his father's wife, so that he does not uncover his father's nakedness."[29]

27. Song argues that theological affirmation of same-sex relationships cannot—and should not—be grounded in the creation narratives (Song, *Covenant and Calling*, chap. 2, Kindle loc. 559–610 of 1831).

28. Gagnon, "Old Testament and Homosexuality," 372; cf. Gagnon, "Bible and Homosexual Practice" 56–57; and Gagnon, *Bible and Homosexual Practice*, 63–70. Loader thinks that we have "another instance of male rape, and this would be similarly understood as a grab for power by setting himself above his father (and his brothers)" (Loader, *New Testament*, 30).

29. Cf. Lev 18:8; and Ezek 22:10: "In you men uncover (*gillāh*) their fathers' nakedness (*'erĕwat*); in you they violate women who are unclean in their menstrual impurity." Block comments on the Ezekiel passage: "In this instance 'to expose the nakedness of one's father' means to violate the nakedness of the person reserved for one's father, viz., one's natural mother or a stepmother" (Block, *Ezekiel*, 710).

But secondly, and more importantly, Ham does not actively "uncover" his father's nakedness. Noah has exposed himself. The brothers do not protest at this abuse of their father; and they resolve the situation simply by *properly* covering him, which seems to indicate that the offense was *seeing* Noah's nakedness ('erĕwat).[30] What Ham "had done" was not rape his father but fail to respect and defend his father's dignity, an offense made worse by the announcement of the fact to his brothers. Presumably the incident is meant to tell us something about the moral character of the Canaanites, but it appears to have no direct relevance for the debate about same-sex relations. Since Noah has become a gardener, a man of the 'ădāmāh (Gen 9:20), the significance of the story perhaps lies in its relation to the description of the man and the woman as "naked ['arûmmim] and not ashamed" (Gen 2:25). The language is different, but outside the legal texts 'erĕwāh may signify opprobrium in a more general sense: "Jerusalem sinned grievously; therefore she became filthy; all who honored her despise her, for they have seen her nakedness ['erĕwat]; she herself groans and turns her face away" (Lam 1:8; cf. Isa 20:4; 47:3). This is a new creation, but an imperfect one. Humanity has been given a fresh start, but the deeply disturbing association of nakedness and disgrace remains in force.

The other two stories are less ambiguous, but still only indirectly relevant. In the first, God hears a "great outcry against Sodom and Gomorrah" and sets out to investigate (Gen 18:20–21). Two angels come to Sodom, and Lot welcomes them into his home. The men of Sodom surround the house and call out to Lot: "Where are the men who came to you tonight? Bring them out to us, that we may know them" (Gen 19:5). Lot protests and offers instead his two daughters for the men to "do to them as you please." The rape of the two "men" and the abuse of hospitality are considered a worse crime than the rape of the two virgin daughters: "Only do nothing to these men, for they have come under the shelter of my roof" (Gen 19:8).

A similar story is told in Judges 19. A Levite and his concubine are returning home. On the way, rather than spend the night in the "foreign" town of Jebus (pre-Israelite Jerusalem) they stop at the Benjaminite town of Gibeah. An old man, who is not from the tribe of Benjamin, offers the two travelers shelter for the night. That evening, while they are "making their

---

30. Cf. Hamilton, *Genesis*, 323: "We are on much safer ground in limiting Ham's transgression simply to observing the exposure of the genitalia and failing to cover his naked father. Otherwise, the other two brothers' act of covering their father's nakedness becomes incomprehensible." See also the extensive discussion in Davidson, *Flame*, 142–45.

hearts merry," worthless men from the city surround the house and beat on the door, demanding that the old man send out the Levite "that we may know him" (Judg 19:22). He implores them not to act so wickedly "since this man has come into my house," and offers the men his virgin daughter and the Levite's concubine: "Violate them and do with them what seems good to you, but against this man do not do this outrageous thing" (Judg 19:24).

The problem that these stories present to the modern reader who wants to understand how same-sex relations are regarded in the Bible is that it is difficult to disentangle homosexual behavior from violent assault, on the one hand, and gang rape from a complex nexus of issues relating to foreignness and hospitality, on the other.[31] Both Lot and the old man in Gibeah are outsiders in their towns, and the men of Sodom revile Lot as a sojourner—an outsider or foreigner—who has set himself up as judge (Gen 19:9). In both stories the reason given for protecting the male visitors is not that same-sex behavior is inherently wrong but that gang rape would be a gross breach of the rules of ancient hospitality.[32] The daughters are offered instead not—it would appear—because heterosexual rape is considered less serious than homosexual rape, but because they are *not guests*, and specifically not *male* guests. The concubine is a guest, but she and the daughter are finally shoved out into the square to be abused all night because in a solidly patriarchal culture they are both of less value than the male Levite. "The differentiating criterion between the Levite and the women," Ken Stone writes, "is the social status of the women as sexual objects."[33] If no women had been available, would a male servant or son have served the purpose? Presumably not. That said, Davidson warns against discounting the force of the demand "that we may know [*nēdĕ'âh*] them/him" (Gen 19:5; Judg 19:22). When Lot says that his two daughters "have not known [*yādĕ'û*] any man," he means that they have not had sexual intercourse, not that they have not been raped. Davidson concludes that the stories imply disapproval of *homosexual intercourse*, not only of homosexual rape.[34]

---

31. Cf. Vines, *God and the Gay Christian*, 66–68.

32. Cf. Loader, *New Testament*, 29: "Both stories assume male rape and reflect its widespread use in the ancient world . . . as a form of subjugation. It not only inflicted pain; it also inflicted disgrace and humiliation on a man by making a woman of him. Both are thus stories about inhospitality expressed through sexual violence."

33. Stone, "Gender," 100.

34. Davidson, *Flame*, 147–48.

Elsewhere in the Old Testament Sodom is a byword for extreme wickedness. Israel is compared with Sodom and threatened with a similar fate (e.g., Deut 29:22–24; Isa 1:9–10; 3:9; Jer 23:14). It is sometimes pointed out that in these passages a wider range of social evils is condemned than those illustrated in the story of Lot. For example, Ezekiel condemns Jerusalem as worse than Sodom: "Behold, this was the guilt of your sister Sodom: she and her daughters had pride, excess of food, and prosperous ease, but did not aid the poor and needy" (Ezek 16:49). Sexual misconduct is not mentioned here, and Vines argues that in Ezekiel's eyes Sodom's sin was not same-sex behavior but a broad spectrum of economic and social injustices.[35] This neatly fits the progressive narrative that the conservative church fusses too much over sexual sin and neglects far weightier matters of social justice. As Vines sees it, the men of Sodom "were not expressing sexual interest in Lot's guests." Rape, perhaps culminating in murder, was rather a means of demonstrating "hostility and dominance."[36] That in both stories women were proposed in place of the male guests shows that these were not predatory "gay men" in the modern sense. Phyllis Bird similarly concludes that the texts "strongly suggest that the ancient Israelites had no experience or conception of male homoerotic relations as consensual or expressive of a committed relationship." The *use* of another male in sexual relations constituted a violation of male honor and did serious harm to male identity.[37]

Ezekiel's account of events, however, is closer to the original story than Vines allows and probably also makes reference to the Leviticus prohibitions. The description of Sodom as wealthy but contemptuous of the poor is likely to be an explanation of the great "outcry" against the two cities, which prompted the visitation of the angels in the first place (Gen 18:20–21). But Ezekiel adds: "They were haughty and did an abomination before me. So I removed them, when I saw it." So the narrative continues: Sodom was guilty of grave social injustices, the angels investigated, the men

---

35. Vines, *God and the Gay Christian*, 63–64; cf. Furnish, "Bible," 19; McNeill, "Homosexuality," 53–54; Vasey, *Strangers*, 125; Soards, *Scripture*, 15–16; Song, *Covenant and Calling*, chap. 4, Kindle loc. 1276 of 1831; Davison, *Amazing Love*, 43–44; Gushee, *Changing Our Mind*, 62–63. Hays dismisses the passage as irrelevant: "The gang-rape scenario exemplifies the wickedness of the city, but there is nothing in the passage pertinent to a judgment about the morality of consensual homosexual intercourse" (Hays, *Moral Vision*, 381).

36. Vines, *God and the Gay Christian*, 66.

37. Bird, "Bible," 148–49; see also Gagnon, "Old Testament and Homosexuality," 368.

of the city committed a gross "abomination" (tô'ēbôt) which was witnessed by the angels (and therefore *seen by the Lord*), and *for that reason* the city was destroyed.[38] The singular "abomination" makes it certain that the intended homosexual gang rape was understood to have been the reason for the destruction of the city. The singular is rare; generally, Ezekiel speaks of multiple "abominations," which more naturally fits the indictment of a city or nation for religious and social failings (e.g., Ezek 18:24; 33:29; 36:31). In Ezekiel 22:11 and 33:26 the singular is used with reference to other sexual relations proscribed in Leviticus 18 and 20: sex with a neighbor's wife, a daughter-in-law, or a sister.[39] In the case of these "abominations" (cf. Lev 18:26), there is no suggestion of coercion or violence, so the conclusion must be that Ezekiel regarded the attack on Lot and his guests as an abomination *for the specific reason that the aggressors threatened homosexual rape*, the penetration of male by male. The men of Sodom precisely modeled—even if they were mistaken in the object of their assault—the sort of behavior that originally rendered the land unclean and which, therefore, had to be strictly avoided by the Israelites (cf. Lev 18:27).

Apart from the Sodom and Gibeah stories there is little direct evidence for the presence of gay and lesbian people in ancient Israel, which conforms with the relative obscurity of the commandment in Leviticus. The intense friendship between David and Saul's son Jonathan has sometimes been thought to border on a youthful homoerotic relationship.[40] David says that the love of Jonathan for him was "extraordinary, surpassing the love of women" (2 Sam 1:26; cf. 1 Sam 18:1–3);[41] and since the love of Amnon for his sister Tamar is later also described as "extraordinary" (from the niphal of the verb *pele'* in both cases, "be surpassing, extraordinary"), there is perhaps a hint of transgression in the use of the word. Tamar

---

38. See Gagnon, "Bible and Homosexual Practice," 57–58; Gagnon, "Old Testament and Homosexuality," 372–73; Davidson, *Flame*, 162–63. Philo says of the people of Sodom: "not only did they go mad after women, and defile the marriage bed of others, but also those who were men lusted after one another, doing unseemly things, and not regarding or respecting their common nature" (*Abraham* 135). In *T. Naph.* 3:4–5 we read that Sodom "changed (*enēllaxe*) the order of its nature" (my translation), but the reference to the Watchers also changing the order of their nature may mean that it is the attempted rape of the angels that is in view, rather than same-sex rape, as in Jude 7.

39. In Ezek 18:12 the nature of the singular abomination is not made explicit.

40. Vasey, *Strangers*, 120–21.

41. Note the sexual connotations that attach to *pele'* in 2 Sam 13:2: "and Amnon was so tormented that he made himself ill because of his sister Tamar, for she was a virgin, and it seemed impossible (*yippālē'*) to Amnon to do anything to her."

speaks of the shamefulness of Amnon's proposition (2 Sam 13:11–13), and Saul reproaches Jonathan for having "chosen the son of Jesse to your own shame, and to the shame of your mother's nakedness" (1 Sam 20:30). But the most this suggests is that the relationship may have been *perceived* by an angry father as scandalous. The curse pronounced by David on Joab that his house would never be without one "who holds a spindle (*pelek*)" may imply the presence in Israel of effeminate men, who failed to "conform to the male stereotype" (2 Sam 3:29; cf. Prov 31:19).[42] But there is evidence that the word may mean "crutches," and the curse of disability perhaps fits better among the other misfortunes listed: "may the house of Joab never be without one who has a discharge or who is leprous or who holds a *pelek* or who falls by the sword or who lacks bread!"[43]

The Leviticus Prohibition

The numerous prohibitions of Leviticus 18 are prefaced by the command not to "do as they do in the land of Egypt, where you lived" or "as they do in the land of Canaan, to which I am bringing you." The people of Israel are to walk in the statutes and judgments of the Lord their God, by which they shall live (Lev 18:3–5). A man is not to "uncover the nakedness" of "any relation of his flesh," which reminds us of the "one flesh" kinship unit constituted when a man forsakes his father and mother and joins himself to his wife (Lev 18:6–18; Gen 2:24). He must not uncover a woman's nakedness "while she is in her menstrual uncleanness" or give the "seed of intercourse" to a neighbor's wife because it will result in uncleanness (Lev 18:19–20). He must not give any of his "seed" (here "seed" means "children") to the god Molech to "profane the name of your God" (Lev 18:21). A man must not "lie with a male as lying down with a woman"; this is an "abomination" (Lev 18:22). He must not make himself unclean by lying with an animal; and a woman must not stand before an animal to lie with it, which is a perversion (Lev 18:23).

There is no compelling reason to think that the prohibition against male homosexuality is restricted to a cultic context as is sometimes suggested in order to limit its application.[44] There are religious practices that are

42. Vasey, *Strangers*, 119; cf. Anderson, *2 Samuel*, 62.

43. McCarter, *II Samuel*, 118.

44. Against, for example, Schuh: "The homosexual acts prohibited in Lev 18 and 20 are described in the immediate context of idolatry and therefore very likely refer to ritual

described as abominations (e.g., Deut 12:31), but not every abomination is a religious practice (Deut 25:13–16). There is the reference to the offering of "seed" to Molech in verse 21, but the prohibitions of Leviticus 18:19–23 appear to have isolated practices in view; and the juxtaposition is missing when it comes to the pronouncement of punishment in Leviticus 20:13. There is no reference to "male cult prostitutes" (qĕdēšim) in this context (cf. Deut 23:17; 1 Kgs 15:12; 22:46). Some scholars argue that "abomination" (tôʿēbāh) is not an ethical term but a "boundary marker" with "a basic sense of taboo."[45] This is perhaps supported by the fact that Moses knew that Israelite sacrifices were "an abomination to the Egyptians" and that they were likely to be stoned as a result (Exod 8:26). Abominations are what *other peoples* do: "When you come into the land that the LORD your God is giving you, you shall not learn to follow the abominable practices [tôʿēbôt] of those nations" (Deut 18:9).[46] In the category of "abomination" are included eating camel and pig meat, a woman wearing a man's garment and a man wearing a woman's cloak (Deut 14:3, 7–8; 22:5). But it is important to note that when Bird, for example, says that "issues of prohibited sexual relations are presented . . . in essentially cultic rather than ethical terms: they defile, and therefore, endanger, the community," her point is not that the Holiness Code only has in view same-sex acts in a cultic context—as in the case of male temple prostitution.[47] It is that *whenever* a man lies with a man as with a woman, the act defiles Israel and jeopardizes its possession of the land.[48]

---

acts of male homosexual prostitution" (Schuh, "Challenging Conventional Wisdom"). Note Loader, *New Testament*, 25: "Most conclude that Lev 18:22 does condemn same-sex anal intercourse between males in general, and is not restricted to particular settings"; Loader, "Homosexuality and the Bible," 22; also Davidson, *Flame*, 151–52; and Paul, *Same-Sex Unions*, 17–18.

45. See Vines, *Gay Christian*, 85; cf. Loader, *New Testament*, 24n48; Gushee, *Changing Our Mind*, 67: "The issue may then be preserving Israel's clear differentiation from its pagan neighbors, especially their idolatrous practices and perhaps also cultic prostitution."

46. Bird says that abomination belongs to "the language of separation and distinctness from the nations that came to expression during the exile and was applied retroactively to earlier stages of Israelite history" (Bird, "Bible," 152).

47. Bird, "Bible," 150.

48. Milgrom suggests that the prohibition applies only within a degree of forbidden relations equivalent to that stipulated for heterosexual relations in verses 6–18, which would mean that "sexual liaisons with males, falling outside the control of the paterfamilias, would be neither condemnable nor punishable" (Milgrom, *Leviticus*, 1569). But the prohibitions of 18:19–23 appear to be of a more general and arbitrary

The "moral logic," if we can call it that, is made clear.[49] The Canaanites made themselves unclean by committing these "abominations," and as a result the land vomited out its inhabitants. The prohibition against male prostitution in Deuteromomy 23:17–18 also has Canaanite practice in view: it is one of the "abominations of the nations that the LORD drove out before the people of Israel" (1 Kgs 14:24). If the people of Israel do these things, they can expect the land to vomit them out likewise (Lev 18:24–28). For this reason, offenders must be "cut off" from the people. Repentance and atonement are not an option; the uncleanness has to be immediately and actually eliminated.[50] The penalties are set out in Leviticus 20:10–21. In the case of male same-sex activity: "If a man lies with a male as with a woman, both of them have committed an abomination; they shall surely be put to death; their blood is upon them" (Lev 20:13). The people of Israel will inherit the land that formerly belonged to the Canaanites, therefore they must not "walk in the customs of the nation that I am driving out before you." "You shall be holy to me, for I the LORD am holy and have separated you from the peoples, that you should be mine" (Lev 20:26). Davidson overstates the matter, however, when he says that the application of the law against homosexuality to the Canaanites and to resident aliens makes it "universal moral law, not just ritual law pertaining only to Israel."[51] The limiting factor, as far as the argument goes, is not the ritual purity of Israel *as a people* but the health of the *land*. The Canaanites and sojourners are implicated because they once were or now are living in the land that God promised to Abraham. The universal perspective is not irrelevant, but in the narrative foreground is the story about a land set apart for God's people.

---

nature, ungoverned by concerns about kinship.

49. Brownson argues that for purposes of interpretation today a distinction needs to be maintained between what is being said in any particular passage and the underlying "moral logic" of Scripture as a whole: "We must discern the deeper and more comprehensive moral logic that undergirds the specific commands, prohibitions, and examples of the biblical text. We do not interpret rightly any single passage of Scripture until we locate the text within this larger fabric of meaning in Scripture as a whole" (Brownson, *Bible*, 9).

50. See Loader, *New Testament*, 24; Gagnon, "Old Testament and Homosexuality," 14–15. There are purificatory remedies for the pollution of the sanctuary (Lev 11–16), but the Holiness Code "provides no countervailing measures for the polluted land. The land stores its defilement nonstop until it vomits out its inhabitants" (Milgrom, *Leviticus*, 1567).

51. Davidson, *Flame*, 155.

The specific rationale for the objection to a man lying with a "male as with a woman," however, is not easy to determine. Milgrom thinks that there must be a reason for the prohibition because the "absolute ban on anal intercourse is unique not only in the Bible but . . . in the entire ancient Near Eastern and classical world."[52] His view is that the "*legal reason for interdicting anal intercourse* . . . is the waste, the nonproductive spilling, of seed."[53] Scholars who wish to generalize the prohibition may argue that same-sex relations were regarded as a violation of the biological complementarity of the creation order: "The use of 'male' (*zaqar*) alongside 'man' and 'woman' (*ish* and *ishshah*) creates an echo of the creation accounts in Genesis 1 and 2; it is plausible to see the serious nature of the offence as reflecting its rejection of God's creation order of 'male and female.'"[54] But the echo is very faint: we do not have the characteristic pairing of "male" and "female"; and elsewhere in Leviticus mention of the "male" (whether or not in conjunction with the "female") entails no reference to the creation accounts. The law concerning a bodily discharge, for example, is "for anyone, male or female . . . and for the man who lies with a woman who is unclean" (Lev 15:33; cf. 27:3, 5–7). However we are precisely to understand the offensiveness of anal intercourse, it has to do fundamentally with the status and condition of the land surrounded by unclean nations.[55] The "end" of the story that is in view, of course, is the exile.

52. Milgrom, *Leviticus*, 1566.

53. Milgrom, *Leviticus*, 1568. Via lists four reasons for the Old Testament's objection to homosexuality: it makes a person unclean and therefore limits association with other people and access to God; it "compromises purity in the production of male heirs to hold the land"; it violates the boundary between Israel and the nations; and according to the values of patriarchal culture it is an "affront to male honor" (Via, "Bible," 8).

54. Paul, *Same-Sex Unions*, 14; cf. Davidson, *Flame*, 155–57; Hill, "Christ," 132–33.

55. Note Loader, *New Testament*, 26: "The language of purity suggests that what lies behind the prohibition is the sense of order, which pervades the laws concerning holiness, and is about community solidarity, not least in the face of the threat of surrounding cultures."

CHAPTER 4

The Greek-Roman Cultural Background

THE BIBLICAL TEXTS CONDEMN same-sex sexual activity among members of the covenant community, but in both the Old Testament and the New Testament this is against a background of ancient cultural assumptions and practices. The Old Testament has in view behavior associated with the Canaanites in particular, the former inhabitants of the land: the homosexual rape of outsiders, male cultic prostitution (cf. 1 Kgs 14:23–24; 15:12; 22:46; 2 Kgs 23:7), and more generally a man lying with a man as with a woman. Apart from the brief biblical references, however, there is little material available from which to construct a satisfactory picture of same-sex sexual activity or how it was evaluated in the Ancient Near East.[1] Bird thinks that what evidence there is generally "supports the view that sexual relations (of all types) were defined and judged according to gender-role prescriptions that identified the male as the active partner and the female as the passive."[2] This was the controlling moral assumption across the region during the period: with few exceptions, it was considered shameful and dishonoring for an adult male to be used as a woman for sexual purposes.

The New Testament has in view the prevalence of homosexual practices in the Greek-Roman world. It will be apparent from Paul's argument in Romans 1:18–32 that his opposition to such behavior formed part of a characteristically Jewish critique of the dominant pagan culture. In order to understand the terms and scope of his censure, therefore, we

---

1. See Bird, "Bible," 158–61, 173–76.

2. Bird, "Bible," 158; cf. Gagnon, "Bible and Homosexual Practice," 60; Davidson, *Flame*, 134–42.

have to take into account not only its relation to the Jewish scriptures but also the likely nature of the phenomenon under consideration.[3] The literary evidence relates mainly to higher levels of Greek and Roman society. We can probably assume that the lifestyle of the rich and famous, real or imagined, was a popular topic of conversation at all levels of society. There is, in any case, no reason to think that homosexual behavior and interest in it were confined to social elites. William Loader notes, for example, that pottery depicting explicit sexual activity, including same-sex sexual activity, was mass-produced and widely used by ordinary people.[4] The frequent appearance of homosexual themes in the comedies of Plautus suggests that "such realities were a fact of life quite familiar to his audience, as familiarly Roman as the references to food, topography, military and political themes, and indeed heterosexual behaviour."[5] Graffiti found at Pompeii point to the existence of a "thriving homosexual subculture" in the city before it was destroyed by the eruption of Vesuvius in 79 AD.[6] But practices and attitudes are much harder to evaluate at this level than is the case with the extensively documented phenomenon of aristocratic pederasty.[7]

THE GREEK IDEAL OF MALE LOVE

Same-sex sexual activity in Ancient Greece is commonly encountered in the context of a pederastic relationship between an adolescent boy (the *erōmenos* or "beloved") and an older man (the *erastēs* or "lover").[8] Pederasty (*paiderastia*) was a more or less institutionalized aspect of a boy's education, at least among the ruling elite. How keen boys were to receive this sort of attention in the first place is unclear, and it appears that fathers might do their best to prevent their sons being seduced.[9] In Plato's *Symposium*, Pausanias observes that "fathers put tutors in charge of their boys when they are beloved, to prevent them from conversing with their lovers," though he maintains that this is an example of doing pederasty "nobly"

---

3. See further Loader, *New Testament*, 32–33, 83–91; Hubbard, *Homosexuality*.

4. Loader, *New Testament*, 89.

5. Williams, "Greek Love," 519.

6. Hubbard, *Homosexuality*, 384.

7. Cf. Scroggs, *New Testament*, 17.

8. For discussion of the definition and parameters of pederasty see Smith, "Ancient Bisexuality," 229–31.

9. See Ruden, *Paul*, 62–63.

(*Symp.* 183C–E). On the other hand, Xenophon has Socrates praise Callias because he invites the father of his beloved Autolycus to their meetings: "For the gentlemanly lover does not conceal any of this from his beloved's father" (*Symp.* 8.11). Kenneth Dover speculates that many boys would have found praise of physical beauty, gifts, and social advancement hard to resist.[10] The relationship would normally end when either the "beloved" attained manhood or the "lover" reached his late twenties, when he was expected to marry. Discussions in ancient medical literature suggest that a continued preference for playing the passive role after the normal period of the pederastic relationship was regarded as a disease, either of the mind or of the body, though some theorists proposed biological or "genetic" explanations for the existence of people who did not conform to the standard types of male and female.[11]

It has been a matter of particular controversy for the interpretation of the biblical prohibitions whether long-term, loving same-sex relationships were known in antiquity and whether Paul, in particular, would have included them in his condemnation along with more obviously dehumanizing forms of homosexual activity. The case for affirming same-sex relationships would be stronger if it could be shown that the apostle could not have had in mind the modern egalitarian ideal.[12] Much of the evidence from the Greek world cited against this line of thought by conservative scholars comes from three philosophical "conversation" texts spanning the period. Plato's *Symposium* (late fourth century BC) famously presents a fictional dialogue among notable men at a drinking party. Speeches are made in praise of Love; three of the speakers (Phaedrus, Pausanias and Aristophanes) put forward a defense of male love.[13] In Plutarch's *Amatorius* (late first century/early second century AD) Protogenes makes the case for pederasty and is opposed by Daphnaeus and Pisias. Finally, in the *Amores* or *Affairs of the Heart* of Pseudo-Lucian (c. 300 AD) Callicratidas and Charicles almost come to blows over the question of whether the love of boys or the love of women is superior.[14]

10. Dover, *Greek Homosexuality*, 89–90.

11. Schoedel, "Same-Sex Eros," 52–59.

12. See DeYoung, *What Does the Bible*, 83–86, for a catalogue of scholars who argue that something like persistent same-sex orientation was known in the ancient world.

13. Xenophon's more frivolous *Symposium*, written perhaps twenty years after Plato's, touches on similar themes of male love but in the context of broader philosophical banter, possibly with satirical intent (see Huss, "Dancing Sokrates").

14. A similar debate in Achilles Tatius *Leuc. Clit.* 2.35–38 (Hubbard, *Homosexuality*,

The discussions are worth listening to in some detail—the topic is frequently summarized but rarely presented in its own terms. They do not constitute exact historical observation, but they give a lively and accessible impression of the place that same-sex relations had in cultured Greek society. The later works are no doubt emulations of Plato to a degree. They have their own biases—Plutarch, for example, sets much greater store by heterosexual married love. But they suggest that the debate remained vigorous in the Greek world for centuries spanning the New Testament period. I will argue that when Paul speaks in Romans about the Greek who does evil or does good (Rom 2:9–10), the "Greek" is not a representative of humanity in general. Paul is thinking specifically of the Greek—or more broadly Greek-Roman—culture that he encountered in the Hellenized cities of the eastern empire. The better we understand that world, the better we will understand Paul. We may also gain some insight into the profound differences between the world in which Jews and Greeks clashed over sexuality and our own.

In brief, the defenders of cultured pederasty put forward three arguments: 1) male love is superior to female love, for the simple reason that the male is superior to the female; 2) pederastic relationships may develop into rewarding lifelong attachments; and 3) pedagogic pederasty—that is, pederasty as a form of mentorship and training—is reckoned to serve the public good.

The Superiority of Male Love

In the *Symposium* of Plato, Pausanias differentiates between two types of love: one that is vulgar, which takes both women and youths as its object, and is associated with the "meaner sort of men," who "are set on the body more than the soul"; another that is noble, which is the love of the male only "in fondness for what has the robuster nature and a larger share of mind" (*Symp.* 181A–D).[15] Men who pursue this higher form of love are attracted to boys "only when they begin to acquire some mind—a growth associated with that of down on their chins." They will not "take advantage

---

484–87) is confined to a discussion of physical appearance and sexual performance.

15. Cf. Xenophon *Symp.* 8.9–10: "Now, whether there is one Aphrodite or two, Celestial and Popular, I do not know. . . . I do know, however, that for each Aphrodite there are separate altars, temples, and sacrifices, those of the Popular rather casual, those of the Celestial more holy. You might conjecture also that different types of love come from the different sources, love for bodies from the Popular and from the Celestial love of souls, friendship, and fine deeds."

of a boy's green thoughtlessness to deceive him and make a mock of him by running straight off to another." Such exploitation of prepubescent boys is the sort of thing that gets pederasty a bad name and should be made illegal, in Pausanias's view, whereas "whatsoever is done in an orderly and lawful manner can never justly bring reproach" (181D–182A). The argument presupposes a society in which significant social interactions are confined more or less exclusively to the domain of the male: "public culture of these centuries was male oriented, and the apposite *intellectual and, indeed, affective partner to a male was another male*."[16] Men may either seek to satisfy wanton sexual cravings by loving the body, whether of young men or of women, or they may develop long-term friendships, grounded in more intellectual pleasures. In the texts the possibility of having a sexually intimate relationship with an intelligent and educated *woman* is barely considered. The conclusion that Dover reaches in attempting to account for the prevalence of homosexuality in classical Greek society is that "the need in question was a need for personal relationships of an intensity not commonly found within marriage or in the relations between parents and children or in those between the individual and the community as a whole."[17]

A similar sentiment is expressed by Protogenes in Plutarch's *Amatorius*. Marriage between men and women is "necessary for producing children" (*Amat.* 750C), but romantic attachment to women and girls falls short of true love. "Love . . . it is that attaches himself to a young and talented [male] soul and through friendship brings it to a state of virtue; but the appetite for women we are speaking of, however well it turns out, has for net gain only an accrual of pleasure in the enjoyment of a ripe physical beauty" (750D). The love of women offers soft and enervated pleasures but is "devoid of manliness and friendship and inspiration." The love of boys, by contrast, is "simple and unspoiled. You will see it in the schools of philosophy, or perhaps in the gymnasia and palaestrae, searching for young

---

16. Scroggs, *New Testament*, 23. Thornton remarks on the link between pederasty and the symposia: "Both were aristocratic cultural institutions whose function was to exploit pederastic eros for the inculcation of aristocratic values" (Thornton, *Eros*, 199).

17. Dover, *Greek Homosexuality*, 201; cf. Vasey's comments on "transgenerational" homosexuality in societies where "the male and female spheres of life are kept radically separate and young boys have to make the demanding transition from the maternal world of their early years" (Vasey, *Strangers*, 75–76). The educated woman may have been less rare in the Roman setting but was nevertheless clearly the exception rather than the rule (Scroggs, *New Testament*, 20–21).

men whom it cheers on with a clear and noble cry to the pursuit of virtue when they are found worthy of its attention" (751A–B).[18] This high-minded apology for male love is somewhat deflated by Daphnaeus, who thinks that Protogenes's talk of "friendship and virtue" is a pretext "because of the law." When night comes, "Sweet is the harvest when the guard's away" (Solon). He does not believe Protogenes's claim that "there is no sexual partnership in paederasty" (752A).

Pseudo-Lucian's proponent of male love, the Athenian Callicratidas, also maintains that Eros is a "twofold god" (*[Am.]* 37). One Eros inspires in the foolish a base and sometimes violent lust for women; the other Eros is the "dispenser of temperate passions who sends his kindly breath into the minds of all," combining pleasure with virtue. He ardently depicts the young man who is not only physically beautiful but also educated in philosophy and all types of knowledge and trained in athletics and war, and exclaims: "Who would not fall in love with such a youth?" (46).[19] The male is more attractive to the cultured Greek because he is in all respects—physically, intellectually, morally—superior to the female.[20] The force of the argument is confirmed by Lycinus's verdict on the debate. Marriage has its use, he admits, but he considers the love of boys to be "the privilege only of philosophy"; for "perfect virtue grows least of all among women" (51). But then Theomnestus dismisses the "highbrow words" of Callicratidas as so much bombast and recommends a more down-to-earth, carnal approach to young boys (53–54). Charicles complains that "it is lovers of youth rather than of wisdom who give honourable names to dishonourable passions and call physical beauty virtue of the soul" (24).

Aristocratic pretension to a higher form of love is a soft target for satire, but it appears to have been the case that, in the earlier period at least, anal sex was frowned upon as degrading for both parties and that somewhat "innocent" forms of physical intimacy were considered normal

18. Cf. Hubbard, *Homosexuality*, 12: the goal of pederasty was not to "objectify and subordinate" the boys but to "advance their socialization into the elite male world of the symposium and athletics, and eventually politics and the life of the mind. Indeed, it was to make them as much like their lover as possible, a true mirror image."

19. Hubbard notes that the *palaestra* (a private wrestling school) was a "favorite gathering place for upper-class adolescent boys and their older admirers" (Hubbard, *Homosexuality*, 3); see also Dover, *Greek Homosexuality*, 68–73.

20. Dover makes the point that among the rich the male was also more accessible: "a young man's opportunities for love-affairs with girls of his own class were minimal, and if he was to enjoy the triumph of leisurely seduction (rather than the flawed satisfaction of purchase) he must seduce a boy" (Dover, *Greek Homosexuality*, 149).

and preferable.²¹ So, for example, Callicratidas cites the view of Socrates that the love of boys is "the greatest of boons" but insists that boys must be loved in the same way that Alcibiades was loved by Socrates, "who slept like a father with him under the same cloak" (Lucian *[Am.]* 49).²² The reference is to a night of unrequited affection that Alcibiades spent wrapped up with Socrates in his cloak: "when I arose I had in no more particular sense slept a night with Socrates than if it had been with my father or my elder brother" (Plato *Symp.* 219D). The incident illustrates the point that homosexual eros, because it is not directed toward procreation, was "significant as a step towards the world of Being" and absolute Beauty, as Dover puts it.²³ Pederastic relationships were rarely chaste, but the intention was to prepare the boy for membership of the same cultural and political elite, not to degrade him to the level of slave or male prostitute. So Thornton writes: "The 'technology' of boy-love . . . requires a delicate balancing act between acknowledging the power of homosexual eros without corrupting the boy who is its object, turning him into the dreaded *kinaidos*."²⁴ The precise meaning of the derogatory term *kinaidos* (or *cinaedus* in Latin) is uncertain, but it seems to have referred to men who for one reason or another were regarded as sexual perverts and pariahs. Thomas Hubbard says that it potentially included "anyone who is perceived as sexually excessive or deviant."²⁵

21. Hubbard notes satirical texts that "take it for granted that these philosophical pretensions were fraudulent covers" (Hubbard, *Homosexuality*, 9), but Scroggs thinks it "unduly skeptical to doubt that the philosophical ideal was often realized" (Scroggs, *New Testament*, 32). By the time we get to Pseudo-Lucian it appears that "both defenders and detractors of pederasty assume the sexual act is anal in nature" (Scroggs, *New Testament*, 35).

22. See Dover, *Greek Homosexuality*, 157–58.

23. Dover, *Greek Homosexuality*, 161–65; see Scroggs, *New Testament*, 24–28, on the Greek ideal of beauty.

24. Thornton, *Eros*, 196. Hubbard also maintains that pederasty would not normally involve penetration or the debasement of the youth (Hubbard, *Homosexuality*, 10–11; cf. Jewett and Kotansky, *Romans*, 178n141).

25. Hubbard, *Homosexuality*, 7.

Life-Long Attachment

Pederastic relationships were by definition short-lived: "Youth's time with its torch is running by."[26] The "beloved" (*erōmenos*) would acquire a beard and perhaps go on to become a "lover" (*erastēs*) himself, and the lover would normally marry.[27] Hubbard relates an encounter in Theocritus's *Idyll* 5 between two shepherds who had previously been in a homosexual relationship: the younger has become "the lover of a boy in his own right" while the older "has graduated to the love of women."[28] Broadly speaking, in a patriarchal honor-shame culture, pederasty could be tolerated only as long as the youthful "passive" partner in the relationship remained *womanlike* in appearance and therefore of a lower status.[29] Nevertheless, the ideal of a virtuous and cultured pederasty, with its emphasis on like-minded friendship, appears to have given rise to the possibility of long-term male same-sex relationships.[30]

Plato's Pausanias thinks it likely that the relationship between a man in his twenties and a boy in his late teens, if it is an expression of the higher form of love, will endure throughout life (*Symp.* 181D). We know from other sources that his relationship with the poet Agathon, who also appears in the *Symposium*, lasted into later life.[31] Aristophanes will offer an elaborate mythological explanation of the persistence of same-sex attraction (189C–192E). Humans originally existed in three forms: male, female and androgynous; but in order to curb their power and ambition Zeus split each form into two, with the result that people are always searching for their other half: so we have male-male pairs, female-female pairs, and

26. Alcaeus of Messene *AP* 12.29 (c. 200 BC) (Hubbard, *Homosexuality*, 291).

27. See Dover, *Greek Homosexuality*, 86; Hubbard, *Homosexuality*, 5–6.

28. Hubbard, *Homosexuality*, 269. See, in particular, Theocritus, *Id.* 5.132–35. Judging by the tone of the piece and the social setting of the two participants in this ribald singing contest, it was not your typical pederastic relationship (cf. *Id.* 5.116–19).

29. Stone, "Gender," 97–98.

30. Citing Dover, Loader says that in both the classical and Hellenistic periods Greek homosexuality "was not always seen as exploitative, and . . . same-sex sexual relations could include lifelong consensual adult partnerships" (Loader, *New Testament*, 324).

31. See Dover, *Greek Homosexuality*, 84, 144; Hubbard, *Homosexuality*, 6. Smith notes, "The focus of Pausanias's speech is that his relationship with Agathon is superior to common pederasty (and to heterosexual relationships), precisely because it has endured and is based on their loving regard for one another's souls" (Smith, "Ancient Bisexuality," 235). Xenophon has Socrates argue that love of the soul is superior to, and will outlast, love of the body (*Symp.* 8.12–15).

male-female pairs. When a man and a woman embrace, they breed; when two males come together, they are physically satisfied and then "turn their hands to their labors and their interest to ordinary life." In this way, the ancient, deeply ingrained desire for another reunites our original nature, "reassembling our early estate and endeavoring to combine two in one and heal the human sore." There are men, therefore, who are born to be lovers of youths. They have no natural inclination to marry and have children, and will do so only because it is expected of them socially; otherwise, "they are quite contented to live together unwedded all their days" (192A–B).[32] In most cases, they will pass from one boy to another as each transitions into adulthood, but when one of them "happens on his own particular half, the two of them are wondrously thrilled with affection and intimacy and love, and are hardly to be induced to leave each other's side for a single moment" (192C). This suggests that unostentatious, lifelong, same-sex cohabitation was not unknown.[33] Callicratidas differentiates between the "cheap thrill" of sexual exploitation and the love of virtuous boys that would endure into old age. "For my part, ye gods of heaven," he exclaims, "I pray that it may for ever be my lot in life to sit opposite my dear one and hear close to me his sweet voice, to go out when he goes out and share every activity with him" (Lucian [Am.] 46). He describes, rather touchingly, how Orestes and Pylades, taking Eros as a witness of their love, "sailed together as it were on the same vessel of life."[34]

With Aristophanes's myth in mind Dover says that "Greek recognition that some people are more homosexual than others need not surprise us"; and Hubbard lists a number of other texts that appear to view "male

32. Philo was unimpressed by the argument: "I pass over in silence the different fabulous fictions, and the stories of persons with two bodies, who having originally been stuck to one another by amatory influences, are subsequently separated like portions which have been brought together and are disjoined again, the harmony having been dissolved by which they were held together" (Contempl. 63).

33. Cf. Schoedel, "Same-Sex Eros," 46–47; Via, "Bible," 15.

34. Gagnon notes two second century AD romances that include "tragic love stories about similar-aged, male lovers": Xenophon of Ephesus An Ephesian Tale 3.2; Achilles Tatius Leuc. Clit. 1.7–8, 12–14, 2.33–34 (Gagnon, "Not To Be Embraced," 68–69). He may have misrepresented the relationships. In An Ephesian Tale Hippothous falls in love with Hyperanthes at school. We are told that the closeness of age removed all suspicion regarding their relationship, and they do not get beyond "kisses and caresses." Hyperanthes was still a "youth" (meirakion) when he tragically died (3.12). In the two stories in Leucippe and Clitophon it appears that an older man loves a "youth" (meirakion: 1.7.1; 2.34.1). The term would normally designate a young man between eighteen and twenty-one (Hubbard, Homosexuality, 5).

sexual passivity" as an "inborn" or "essential" aspect of human identity, attributable to faulty conception, congenital defects, childhood abuse, or divine bungling. In the early first century AD Phaedrus attributed the existence of lesbians and "effeminate males" (*tribadas et molles mares*) to the ineptitude of the god Prometheus when drunk, who fitted male parts to some women and female parts to some men: "Hence lust now gratifies itself with a perverted pleasure" (*Fables* 4.16.14).[35] The Greek novelist Longus (second/third century AD) says of a character that he was a "pederast by nature" (*physei paiderastēs*) (*Daphn.* 4.11.2, my translation). Astrological texts offered their own distinctive explanations: different alignments of the planets will produce men who "have relations with both males and females, but no more than moderately inclined to either," or who are "infected only with love of boys" or "with males of any age" (Ptolemy *Tetrabiblos* 4.5.188). Brooten concludes that astrologers in the Roman world would have understood our modern idea of sexual orientation but would not have limited it to homosexual and heterosexual: "these ancient writers believed that configurations of the stars created a broad range of sexual inclinations and orientations."[36]

To what extent a pattern of stable homosexual relationships emerges in the Greek cultural context apart from the standard pederastic arrangement is unclear. Mark Smith suggests that there is abundant "literary evidence for non-pederastic homosexual practices," but the examples he gives are questionable.[37] The relationship between Critobulus and Cleinias may not have been the normal pederastic one, but Critobulus becomes infatuated with Cleinias while at school; they are both barely bearded (Xenophon *Symp.* 4.23). In Plato's *Euthydemus* Cleinias (again) and Ctesippus belong to a group of pupils; Cleinias, in fact, is followed by a "whole troop of lovers (*erastai*)"; he is described as the "favorite" (*paidika*) of Ctesippus (*Euthyd.* 273A–B, 274C). Charmides is a young man, also pursued by a bevy of "lovers" (*erastai*), greatly admired for his physical beauty (Plato *Charm.*

---

35. Dover, *Greek Homosexuality*, 62; Hubbard, *Homosexuality*, 2; and page 390 for Phaedrus. Aristotle *[Probl]* 4.26 offers a medical explanation of why "some men enjoy being the passive partner in the sexual act" (in Hubbard, *Homosexuality*, 262–64). Hippocrates attributes effeminacy (and "mannishness" in women) both to genetic factors and to upbringing (*On Regimen* 1.28–29, in Hubbard, *Homosexuality*, 261–62). "Petronius' Encolpius . . . and Juvenal's Virro . . . are men who seem genuinely incapable of erectile performance with women" (Hubbard, *Homosexuality*, 386).

36. Brooten, *Love Between Women*, 140.

37. Smith, "Ancient Bisexuality," 235–36.

154B–C). Philolaus "became the lover (*erastēs*) of Diocles the winner at Olympia," which presumably means that Diocles was young, even if they went on to set up home in Thebes and were buried together (Aristotle, *Pol.* 1274A). We are not here far outside the bounds of pederastic convention, if at all. Beautiful adolescent youths are attractive to, and loved by, either their peers or young men.

Three other texts that Smith mentions barely disturb this conclusion. As part of his training, personified Virtue accuses Heracles of forcing lust "when there is no need, by all kinds of tricks and by using men as women," and encouraging his friends to run riot at night (Xenophon, *Mem.* 2.1.30), but there is clearly nothing reputable about this behavior. That Menon, while still beardless, had a "bearded favorite" is considered shocking and exceptional (Xenophon, *Anab.* 2.6.28). Whatever the nature of the same-sex relations practiced among the soldiers of the Theban Sacred Band, it does not constitute a model for normal social relationships. Plutarch says only that the Band was supposedly composed of men bonded in friendship pairs as lover and beloved (*Pel.* 18.1–3). These texts would appear, in fact, to be exceptions that prove the rule that Greek homosexual attraction, insofar as it was socially acceptable, centered on the beautiful youth, sometimes leading to relationships that continued outside the pedagogic setting.

Public Benefit

Male love is defended in these texts not only as an expression of cultured friendship but also on the grounds of public benefit. In Plato's *Symposium* Phaedrus regards pederasty as a guarantee of political integrity: "if we could somewise contrive to have a city or an army composed of lovers and their favourites, they could not be better citizens of their country than by thus refraining from all that is base in a mutual rivalry for honour" (178E–79A). Pausanias argues that male love, as an aspect of the wider Greek "training in philosophy and sports," is a defense against tyranny (182B–C). Aristophanes repudiates the charge that male love is shameless by claiming that "their behaviour is due not to shamelessness but to daring, manliness, and virility, since they are quick to welcome their like." The proof of the claim, he says, lies in the fact that "on reaching maturity these alone prove in a public career to be men" (192A). Socrates relates the argument of the wise woman Diotima that male love is superior because it begets not physical children but social virtues. A young man learns sobriety and justice as a youth. Upon reaching manhood he seeks a boy who is beautiful both in body and soul and takes responsibility for his education. In this way together they raise a superior "family": "men in this condition enjoy a far fuller community with each other than that which comes with children, and a far surer friendship, since the children of their union are fairer and more deathless" (209A–D). Pederasty is thus lauded as an ideal fusion of *eros* and philosophical education undergirding the moral and political character of the state; and it is again apparent that the practice was an integral component of an almost exclusively male public life.[38]

In Plutarch's *Amatorius* Pisias is at first impressed by Daphnaeus's rejection of the cultured defense of pederasty, but on reflection he sees no reason why love should be banished from the gymnasia and open spaces and confined "in brothels with the vanity-cases and unguents and philtres of disorderly females" (*Amat.* 752C). Male love flourished because Greek society was sharply divided between the male public sphere and the female private sphere. Pseudo-Lucian, finally, has Callicratidas defend same-sex relations as the product of a progressive and sophisticated Greek culture. Ancient societies could not afford the luxury of male love: it was all hands to the pump just to keep the species afloat. "But the manifold branches of wisdom and men's desire for this virtue that loves beauty were only with difficulty to be brought to light by time which leaves nothing unexplored, so that divine philosophy and with it love of boys might come to maturity" (Lucian, *[Am.]* 35).

An Enduring Ambivalence

The propriety or relative merit of male love does not go unchallenged in these dialogues.[39] We have heard Daphnaeus and Theomnestus pour scorn

---

38. Cf. Dover, *Greek Homosexuality*, 202: "the philosophical *paiderastiā* which is fundamental to Plato's expositions in *Phaedrus* and *Symposium* is essentially an exaltation, however starved of bodily pleasure, of a consistent Greek tendency to regard homosexual eros as a compound of an educational with a genital relationship." Dio Chrysostom (AD c. 40–120) had a quite different take on the relation between pederasty and public advancement. A man with an insatiable sexual appetite will scorn the easy conquest of the female and will "turn his assault against the male quarters, eager to befoul the youth who will very soon be magistrates and judges and generals, believing that in them he will find a kind of pleasure difficult and hard to procure" (*Ven.* 151–52).

39. Xenophon's *Symposium* is more critical of pederasty (Hubbard, *Homosexuality*, 164, 207–21).

on the high-minded pretension that pederasty has little to do with the satisfaction of ordinary sexual appetites. It could also be seen as damaging to natural and necessary heterosexual relations, by which mortal mankind is immortalized "by kindling afresh through new generations our being, prone as it is to extinction" (*Amat.* 752A). Charicles regards male love as degenerate—a decline from the original state of humanity—and a transgression of the laws of nature. They sow their seed on barren rocks, they "bought a little pleasure at the cost of great disgrace" (Lucian *[Am.]* 20). "If each man abided by the ordinances prescribed for us by Providence, we should be satisfied with intercourse with women and life would be un-corrupted by anything shameful" (*[Am.]* 22).

The impression is given, nevertheless, allowing for fluctuations in public mood over time, that cultured Greek male society in the period from Plato to Pseudo-Lucian was broadly bisexual.[40] The debates in themselves are evidence that Greek society was never entirely comfortable with the practice. There is ambivalence, but not outright condemnation. The ped-erastic relationship between an unmarried man and an adolescent youth represented in the eyes of many an ideal fusion of sexuality and cultured friendship that could not be found in heterosexual relationships, which was foundational not only for personal development but also for civic virtue and the well-being of the state. The naturalness and potential longevity of these relationships, moreover, were a crucial part of the defense, though in this respect they begin to sound more like "Platonic" friendships than sexual unions.

THE DARK SIDE OF SAME-SEX RELATIONS IN THE GREEK-ROMAN WORLD

Outside the bounds of a civilized pederasty a vulgar, dissolute, and damag-ing same-sex ecology appears to have flourished in both parts of the Medi-terranean world.[41] Plutarch's Daphnaeus disapproves of consorting with males "whether without consent, in which case it involves violence and brigandage; or if with consent, there is still weakness and effeminacy on the part of those who, contrary to nature, allow themselves in Plato's words "to be covered and mounted like cattle"" (*Amat.* 751D–E). Adult Greek men

---

40. Scroggs, *New Testament*, 27; and Smith, "Ancient Bisexuality," 243: "if there was any sexual 'model' in ancient Greece and Rome, it can best be described as bisexual."

41. Cf. Soards, *Scripture*, 48–50.

who took the passive role in anal sex were judged to have made women of themselves and were liable to ridicule and censure. "To choose to be treated as an object at the disposal of another citizen," Dover says, "was to resign one's own standing as a citizen."[42] Male prostitutes and related classes of men such as the *kinaidoi* were viewed with contempt, though that did not stop men using them. "I pity the boys," wrote Clement of Alexandria, "possessed by the slave-dealers that are decked for dishonour" (*Paidagogos* 3.3).

In the Roman context the basic division was between the dominant, active, masculine role and the submissive, passive, feminine role. The Greek pederastic model of romantic and sexual relations *with free-born youths* was viewed with disgust, though in the words of the French historian Paul Veyne: "Rome never opposed love of women to love of boys: she opposed activity to passivity; to be active is to be a male, whatever the sex of the passive partner."[43] Sex was not so much a shared activity or expression of mutuality—even between husband and wife—as something that a man *did to someone else*, either to satisfy sexual desire or to assert dominance. Craig Williams notes the prevailing assumption among Romans that "men normally experience desire for both female and male bodies, and that any given man might act out those desires with persons of one or the other sex, or both."[44] This could be attributed to an excess of sexual passion or a lack of self-control. "The usual supposition of writers during the Hellenistic period," Richard Hays says, "was that homosexual behavior was the result of insatiable lust seeking novel and more challenging forms of self-gratification."[45] The Roman Stoic philosopher Musonius Rufus (first century AD) condemns male same-sex behavior as "a monstrous thing and contrary to nature," but he sees it as an example of "sexual excess," symptomatic of "the life of luxury and self-indulgence."[46] The only legitimate alternative is heterosexual sex in marriage "for the purpose of begetting children." The possibility that a couple might engage in monogamous sexual relations

---

42. Dover, *Greek Homosexuality*, 104.

43. Veyne, "La Famille," 50 (my translation). Playing the active role, Williams says, "can justly be called the prime directive of masculine sexual behaviour for Romans, and it has an obvious relationship to hierarchical social structures" (Williams, *Roman Homosexuality*, 18).

44. Williams, *Roman Homosexuality*, 23. See also Paris, *End of Sexual Identity*, 64–66; Vines, *God and the Gay Christian*, 34–36.

45. Hays, "Relations," 200; cf. Vasey, *Strangers*, 132–33.

46. Musonius, *Discourse 12: On Sexual Indulgence* (Lutz, *Musonius Rufus*, 87); also Dover, *Greek Homosexuality*, 185–86.

for reasons other than procreation or that same-sex relations might be the expression of something other than licentiousness and self-indulgence is hardly considered. Scholars mostly agree that neither Jews nor pagans in the ancient world would have understood the modern distinction between heterosexual and homosexual people. The Greeks and Romans had no language to differentiate between heterosexual and homosexual, straight and gay, Smith says. "From their point of view humans are simply sexual, and they have expressed that sexuality in many different ways, with their own sex or the opposite or, perhaps more commonly, if pederastic practices tell us anything, with both at different times, maybe even at the same time."[47]

Penetrative sex was also a means of asserting dominance: "There is little dispute that in Rome sexual penetration was perceived as a mark of true masculinity, and so as a way of establishing or reiterating power over the one penetrated. A slave owner might routinely engage in anal intercourse with his male slaves to demonstrate his ownership."[48] It was acceptable for a freeborn Roman male to engage in penetrative sex with other men provided that he took the dominant role and that his partner was not also a freeborn Roman male. The submissive partner was likely to be a slave, prostitute, or entertainer. There was a natural preference for youths between the ages of twelve and twenty, though it appears that the Romans were less fussy about age than the Greeks.[49] As with the *kinaidoi* in the Greek world, there may have been a class of *cinaedi* in Rome who habitually took the passive role, who were deemed permanently degraded and subjected to something like our modern homophobia.[50] Roman law strictly prohibited same-sex intercourse between citizens.[51] For a freeborn Roman male to allow himself to be penetrated was an affront not only to his own dignity and status as a citizen but to the patriarchal-conquest ideology on which Roman power was founded.

---

47. Smith, "Ancient Bisexuality," 243–44; cf. Williams, *Roman Homosexuality*, 4; Paris, *End of Sexual Identity*, 41: "Most cultures that have ever been present on the earth, including biblical ones, didn't have heterosexuals. They didn't have homosexuals either, because heterosexuality requires homosexuality; each makes sense only with reference to the other."

48. Holmes, "Listening," 176; cf. Wilson, *Letter*, chap. 3, Kindle loc. 1003 of 3155.

49. Loader, *New Testament*, 90n94.

50. See Hubbard, *Homosexuality*, 7.

51. Loader, *New Testament*, 86.

GAY "MARRIAGE" IN THE ROMAN WORLD

Probably not all same-sex sexual relationships in the Roman world were abusive. It is a major part of Smith's critique of Robin Scroggs's thesis that Paul would have known that homosexual partnerships existed that were neither pederastic nor abusive.[52] Again, however, the evidence is of limited value. Dio Cassius gives a brief illustration of Caligula's bisexuality: "Drusilla was married to Marcus Lepidus, at once the favourite (*paidika*) and lover (*erastēs*) of the emperor, but Gaius also treated her as a concubine" (Dio Cassius, 59.11.1; cf. Suetonius, *Cal.* 36). The conspirator Catiline had a reputation for engaging in sordid homosexual liaisons (Cicero, *Red. sen.* 10–12); Cicero notes that one Consul claimed to have been Catiline's "lover" (*amatorem, delicias*) (*Red. sen.* 10; *Dom.* 62).[53] We can only guess at the nature of these "relationships," but it seems clear that they were subject to powerful political dynamics.

We find occasional reference to same-sex "marriage," after a fashion. The best known example, according to Smith, comes from Cicero's attack on Mark Antony, who was rescued from male prostitution by Curio, given a "married lady's robe as it were," and settled in "steady wedlock" (Cicero, *Phil.* 2.18.44–45). But the "as it were" (*tamquam*) rather suggests that "matrimony" is only a metaphor for the prolonged relationship, which in any case Cicero regarded as a matter of "shame and debauchery" (*stupra et flagitia*) (2.19.47). Nero had a boy called Sporus castrated and then "married him with all the usual ceremonies, including a dowry and a bridal veil, took him to his house attended by a great throng, and treated him as his wife" (Suetonius, *Nero* 28.1). Nero was later "married" as a wife to a certain Doryphorus "in the same way that he himself had taken Sporus, going so far as to imitate the cries and lamentations of a maiden being deflowered" (29).[54] Tacitus describes a dissolute entertainment at which Nero

52. Scroggs's argument is that the only model of same-sex behavior Paul could have had in mind was pederasty, which was typically exploitative and dehumanizing, raising the question of the "legitimacy of using New Testament judgments about a particular form and model of homosexuality to inform decisions about the acceptability of a contemporary form of homosexuality, which projects an entirely different model" (Scroggs, *New Testament*, 122). For a thorough critique see Smith, "Ancient Bisexuality," 226–32; also DeYoung, "Meaning of 'Nature'"; Soards, *Scripture*, 46–50; Brooten, *Love Between Women*, 256–57.

53. Smith, "Ancient Bisexuality," 237.

54. Smith says that there is no mention of Doryphorus being a slave; Suetonius describes him as a "freedman" (*liberto*).

became, with the full rites of legitimate marriage (*in modum sol-lemnium coniugiorum*), the wife of one of that herd of degenerates, who bore the name of Pythagoras. The veil was drawn over the imperial head, witnesses were despatched to the scene; the dowry, the couch of wedded love, the nuptial torches, were there: every-thing, in fine, which night enshrouds even if a woman is the bride, was left open to the view. (*Ann.* 15.37).

But this is merely play-acting. Juvenal (late first to early second century AD) is scandalized that "a man illustrious in family and fortune is handed over in marriage to another man"—complete with dowry, contract, a huge wedding feast, and wearing "the bride's flounces, long dress, and veil" (*Sat.* 2). Or consider these lines from the first-century AD Roman poet Martial: "Bearded Callistratus married rugged Afer in the usual form in which a virgin marries a husband. The torches shone in front, the wedding veil covered his face. . . . Even the dowry was declared. Are you still not satisfied, Rome? Are you waiting for him to give birth?" (*Ep.* 12.42; cf. 1.24). We are left with the distinct impression that these "marriages" were more often than not entered into in a frivolous, satirical, or subversive fashion and confined to a very small social-political elite. To what extent such unconventional practices entered into the ethical calculations of Jewish commentators such as Paul is difficult to say (we will revisit this matter), but the shock expressed by the satirists at such decadence ("O father of Rome," Juvenal exclaims, "where has it come from, this appalling outrage that afflicts the shepherds of Latium?") parallels Paul's narrative of the degradation of idolatrous "Greek" culture.

LESBIANISM

Considerably more is said about male than female homosexuality in the literature.[55] We have already noted Aristophanes's finely symmetrical thesis regarding the origins of male and female same-sex attraction presented in Plato's *Symposium* (*Symp.* 189C–192E). The conclusion is reached: "All the women who are sections of the woman have no great fancy for men: they are inclined rather to women, and of this stock are the she-minions (*hetair-istriai*)" (191E). In language that foreshadows Paul's argument in Romans

---

55. Dover remarks on "the paucity of women writers and artists in the Greek world and the virtual silence of male writers and artists on these topics" (Dover, *Greek Homo-sexuality*, 171).

1:26–27, Plato has the Athenian express the view that "when male unites with female for procreation the pleasure experienced is held to be due to nature, but contrary to nature when male mates with male or female with female, and that those first guilty of such enormities were impelled by their slavery to pleasure" (*Laws* 636C). Speaking about the practice of pederasty in Sparta, Plutarch notes that "this sort of love was so approved among them that even the maidens found lovers in good and noble women" (Plutarch, *Lyc.* 18.4). The Jewish moralist known to us as Pseudo-Phocylides warns not to let women "imitate the sexual role of men" (Ps.-Phoc. 192). Clement of Alexandria, toward the end of the second century AD, complains bitterly that luxury has corrupted sexual relations: "Men play the part of women, and women that of men, contrary to nature (*para physin*); women are at once wives and husbands" (*Paidagogos* 3.3).[56]

Loader says that "love between women was deemed unnatural, even in the animal world . . . and offensive."[57] Ovid tells the story of Iphis, a girl brought up as a boy, who falls in love with Ianthe, daughter of the Cretan Telestes, and is transformed into a real boy by Isis on the eve of her wedding. Before that happy outcome Iphis laments her "strange and monstrous love": "Cows do not love cows, nor mares, mares; but the ram desires the sheep, and his own doe follows the stag. So also birds mate, and in the whole animal world there is no female smitten with love for female. I would I were no female!" (*Metam.* 9.731–35; cf. Ps.-Phoc. 190–91). Hubbard notes that in the early imperial period references to lesbianism are almost always "deeply hostile and couched in terms of women taking on men's roles."[58] "Unlike the sources on male-male couplings," Brooten says, "some of which promote and some of which reject such couplings, the ancient sources nearly uniformly condemn sexual love between women."[59] Some scholars argue, however, that a measure of female emancipation was underway in

56. Hubbard, *Homosexuality*, 269–71; but note Loader, *New Testament*, 84–85, n62. Lucian of Samosata (second century AD) relates a salacious conversation about a manlike woman from Lesbos called Megilla who is supposedly married to a woman from Corinth called Demonassa (*Dialogues of the Courtesans* 5). Megilla explains her sexuality: "I was born with a body entirely like that of all women, but I have the tastes and desires of a man." Ptolemy of Alexandria, *Tetrabiblos* 3.14 (second century AD): "the females are lustful for unnatural congresses, cast inviting glances of the eye, and are what we call *tribades*; for they deal with females and perform the functions of males. . . . sometimes they even designate the women with whom they are on such terms as their lawful 'wives.'"

57. Loader, *New Testament*, 89; also Jewett and Kotansky, *Romans*, 174–75.

58. Hubbard, *Homosexuality*, 385; see further pages 16–17.

59. Brooten, *Love Between Women*, 359; cf. Jewett and Kotansky, *Romans*, 175.

the Roman world that may have given greater scope for female same-sex sexual activity.[60] Smith concludes that "the most prevalent form of female homosexual practice involved mutually consenting women of roughly equal age"—the significance of which is that it will be harder to claim that Paul condemned only abusive, non-consensual same-sex relations.[61]

JEWISH ATTITUDES

Jewish writings from the Greek-Roman period uniformly condemn same-sex activity as a leading example of Gentile depravity, typically in the form of pederasty, male prostitution, and generally dissolute behavior.[62] According to one apocalyptic text, the Jews do not "engage in impious intercourse with male children, as do Phoenicians, Egyptians, and Romans, spacious Greece and many nations of others, Persians and Galatians and all Asia, transgressing the holy law of immortal God, which they transgressed." These peoples will incur "disaster and famine and woes and groans and war and pestilence and lamentable ills, because they were not willing to piously honor the immortal begetter of all men, but honored idols made by hand, revering them" (*Sib. Or.* 3:596–603; cf. 3:184–85, 764; 4:34). Another oracle denounces the "Effeminate and unjust" city of Rome, "unclean in all things," notorious for its adulteries and "illicit intercourse with boys (*paidōn*)" (*Sib. Or.* 5:166–67). Pseudo-Aristeas (mid-second century BC) is appalled that countries and cities pride themselves on "intercourse with men," among other vices (*Let. Aris.* 152, trans. Evans). In a vision of the last days in the *Apocalypse of Abraham* (first to second century AD) are depicted "naked men, forehead to forehead, and their shame and the harm (they wrought) against their friends and their retribution" (*Apoc. Ab.* 24:8). We will see that Paul shares something of the keen apocalyptic perspective illustrated by these texts.

Same-sex sexual activity was commonly attributed by Jewish writers to disordered desire on the part of men who would normally engage in heterosexual relations, licit or otherwise.[63] The basic objection was to heterosexual men departing from "natural" sexual relations with women

---

60. Ward, "Why Unnatural?," 279–84; cf. Scroggs, *New Testament*, 20–21.

61. Smith, "Ancient Bisexuality," 243.

62. See Loader, *New Testament*, 32–33, for a concise summary of the evidence.

63. Josephus tells the story of how Mark Antony was sexually attracted both to Mariamne, Herod's wife, and to her brother Aristobulus (*Ant.* 15.25–30).

(within the bounds of social convention) to engage in homosexual acts, either for cultic purposes or more typically in order to satisfy an excessive sexual appetite.[64] Philo judged pederasty to be an evil not because of the age difference between the partners but because it resulted in the feminization of the passive partner.[65] He complains of Plato's *Symposium* that "the greater part of the book is occupied by common, vulgar, promiscuous love, which takes away from the soul courage, that which is the most serviceable of all virtues both in war and in peace, and which engenders in it instead the female disease, and renders men men-women (*androgynous*), though they ought rather to be carefully trained in all the practices likely to give men valour" (*Contempl.* 60). Like Pseudo-Aristeas he expresses horror at the evil which has been "let loose upon cities, namely, the love of boys," which inflicts on boys the shame of being transformed both visually and functionally into women and renders them useless for the normal male business of "acts of courage" and propagation of the species (*Spec. Laws* 3 37–39).[66] He considers it reasonable for Law-abiding Jews to have a "murderous" (*phonan*) attitude toward such people "since the Law commands that the man-woman (*androgynon*) who falsifies the coinage of nature should die with impunity, not permitting him to live one day or even an hour, being a disgrace to himself, family, and country, and to the whole race of humankind" (*Spec. Laws* 3 38, my translation).

CONCLUSIONS

As far as appraisal of the New Testament prohibitions is concerned, there are two very different patterns of male same-sex behavior to be considered: the Greek model of pederastic male-love as a semi-respectable component of the education and socialization of high status boys; and a range of promis-cuous, orgiastic, debauched, subversive, abusive, and exploitative practices that were either judged morally unacceptable or regarded as unavoidable in male-dominated, hierarchical, slave-owning cultures. The first pattern gave

64. See Vines, *God and the Gay Christian*, 33–34; Jewett and Kotansky, *Romans*, 176.

65. On Philo see Schoedel, "Same-Sex Eros," 49–52.

66. See also his comments on the corruption of the men of Sodom, who "became accustomed to be treated like women, and in this way engendered among themselves the disease of females, and intolerable evil; for they not only, as to effeminacy and delicacy, became like women in their persons, but they made also their souls most ignoble, corrupting in this way the whole race of man, as far as depended on them" (Philo, *Abraham* 136).

rise to some notion of same-sex sexual behavior as natural, consensual, and occasionally enduring, which begins to look like the modern phenomenon of loving, lasting relationships between people who are innately same-sex attracted. But such developments remained firmly within the sphere of an aristocratic homosocial order, and for the most part pederasty was acceptable insofar as the boy was aesthetically and socially woman-like. Lesbianism was a category apart—neither socially sanctioned nor a direct affront to patriarchy, just strange and repulsive to men.

Both patterns of male same-sex behavior in the Greek-Roman world can be seen as the product of an entrenched and unquestioned patriarchalism. Either it was an assertion of status, an expression of domination, and a means of extreme sexual gratification, or it presupposed a male social order that discounted women as intellectual companions and relegated normal heterosexual relations to a lower form of "love." Both types are routinely condemned in the Jewish literature of the second temple period on the grounds that same-sex sexual activity is contrary to nature, physically repugnant, morally degrading, self-indulgent, condemned by the Law, and an abomination in the sight of God. No fine distinctions are made by the Jewish writers between pederasty and male prostitution or the sexual exploitation of slaves, perhaps with some justification. The classical scholar Sarah Ruden pours scorn on pederasty as merely an aristocratic version of the degrading abuse of the weak and powerless that characterized all same-sex behavior in the ancient world: "Readers may think that I am exaggerating, that the day-to-day culture of homosexuality could not have been so bad. They may have heard of Platonic homoerotic sublimity or festive or friendly couplings. None of the sources, objectively read, backs any of this up."[67] It seems to me that she *is* exaggerating, but we should not imagine that the institution of pederasty was above reproach.

The more positive side to the uncompromising Jewish opposition, however—at least from a modern point of view—is that it functioned as a means of resisting patriarchalism, whether as a sanction for the abuse of other males or as the cultured denigration of women and marriage. In other words, what delimited the negative Jewish attitude toward same-sex sexual activity was not simply that it was degrading and unjust. Non-affirming critics such as Gagnon are right to say that there is evidence for mutually respectful, long-term same-sex relationships. What delimited, and perhaps partly accounted for, the negative Jewish attitude was a callous,

67. Ruden, *Among the People*, 48–49.

amoral pagan patriarchalism that, in different ways, framed both patterns of behavior. We may then ask whether in a largely *egalitarian* culture, which does not retard the intellectual development of women and which no longer regards same-sex attraction as contrary to nature, opposition to homosexuality carries the same corrective weight.[68] Clearly there remains a solid moral argument against abusive and degrading sexual relations of any orientation. But if lifelong, loving, same-sex relationships are no longer the product of an elitist homosocial order, indeed are grounded in a quite different set of modern egalitarian assumptions, then we may perhaps come to the conclusion that in our context the ancient Jewish antipathy is inappropriate and even counterproductive. Anyway, let us see what Paul had to say on the matter.

---

68. See Balch, "Concluding Observations," 292–93: "Torah's prohibition of same-sex acts began human liberation from unrestrained sexuality and women's liberation from being peripheral to men's lives." Jewett makes a similar point: "Paul and his audience were resisting an aggressively bisexual society whereas the current debate takes place in a predominantly heterosexual society" (Jewett, "Social Context," 240).

CHAPTER 5

Homosexuality and the Kingdom

IN THE NEW TESTAMENT explicit reference to same-sex relations is confined to three passages in Paul's letters: Romans 1:26–27, 1 Corinthians 6:9–10, and 1 Timothy 1:8–11. A couple of stories in the Gospels that are sometimes thought to have a bearing on the subject can be discounted.[1] Jesus's saying about causing "one of these little ones who believe in me to sin" (Matt 18:6; Mark 9:42; cf. Luke 17:2) has been understood as a condemnation of pederasty, but "little ones" is more likely a reference to the disciples than to children (cf. Matt 10:42).[2] There is no good reason to suppose that the centurion had same-sex relations with the slave whom Jesus healed (Matt 8:5–13; Luke 7:1–10). It is hard to believe that he would have been on such good terms with the conservative elders of the synagogue in Capernaum if it was known that he used his slave for sexual gratification.[3]

Some scholars have noted Jesus's reference to the "sexual immoralities" (*porneiai*) that come from the human heart (Matt 15:19; Mark 7:21) and argue that to the Jewish mind this would have included homosexual immorality. Gagnon maintains that "no first-century Jew could have spoken of *porneiai* . . . without having in mind the list of forbidden sexual offenses in Lev 18 and 20, particularly incest, adultery, same-sex intercourse, and

1. See Loader, "Homosexuality and the Bible," 32–33.

2. See Hagner, *Matthew 14–28*, 522. If the saying is indeed about causing children to sin, then both the Galilean Jewish setting and the restriction of the condemnation to children "who believe in me" make a reference to pederasty very unlikely.

3. Vasey lends some credence to Theissen's fictional reconstruction: "Everyone knows that most of these Gentile officers are homosexual. Their orderlies are their lovers" (Vasey, *Strangers*, 120).

bestiality."[4] But the *porneia* word-group is used in the Septuagint version of Leviticus only with reference to a female prostitute (Lev 21:7, 14), so arguably the list of offenses in Leviticus 18 and 20 is precisely *not* what would have come to the mind of a first-century Jew. Ian Paul thinks that the plural form means that the category includes different *types* of sexually immoral behavior, including homosexual immorality.[5] But *all* the sins mentioned are in the plural. Jesus's point is that from the heart come many *acts* rather than many *types* of murder, adultery, sexual immorality, and so on. In Hellenistic-Jewish writings *porneia* and related words appear not to have been used in explicit connection with same-sex sexual relations.[6]

Finally, it is said in Jude 7 that Sodom, Gomorrah and the surrounding cities "practiced sexual immorality (*ekporneusasai*) and departed after other flesh (*sarkos heteras*)" (my translation). This must be a reference to the attempted gang rape of Lot's *angelic* visitors: by definition *same*-sex rape cannot be described as a departure after *other* flesh.[7] There are two offenses here: sexual immorality (fornication) *and* the attempted assault on the angels. The men of Sodom, of course, were unaware of the true identity of the visitors, as Gagnon points out, but the author is uninterested in the *same-sex* aspect of their behavior.[8] It is likely that there is a parallel allusion to the event in 2 Peter. Lot was oppressed by the "licentiousness" (*aselgeiai*)

---

4. Gagnon, "Bible and Homosexual Practice," 72. The proposal made by James that Gentile Christians should abstain from "sexual immorality" (*porneia*) certainly constitutes an appeal to the holiness code (Acts 15:20, 29; 21:25). Fitzmyer argues from the association of the word with the Hebrew *zĕnuĕt* that what is in view here is polygamy and divorce, on the one hand, and marriage within close degrees of kinship, on the other (Fitzmyer, *Acts*, 557–58). The word is thus confined to heterosexual immorality.

5. Paul, *Same-Sex Unions*, 19.

6. Miller argues that in 1 Cor 6:9 the *pornoi* and *moichoi* are distinct from the *malakoi* and *arsenokoitai*, and that when Paul uses the *porneia* word group elsewhere, "the reference, whenever the application is discernible, is always to heterosexuals" (Miller, "More Pauline References," 130). Dover notes that we find "a masculine form *pornos* applied to men or boys who submit to homosexual acts in return for money (Xenophon, *Mem.* i 6.13, Ar. *Wealth* 153–9; first in an archaic graffito on Thera, *IG* xii. 3. 536)" (Dover, *Greek Homosexuality*, 20). The word group has been extended specifically to denote the male *prostitute*, not the homosexual.

7. For example, Bauckham: "σαρκὸς ἑτέρας, 'strange flesh,' cannot, as many commentators and most translations assume, refer to homosexual practice, in which the flesh is not 'different' (ἑτέρας); it must mean the flesh of angels" (Bauckham, *Jude, 2 Peter*, 54; cf. Scroggs, *New Testament*, 100n3).

8. Gagnon, "Bible and Homosexual Practice," 58–59.

of the conduct of the wicked, who "go after flesh in a lust of defilement (*miasmou*)" (2 Pet 2:7, 10, my translation).[9]

WHAT WOULD JESUS HAVE DONE?

Many would argue—particularly among those engaged in missional and pastoral work—that Jesus modeled a form of radical openness that applies just as much to the gay or lesbian person as to the tax collector, the leper, the prostitute, or the adulteress. In the words of Gudorf: "Many find it difficult to justify the exclusion of those with homosexual orientation from the church or from ministry in the face of Jesus's inclusion of various marginalized groups of the unclean, sick, sinners, women, and children. For such Christians homosexuals seem to be the lepers of today."[10] Likewise, David Runcorn argues that a properly Christian approach to ethical questions will imitate Jesus's actions and will, therefore, be "marked by unexpected welcome, healing, and scandalous inclusion"—without preconditions.[11] But it is not the "preconditions" that are the problem. It is the post-conditions. Appeal is often made to the story of the woman caught in adultery in John 8:2–11. Jesus first exposes the hypocrisy of the male religious leaders who brought the woman to him, then he assures the woman that there is no one to condemn her, then he tells her to go and sin no more. Like the woman, gay and lesbian people may have acted contrary to the Law, but none of us is without sin; we are in no position to condemn; we must learn to embrace and love, as Jesus did, before asking anyone to sin no more. There is a lesson here, certainly, for the church as it seeks to engage missionally with LGBT people, but it is important to keep in mind that Jesus expressed compassion for *sinners*. "I believe that Jesus was very intentional in the way he ordered his words," Deb Hirsch writes. "He offered her access to himself. Knowing that he was the living water, he was the only one who could quench her thirst. Once she knows this, he then tells her to sin no more. Acceptance preceded repentance. This is the type of redemptive love Jesus models for us, the kind he expects we will have for one another."[12]

---

9. Wisdom of Solomon catalogues the ills that stem from pagan idolatry, among them: "defilement (*miasmos*) of souls, confusion of lineage, disorder in marriages, adultery and debauchery (*aselgeia*)" (Wis 14:26, my translation).

10. Gudorf, "Bible and Science," 136.

11. Runcorn, "Evangelicals." He appeals to Burridge, *Imitating Jesus*, 78.

12. Hirsch, *Redeeming Sex*, chap. 11, Kindle loc. 2914–17 of 3671. Hvalvik notes

The "what would Jesus have done?" model applied to members of the people of God who fell short of the standards of righteousness defined by the Jewish Law. They were welcomed and embraced by Jesus, but they were *restored to Abraham by repentance, healing and transformation*: the tax collector restored what he had defrauded, the leper was healed and made clean, the prostitute left her former life to serve Jesus, the adulteress was told to sin no more. Between the conservatives who maintain a form of purity but fail to love their neighbor and the liberals who pursue compassion at the expense of biblical truth is the difficult but *reformative* way of Jesus. The model does not work as well when it is applied *outside* the sphere of the people of God. On the one hand, it is difficult to find in the New Testament the same compassion modeled in the pagan context—consider Jesus's begrudging response to the Syro-Phoenician woman, for example (Matt 15:26; Mark 7:27). The mission to Israel, which was fundamentally about the renewal of the people of God, and the mission to the Greek-Roman *oikoumenē* were rather different enterprises. On the other hand, Western society no longer tolerates the classification of LGBT people as "sinners" or in any other sense "unclean." They are not pariahs to be compassionately embraced by followers of Jesus in defiance of religious and social convention. They are just people.

THE *MALAKOI* AND *ARSENOKOITAI*

Paul writes in 1 Corinthians 6:9–10 that neither *malakoi* nor *arsenokoitai* "will inherit the kingdom of God." The word *malakos* can mean "soft, fancy," and presumably signifies the feminized or submissive partner in a same-sex relationship, typically male prostitutes, though it may refer more broadly to effeminate men.[13] Socrates approves of Callias's love for the athlete Autolycus because Autolycus "doesn't revel in luxury or grow sissified in softness (*malakiai*) but shows the world physical strength and stamina, virile courage and self-control" (Xenophon, *Symp.* 8.8). Philo uses the noun *malakia* ("softness, weakness") with reference to the feminized men (*androgynous*) of some nations who flaunt themselves in the marketplaces and lead the processions at festivals—there is perhaps something rather

---

that the message of Jesus is both unconditional acceptance and a refusal to condone sin (Hvalvik, "Present Context," 157).

13. See Gagnon, "Bible and Homosexual Practice," 82–83.

flamboyant and "camp" going on here (*Spec. Laws* 3 40).[14] Scroggs concludes that the word "would almost certainly conjure up images of the effeminate call-boy, *if* the context otherwise suggested some form of pederasty."[15] In this particular instance, the context is probably determined by the word immediately following.

The rare word *arsenokoitēs*, unknown before Paul and apparently a Hellenistic-Jewish coinage, would then refer to the dominant homosexual partner. It probably derives from the juxtaposition of *arsenos* ("male") and *koitēn* ("bed") in the Greek translation of Leviticus 20:13, by analogy with other compound words such as *doulokoitēs* ("a man who beds a slave") and *mētrokoitēs* ("a man who beds his mother").[16] It seems likely, then, that the term is not used narrowly for men who hire effeminate call-boys but has the general semantic scope of the Old Testament prohibition. Loader concludes from the limited literary evidence that the term "might refer to men who exploit other men for sex, including male prostitutes, but also through male rape and pederasty, and certainly not limited to the latter."[17] The *malakoi* are the ostentatiously effeminate, including those who make themselves available for sex; the *arsenokoitai* are the men who avail themselves of other men, including the effeminate, for sex. Since the *malakoi* and *arsenokoitai* are differentiated in 1 Corinthians 6:9 from the *pornoi*, which must refer to the *heterosexually* immoral, it may be that, when listed alongside *porneia* (e.g., Gal 5:19; Eph 5:3; Col 3:5), "uncleanness" (*akatharsia*) entails at least an allusion to same-sex sexual activity. Ed Miller finds support for this proposal in a number of Hellenistic texts where *akatharsia* carries strong

---

14. Dionysius of Halicarnassus says of the tyrant Aristodemus that he was known as "Malacus" or "Effeminate" by the citizens, "either because when a boy he was effeminate (*thēlydrias*) and allowed himself to be treated as a woman . . . or because he was of a mild nature and slow to anger" (*Ant. rom.* 7.2.4). It is unclear, though, whether "allowed himself to be treated as a woman" (*ta gynaixin harmottonta epaschen*) is meant to have sexual overtones. The Latin translation of a second-century-AD Greek medical text by Soranus of Ephesus has the section heading "Concerning soft or passive (*mollibus sive subactis*) men whom Greeks call *malthakoi*" (see Halperin, *One Hundred Years*, 22; Schoedel, "Same-Sex Eros," 63).

15. Scroggs, *New Testament*, 65.

16. Modern translations sometimes obscure the distinction between *malakoi* and *arsenokoitai*: "men who practice homosexuality" (ESV); "men who have sex with men" (NIV). See Wright, "Homosexuality," 297–98; Hays, "Awaiting the Redemption," 7; Hays, *Moral Vision*, 382; Via, "Bible," 12–13; Song, *Covenant and Calling*, chap. 4, Kindle loc. 1310 of 1831; Hvalvik, "Present Context," 152–53; Thiselton, *First Corinthians*, 448.

17. Loader, *New Testament*, 330–31; against Scroggs, *New Testament*, 107–9.

connotations of "bodily filth."[18] We may at least suspect that "uncleanness," rather than *porneia*, is the general ethical category into which same-sex relations were subsumed.

It may also be that Paul has homosexuality in view later in the letter when he asks, "Does not nature itself teach you that if a man wears long hair it is a disgrace for him?" (1 Cor 11:14). Jerome Murphy-O'Connor quotes Pseudo-Phocylides: "If a child is a boy, do not let locks grow on his head. Braid not his crown nor make cross-knots on the top of his head. Long hair is not fit for men, but for voluptuous women. Guard the youthful beauty of a comely boy, because many rage for intercourse with a man" (Ps. Phoc. 210–14); and Philo's disgust at the way boys who are the object of pederastic attention have "even the hair of their heads conspicuously curled and adorned" (*Spec. Laws 3* 37). In a later age, Clement of Alexandria depicts, with some contempt, the type of person who may have been familiar to the Corinthians: "inclining to voluptuousness (*malthakōteron*), they become effeminate (*gynaikizontai*), cutting their hair in an ungentlemanlike and meretricious way, clothed in fine and transparent garments . . . adulterers and effeminate (*androgynous*), addicted to both kinds of venery, haters of hair, detesting the bloom of manliness, and adorning their locks like women" (*Paidagogos* 3.3).[19] Murphy-O'Connor suggests that the "consistent infantilism of the Corinthians rubbed him on the raw, and the hair-dos raised the disquieting question of homosexuality within the community." Paul had no certain evidence, but the "possibility worried him."[20]

The proscription is stated in more general terms in 1 Timothy 1:8–11.[21] On the one hand, the Jewish Law was put in place for the unrighteous, including men who engage in sexual relations with men (*arsenokoitais*); on the other, such behaviors are "contrary to sound doctrine, in accordance

18. Miller, "More Pauline References," 132.

19. The word *malthakōteron* derives from *malthakos*, which is the poetic equivalent of *malakos* (*LSJ* s.v. μαλθἄκ-ός).

20. Murphy-O'Connor, "Sex and Logic," 485–86, 490; cf. Thiselton, *First Corinthians*, 845. Equally, lack of hair on a man's body makes him woman-like: "Woman is born smooth and dainty by nature, and if she is very hairy she is a prodigy, and is exhibited at Rome among the prodigies. But for a man not to be hairy is the same thing, and if by nature he has no hair he is a prodigy, but if he cuts it out and plucks it out of himself, what shall we make of him? Where shall we exhibit him and what notice shall we post? 'I will show you,' we say to the audience, 'a man who wishes to be a woman rather than a man'" (Epictetus, *Diatr.* 3.1.27–28).

21. For the sake of simplicity the whole canonical Pauline corpus is treated as the work of Paul.

with the gospel of the glory of the blessed God."[22] Paul's "gospel," both generally and in the Pastorals, is that Christ died for the sins of Israel in the first place, was raised from the dead, is seated at the right hand of God, and *in the future will judge and rule over the nations*, on which basis the God of Israel will be glorified (cf. Rom 1:1–4; 2:16; 15:8–12; Phil 2:9–11; 2 Tim 1:8–10; 2:8–13). He addresses the issue from the perspective of a Jew who both upholds the validity of the Old Testament prohibitions and sees pressing *eschatological* reasons why there can be no place in the churches for those who practice same-sex relations.[23]

Since "eschatology" will come up a few times in the following chapters—perhaps to the surprise of some—I should explain how the word is being used in the context of a *narrative-historical* reading of the New Testament. In systematics "eschatology" is that part of a general theology that has to do with "final things" or *what happens at the end of everything*. That is fine as far as it goes, but I suggest that, within the framework of an approach to Scripture that emphasizes both narrative and history, a more useful way to think about eschatology is simply to ask how people in the Bible thought about *decisive future outcomes from their particular historical perspective*—in other words, to regard it as an aspect of prophecy. What did they expect to happen, within a meaningful and foreseeable future—within

---

22. It has been argued from the fact that in 1 Tim 1:10 the word occurs between *pornoi* ("sexually immoral people") and *andrapodistais* that *arsenokoitais* refers to men who make use of "boy prostitutes" who are being pimped (e.g., Brownson, *Bible*, 274; DeFranza, "Journeying," 78–79; Gushee, *Changing Our Mind*, 78–79). This is probably reading too much into the simple juxtaposition; in this context the masculine *pornos* is the heterosexually promiscuous male rather than the "male prostitute" (cf. 1 Cor 5:9; Sir 23:17), and *andrapodistēs* has the broader sense of "slave-trader" (cf. Philo *Spec. Laws* 4 13). Martin argues from the context that *mē arsenokoitein* in Sib. Or. 2:73 has reference to "some kind of economic exploitation, probably by sexual means: rape or sex by economic coercion, prostitution, pimping, or something of the sort" (Martin, "Arsenokoités," 121). But the passage is part of the excerpt from Pseudo-Phocylides; the redactor has inserted *mē arsenokoitein* and the prohibitions against slandering and killing, perhaps on the strength of a figurative interpretation of "do not steal seeds." So the economic context may be of little relevance. The argument from the second-century Acts of John is perhaps more convincing: "and let the murderer know that the punishment he has earned awaits him in double measure after he leaves this (world). So also the poisoner, sorcerer, robber, swindler, and *arsenokoités*, the thief and all of this band" (*Acts John* 36).

23. There is a possible allusion to the exclusion of male prostitutes from the kingdom of God at the *parousia* in Rev 22:15: "Outside are the dogs and sorcerers and the sexually immoral and murderers and idolaters, and everyone who loves and practices falsehood." It is assumed that in Deut 23:17–18 "the wages of a dog" refers to money earned by a male prostitute. See Aune, *Revelation 17–22*, 1222–23; Davidson, *Flame*, 635–36.

a generation, say? What did they think God was going to do? In particular, what was he going to do to *resolve a crisis*, not at the personal level but with regard to the condition of his people and their place in the world? How was he going to fix things? How would he prove himself just and faithful? What would be different? What was to be feared? What was to be hoped for? This approach takes account of the fact that a great deal of Jewish prophetic-apocalyptic expectation was directed not toward the end of the world but toward momentous events *in the course of history* which would impact the people of God and establish his reputation among the onlooking nations—the exile, the return from exile, the crisis of Hellenization in the early second century BC, the war against Rome, the clash with pagan imperialism, and so on. So when Paul says that neither *malakoi* nor *arsenokoitai* "will inherit the kingdom of God," we should ask under what actual circumstances or in what way—and indeed *when*—he imagined this being realized. At the very least, we need to ask how it relates to the narrative about the wrath of God against Greek-Roman paganism presented in Romans 1:18–32.

PAUL'S CRITIQUE OF GREEK CULTURE

> Therefore, God gave them up in the desires of their hearts to un-
> cleanness in order that they might dishonor their bodies among
> them—those who exchanged the truth of God for the lie and
> worshiped and served the creature rather than the creator, who is
> blessed forever, amen. For this reason God gave them up to dis-
> honorable passions, for their females exchanged the natural usage
> for that which is against nature. Likewise also the males, abandon-
> ing the natural usage of the female, were burned up in their appe-
> tite for one another, males in males committing the shameless act
> and receiving in themselves the necessary penalty for their error.
> (Rom 1:24–27, my translation)

Therefore, God Gave Them Up

A quite elaborate theological rationale for the negative attitude toward same-sex relations is found in Paul's very Jewish critique of paganism in Romans 1:18–32.[24] This is by far the most important of the biblical texts.

24. See in particular Wis 13–14; *Sib. Or.* 3:596–603. The connection between idola-try and sexual wrongdoing is also found in 1 Thess 4:7 and 1 Cor 10:7–8 (Loader, *New*

A world that "exchanged the truth of God for the lie and worshiped and served the creature rather than the creator" (Rom 1:25) has been *given over* to sexual practices that dishonor the body. There is a sense in which, to Paul's mind, the creator God has *abandoned* pagan culture to the degrading and damaging consequences of its idolatry, as the current expression of a "wrath" that would be enacted at some point in the future (Rom 1:18; 2:5–11). In his commentary on Romans Ernst Käsemann argued that "Paul paradoxically reverses the cause and consequence: Moral perversion is the result of God's wrath, not the reason for it."[25] There is some point to this, but it does not alter the fact that Paul expected the pagan world *as he knew it* eventually to be held accountable for its longstanding mutiny against the creator God. Robert Jewett gives a better account of the whole process. Believing that heterosexuality was essential to human identity and intrinsic to the created order, Paul "presents deviations from traditionally Judaic role definitions as indicative of an arrogant assault on the Creator and as a sign of current and *forthcoming wrath*."[26] The handing over to depravity is evidence not simply that "God's wrath and judgment are already at work in the world," as Hays puts it, but that the pagan world will be *judged in the future* for its rejection of the creator.[27]

Given this, we should probably assume that homosexual behavior was not "of a secondary and illustrative character in relation to the main line of

---

Testament, 299). Cf. Paul, *Same-Sex Unions*, 23: "Paul is deploying a characteristic Jewish critique of Gentile society . . . which Jewish readers would have recognized, and for which we have a number of parallels."

25. Käsemann, *Romans*, 47; cf. Hays, "Awaiting the Redemption," 8; and Brooten, *Love Between Women*, 221: "This would mean that God's handing idolaters over to wretched deeds *is* the revelation of God's wrath against those who suppress the truth."

26. Jewett and Kotansky, *Romans*, 177 (emphasis added). This is a more convincing statement than Jewett's argument in an earlier essay that Paul lands on same-sex relations as merely a "most egregious" example of "dishonorable passions," which is dismissed as a regrettable rhetorical ploy: "The depiction of a particularly unpopular example for the sake of an effective argument leads him to highly prejudicial language, particularly to the modern ear" (Jewett, "Social Context," 230–31). Cf. Gagnon, *Bible and Homosexual Practice*, 250, who assumes a universal eschatological frame, but recognizes that the present revelation of God's wrath is intended as "clear and convincing proof of the certainty of a future, more cataclysmic judgment."

27. Hays, "Relations," 190–91. Via speaks of the wrath that has been revealed as the "anticipation of that final judgment, which happens regularly throughout the historical process" (Via, "Bible," 13). But the "theological horizon" of Paul's thought, according to Via, is the universal one: this is a story about humanity, not about Greek-Roman culture.

argument."[28] Rather, the widespread and notorious departure from natural sexual relations among the Greeks was in Paul's view *the leading and defining measure of the eschatological instability of the culture*—not one example among many that he might have chosen, but the hallmark and outstanding token of their decadence and inevitable destruction.[29] Homosexuality was obviously not confined to the Greek world, but it had a cultural prominence here that required explanation. In the preceding chapter I highlighted the connection with an entrenched patriarchal and homosocial culture. Dover has a more precise explanation: the "overt and unrepressed homosexuality" that was such a conspicuous feature of Greek life from the fourth century BC onwards is to be attributed ultimately to the "political fragmentation of the Greek world" and the necessary concentration of political and military power in the hands of a competent and close-knit male elite. So "the inadequacy of women as fighters promoted a general devaluation of the intellectual capacity and emotional stability of women; and the young male was judged by such indication as he afforded of his worth as a potential fighter."[30] The distinctive patterns of Greek sexuality, therefore, Dover thinks, evolved to serve this arrangement. Paul the apostle understood matters differently: the overt and unrepressed homosexuality of the Greeks was theologically the direct consequence of the culture's alienation from the creator God.

It is the signal character of same-sex relations in Paul's analysis that makes it difficult to accept the argument of some scholars that he opposed only forms of homosexual behavior that were patently abusive, exploitative, degrading, licentious or promiscuous. DeFranza, for example, thinks that

28. Hays, *Moral Vision*, 386; cf. Hays, "Awaiting the Redemption," 8: "Paul singles out homosexual intercourse for special attention because he regards it as providing a particularly graphic image of the way in which human fallenness distorts God's created order." Soards, *Scripture*, 35: the references to homosexuality are "mere illustrations of the sinful behavior of idolatrous humanity." Wright, *Romans*, 433: Paul has highlighted homosexuality both because "Jews regarded homosexual practices as a classic example of pagan vice" and because it exemplified "what humans in general have done in swapping God's truth for a lie." Loader thinks that Paul might have highlighted a different "example of human depravity," such as drunkenness or "wild revelry" (Loader, *New Testament*, 293). DeYoung says that Paul's point is "more illustrative than evaluative" (DeYoung, *What Does the Bible*, 52). Smith maintains that Paul "does not place any special emphasis on censuring homosexual activity; rather, the opposite is the case" (Smith, "Ancient Bisexuality," 247).

29. The argument may be different in 1 Thess 4:3–7, where the "passion of lust" (*pathē epithymias*) of Gentiles who "do not know God" and who exist in a state of "uncleanness" (*akatharsiai*) seems to be more broadly understood as *porneia*.

30. Dover, *Greek Homosexuality*, 1, 201–2.

the forms of same-sex partnership common in the period were marked by sharp differentials of power:

> Upper-class men over lower-class men, boys, eunuchs, slaves; wealthy "johns" exploiting the poverty of those pressured into prostitution through economic need; aristocrats grown tired of the ordinary, searching for more exotic pleasures, and supplied by those looking to profit from human trafficking. . . . And it is these kinds of exploitative relationships which make the best sense of the tone which Paul uses in his warnings to the Christians in Corinth, Ephesus, and Rome.[31]

These scholars would say that Paul could not have reckoned with the very different modern point of view, which is that a small section of the population has an innate and unalterable same-sex orientation, and that such people have the fundamental human right to form same-sex relationships that are not abusive or exploitative. Such a development was simply beyond the historical horizon of the biblical communities. Ken Wilson firmly makes the point: "the evidence adds up to a very strong probability that the texts are not addressing the morality of what happens between same-gender couples who love each other as equals and express their sexuality in the context of a loving, monogamous relationship."[32] Those aspects of modern LGBT culture and practice that fit the ancient biblical categories (homosexual rape, male prostitution, pederasty, sexual incontinence, promiscuity, domination, etc.) are still to be regarded as sin. But we have to recognize, it is argued, that modern anthropology, on the one hand, and modern rights-based morality, on the other, have generated

---

31. DeFranza, "Journeying," 53. Cf. McNeill, "Homosexuality," 56: "Scriptural authors never deal with homosexual orientation, and when they do treat homosexual activities, they never do so in the context of a loving relationship. They presuppose that they are dealing with lustful activity freely chosen by heterosexuals (as in Rom 1), or they deal with a humanly destructive activity in the context of idolatry, prostitution, promiscuity, violent rape, seduction of children, or violation of guests' rights."

32. Wilson, Letter, chap. 3, Kindle loc. 1014–16 of 3155; cf. Gushee, Changing Our Mind, 88–89; Loader, "Homosexuality and the Bible," 45: "If . . . we need to acknowledge that Paul's understanding about the nature of human sexuality was limited, we cannot simply apply his judgments to the situations where people are genuinely gay"; and Runcorn, "Same Sex Marriage": "Those texts traditionally presumed to be teaching against homosexual relationships in every case describe subjugation, rape or violence, excessive lustful activity, patterns of coercive male dominance and a total disregard of acceptable norms of social, religious and sexual behaviour. So it is more accurate to say that these Bible texts condemn abusive sexual behaviour *of any kind*."

a wholly new situation, for which a new set of theological guidelines is required.

The general historical observation may be valid: the modern evaluation of homosexuality is now very different to the ancient. We will return to this. What Paul condemned, however, was not a particular form of sexual abuse—why not highlight *heterosexual* depravity?—but a distinctive pattern of sexual conduct that could be said to have characterized a whole civilization for centuries. This had to include not only depraved and deplorable practices but also the "enlightened" aristocratic—and therefore salient and representative—culture of pederasty and whatever long-term affective relationships may have emerged from it. In its level of acceptability Greek pederasty was at least comparable to modern same-sex marriage.

In the Desires of Their Hearts to Uncleanness

Those who have "exchanged the glory of the immortal God for images resembling mortal man and birds and animals and creeping things," Paul says, have been given up "in the desires of their hearts" to uncleanness (*akatharsia*) in order that they might dishonor their bodies "among them" (*en autois*), in a state of sharp separation or quarantine from God's own people. The phrase "in the desires of their hearts" may be a reference to the underlying predisposition toward idolatry rather than to sexual desires, as usually understood: it precedes the being given over to uncleanness and the dishonoring of their bodies. We read in Wisdom of Solomon that the Jews were not led astray by the visual allure of pagan idols, figures "stained with varied colours, whose appearance arouses yearning in fools so that they long for the unbreathing form of a dead image" (Wis 15:5). These were the desires of "foolish hearts" that had been darkened, with the result that such people worshiped idols (cf. Rom 1:21–23). This reading does not much affect the overall meaning of the passage, but it reinforces the connection with the practice of idolatry, which easily gets overlooked by modern readers who habitually dissociate ethics and religion.

Elsewhere in Paul *akatharsia* tends to occur in "vice lists," alongside other such instances of Gentile sinfulness as sexual immorality, sensuality, covetousness, passion, and evil desire (cf. 2 Cor 12:21; Gal 5:19; Eph 4:19; 5:3; Col 3:5); and we noted Miller's suggestion that homosexual behavior was a type of uncleanness rather than of sexual immorality as such. In this context, it is said that the Gentiles have actively "given themselves up to ... every impurity (*akatharsias pasēs*)" (Eph 4:19), rather than that they have been *given up by God*. But *akatharsia* can also refer more generally to the condition of Gentiles who have not been called by God and who do not have the Law: "God has not called us for impurity (*akatharsiai*), but in holiness" (1 Thess 4:7); "you once presented your members as slaves to impurity (*akatharsiai*) and to lawlessness leading to more lawlessness" (Rom 6:19). In the argument of Romans 1:24–27 "uncleanness" is introduced ahead of the specification of sexual misconduct: they desired idols in their hearts, therefore they were given over to uncleanness, and in that setting they dishonored their bodies among them. Either uncleanness already existed in the world and they were consigned to it, or the fundamental ethical-religious division between clean and unclean was instituted in order to maintain the clear and effective separation of Jews, as a priestly people, from the idolatrous and sexually immoral nations. This seems to make better sense than to suppose that "among them" (*en autois*) in verse 24 refers to mutual sexual activity. The phrase is not normally reflexive ("among themselves"); and it is difficult to see how being handed over to *uncleanness*, rather than to corrupted desires, would lead to dishonorable behavior.[33] In effect, "among them" is explained by the following *hoitines* clause: among that section of humanity ("whoever") which worships and serves idols. If "among themselves" seems necessary in English, the thought would still be: among themselves as a pagan civilization rather than among the Jews.

For the pious Jew the distinction between clean and unclean was not a theological abstraction, even if in the context of Paul's ministry it was more an ethical than a cultic idea.[34] The boundary was heavily marked by ingrained ethnic practices, policed by social custom, and deeply colored by emotion, not least disgust. The debacle at Antioch illustrates the point (Gal 2:11–13).[35] Paul's argument is that same-sex sexual activity among the Greeks, arising from the corruption of passion and the inflammation of desire, has been strictly confined by God to the sphere of uncleanness in order to safeguard the sanctity or cleanness of his people.[36] We are made aware,

33. A few MSS have *heautois*; Dunn notes the view of Metzger that *autois* could be reflexive (Dunn, *Romans 1–8*, 53).

34. Dunn, *Romans 1–8*, 62.

35. Jewett and Kotansky, *Romans*, 168, note, "Although the ritual aspects of impurity were redefined and partially abandoned in the NT, the deep sense of revulsion about polluting behavior remains."

36. Taking *tou atimazesthai* as a genitive of purpose rather than (as, e.g., Jewett and

here, of the continuity in the logic between the Old Testament and the New. On the one hand, Israel was not to tolerate same-sex sexual activity because it would return the land to the unclean state that it had been in before they took possession of it from the Canaanites. So we read in 1 Esdras 8:66: "The nation of Israel and the rulers and the priests and the Levites have not put away from themselves the alien nations of the land as their uncleanness (*akatharsias*) requires" (translation modified). On the other, the idolatrous nations have been consigned to a sphere of uncleanness, where they indulge their dishonorable passions by engaging in same-sex sexual activity, as a concrete sign for now that they are subject to, and will be liable to, the wrath of God. The point to stress is that "uncleanness" is not merely another way of talking about sexual impurity: it invokes the powerful logic of segregation, which is echoed in the strict exclusion of the *malakoi* and *arsenokoitai* from the future kingdom of God (1 Cor 6:9).

Drawing on the work of Mary Douglas, Brooten argues that both in ancient Israel and in the Roman world the *uncleanness* of same-sex sexual activity was attributable to the fact that it was perceived as a category transgression. Certain animals are unclean because they are "imperfect members of their class." "Homoerotically involved women do not conform to the class of women, since they take on the active sexual roles that many authors of the Roman period describe as unnatural or monstrous for women."[37] When impurity is applied to gender it means that "people are not maintaining clear gender polarity and complementarity." But the approach taken here suggests that Paul is working with an understanding of "uncleanness" that primarily reflects the separation of Israel from the nations—in the first place, implicitly, from the peoples of Canaan; then more pertinently, from the world under the social-religious influence of Hellenism. At the forefront of Paul's mind are not creational norms but a political narrative that is rapidly becoming an apocalyptic narrative.

God Gave Them Up to Dishonorable Passions

The "dishonorable passions" are explained directly (*gar*) by the observation that "their females exchanged natural usage for that which is against nature; likewise also the males, abandoning the natural usage of the female, were burned up in their appetite for one another (*eis allēlous*), males in males

---

Kotansky, *Romans*, 168) as epexegetic ("consisting in being dishonored").

37. Brooten, *Love Between Women*, 235; cf. Brownson, *Bible*, 184–87.

committing the shameless act" (Rom 1:26–27, my translation). The only form of "dishonorable passions" that Paul considers is that which leads a woman or man to exchange natural for unnatural sexual practice. As far as his argument goes, there are no dishonorable passions that are expressed in other forms of unacceptable behavior and there is no same-sex sexual activity which is not the concrete expression of dishonorable passions. "Paul's wholesale attack on Greco-Roman culture makes better sense," Schoedel writes, "if, like Josephus and Philo, he lumps all forms of same-sex eros together as a mark of Gentile decadence."[38] Hvalvik argues, not unreasonably, that Paul was sufficiently cosmopolitan to have been familiar with the broad spectrum of same-sex arrangements to be found across the Roman Empire, including those forms that were quite close to the modern concept of a stable relationship between people of innate same-sex orientation.[39] Paul does not entertain the possibility that same-sex sexual activity may sometimes arise from *uncorrupted* desire or *honorable* passion—as perhaps in the Greek ideal of male love. But the act is inseparable from the debased and inordinate passions: they are together the consequence of having been handed over to uncleanness, which was itself the consequence of idolatry.[40] Heterosexual immorality generally (*porneia*), notably prostitution, posed a threat to the integrity of the church (cf. 1 Cor 6:15–18), but the argument with respect to the Greeks is quite different: homosexuality was the outstanding and defining mark of the estrangement of this civilization from the living creator God.

38. Schoedel, "Same-Sex Eros," 68. Cf. Jewett and Kotansky, *Romans*, 179: "Neither distinguishing pederasty from relationships between adult, consenting males, nor distinguishing between active and passive partners as Roman culture was inclined to do, Paul simply follows the line of his Jewish cultural tradition by construing the entire realm of homosexual relations as evidence that divine wrath was active therein."

39. Hvalvik, "Present Context," 153–56. Thiselton considers the argument that what Paul would typically have encountered was "abusive pederasty" but agrees with Wolff that this was not the case: "Paul witnessed around him both abusive relationships of power or money and examples of 'genuine love' between males. We must not misunderstand Paul's 'worldly' knowledge" (Thiselton, *First Corinthians*, 452).

40. Loader insists that "Paul sees both the action and the attitude, homosexual passion, as sin. It is not the case that he sees only the act as sin, nor that he sees it as sin only when accompanied by excessive passion, as though moderate passion and its expression would be tolerable" (Loader, "Homosexuality and the Bible," 42). Against this says Hill: Paul "is highlighting lust and its culmination, not the sort of 'pre-behavioral' inclination toward one sex or another, which still exists even in the absence of passionate fantasizing and genital intimacy" (Hill, "Christ," 56).

Their Females

The mention of "unnatural" female sexual activity is unusual, not least because it precedes the statement about unnatural male sexual activity. Some commentators have argued that the reference is to other forms of unnatural practice than lesbianism, but most infer from "likewise" (*homoiōs*) at the beginning of 1:27 that Paul had in mind same-sex sexual activity in both cases.[41] Jewett suggests that there is a "strikingly egalitarian note in Paul's treating same-sex intercourse among females as an issue in its own right and holding women to the same level of accountability as men." But "*their females*" reminds us that this is a patriarchal culture; and it is, of course, a negative equality: lesbian and gay sexual relations are equally unacceptable.[42] Brooten suspects that an intense cultural reluctance to speak about "female shame" may explain "why Paul mentions women first and why he does not spell out the exact form of their sexual contact."[43]

Exchanged the Natural Usage for That Which Is Against Nature

We will look closely at the place of "nature" in Paul's argument in the next chapter. For now, the phrase "natural usage" (*physikēn chrēsin*) reflects a common way of referring to sexual intercourse.[44] Xenophon speaks of the "usage of the body" (*tēn tou sōmatos chrēsin*) as a baser form of pleasure than the "friendship of the soul" (*Symp.* 8.28–29). Plato has the expression

41. See the detailed discussion in Fitzmyer, *Romans*, 285–86; Brooten, *Love Between Women*, 248–54; Jewett, "Social Context," 233; Jewett and Kotansky, *Romans*, 176; Loader, *New Testament*, 310–11. Ruden thinks that lesbianism was "such a rare or little-noticed phenomenon . . . that it is likely he instead means anal penetration of women by men" (Ruden, *Among the People*, 54). Wilson wonders whether Paul has bestiality in mind, given the proximity of Lev 18:23 to the prohibition against male same-sex relations (Wilson, *Letter*, chap. 3, Kindle loc. 1252 of 3155). Ward finds an explanation for the inclusion of female same-sexuality in an "antipleasure, pro-procreation argument" which he traces back through Pseudo-Phocylides and Philo to Plato's *Timaeus* (Ward, "Why Unnatural?"). In most cases, these texts oppose both male and female same-sex behavior, speak of it as "against nature," present a negative view of pleasure or passion, connect the opposition to creation, and use the words *arsēn* and *thēlys* (277).

42. Cf. Brooten, *Love Between Women*, 241: "This qualifying of women underscores their subordinate status within this culture"; and Jewett and Kotansky, *Romans*, 176.

43. Brooten, *Love Between Women*, 240.

44. According to Fredrickson *chrēsis* "emphasizes the instrumentality of the object of sexual desire and does not draw particular attention to the gender of the persons involved" (Fredrickson, "Natural and Unnatural," 202).

"the usage of those indulging lust" (*tēi tōn aphrodisiōn chrēsei*) (*Laws* 841A, my translation). Pseudo-Lucian has Charicles attempt to persuade Callicratidas that "the usage of a woman is far superior to the usage of a boy (*paidikēs chrēseōs*)" (Lucian [*Am.*] 25, my translation). The element of instrumentality in the expression perhaps underscores the point that Paul is not thinking of "homosexual" people in the modern sense: that is, people who have an innate same-sex orientation and who may desire *mutually* loving relationships. What he condemns is the general Greek tolerance of men and women who engage in same-sex sexual activity.

Since it is only women who explicitly have replicated the *exchange* (*metēllaxan*) of the "creator" for the "creature" (Rom 1:23, 25) at the level of sexual behavior, one wonders if there is not perhaps a sly reference here to the *use* of *unnatural* manufactured items in lesbian sex—a play both on "exchanged" and "usage." This may offer a better explanation of why Paul mentions female homosexuality ahead of male homosexuality: the "joke" would have been lost if male behavior had been discussed first. The practice was not unknown. Pseudo-Lucian's Charicles, with trenchant irony, urges a future legislature to support male homosexuality but to "bestow the same privilege upon women, and let them have intercourse with each other just as men do. Let them strap to themselves cunningly contrived instruments of lechery, those mysterious monstrosities devoid of seed, and let woman lie with woman as does a man (*koimasthōsan gynē meta gynaikos hōs anēr*)" ([*Am.*] 28).[45] That could be read as a quite precise gloss on Paul's statement about exchanging what is natural and God-given for what is unnatural and created. The last clause stands as the lesbian equivalent of the Old Testament prohibition (*meta arsenos ou koimēthēsēi koitēn gynaikos*: Lev 18:22 LXX) and, therefore, of Paul's *arsenokoitai*. But perhaps we must think that the apostle would not have sunk to such off-color innuendo.

Likewise Also the Males . . . Were Burned Up in Their Appetite

Whereas Greek women have merely exchanged natural for unnatural sexual behavior, Paul is more precise about the corruption of male sexuality: they are burned up or consumed by their appetite for one another, and men with men, or men *in* men, commit the "shameless deed" (*tēn aschēmosynēn*). To

---

45. In Herondas' *Mimiamb* 6.17–19 (third century BC) a woman wants to know who made her friend's "dildo, The beautifully stitched red leather one." See Hubbard, *Homosexuality*, 289.

say that men were "burned up (*exekauthēsan*) in their appetite for one another" attributes same-sex sexual activity to an *inordinate and uncontrolled* passion rather than to more moderate affections. According to Jewett the wording "implies an irrational bondage to an egoistic, empty, and unsatisfying expression of animalistic sexuality," though he probably overinterprets the psychological intent of Paul's language.[46] Josephus is quite fond of the image: a certain Alexander "was all on fire (*exekaieto*), from his youth and jealousy" when he was led to believe that Herod was enamored of his wife (*Ant.* 16.207. cf. 5.137. *J.W.* 1.436). Philo says that adultery is driven by a love of pleasure that destroys the soul, "consuming (*kataphlegousa*) every thing that it touches, like unquenchable fire, and leaving nothing which affects human life uninjured" (*Decalogue* 122); and following an account of the orgies that Tiberius held on Capri, the Roman historian Suetonius says of the emperor: "He burned with even greater and more repulsive lust than before . . ." (Suetonius *Tib.* 43–44).[47]

For One Another

It is sometimes argued that being consumed in their appetite "for one another" (*eis allēlous*) points to a degree of mutuality that would include the modern idea of consensual same-sex sexual activity. Loader thinks that here "the focus is not pederasty or the exploitation of one by another, but mutual passion ('for one another'), what we would call consensual adult homosexual acts."[48] Given the general and condensed character of the argument and the likelihood that "shameless act" refers specifically to the hierarchically configured act of anal sex, the point may only be that same-sex behavior was exhibited in various ways *among men*.[49] We should reckon with the fact, in any case, that in a patriarchal, slave-owning culture even "consensual" homosexual sex was likely to have been a one-sided and exploitative business.

46. Jewett and Kotansky, *Romans*, 178–79.

47. For the translation Hubbard, *Homosexuality*, 387–88.

48. Loader, "Homosexuality and the Bible," 38; cf. 104. Gagnon says that it "stresses mutuality of affections rather than a coercive master-slave relationship" (Gagnon, "Book Not to Be Embraced," 67).

49. I make the same argument regarding submission "to one another" (*allēlois*) in Eph 5:21 (Perriman, *Speaking of Women*, 52–53). The patterns of relationship in the household codes (wife to husband, child to parent, slave to master) are too hierarchical for this to be construed as mutual submission.

Males in Males Committing the Shameless Act

The "shameless act" (*tēn aschēmosynēn*) likely refers in this context to the act of anal penetration—rhetorically balancing any allusion to the instrumentation of female love. As J. D. G. Dunn says, "The whole phrase ('committing the shameless act') indicates clearly that not merely homosexual tendency or desire is in view, but the genital act itself."[50] The word *aschēmosynē* occurs frequently in the Greek version of Leviticus 18 and 20 as a translation of the Hebrew ʿerĕwāh in the expression "uncover the nakedness of": for example, a person "shall not approach any of the household of his flesh to uncover shame (*aschēmosynēn*)" (Lev 18:6, LXX). The expression is not used with reference to same-sex intercourse: instead, a man lies "with a male as lying down with a woman." But presumably Paul has used *aschēmosynē* by association in order to make discreet reference to the unspeakable act of penetration.

Receiving in Themselves the Necessary Penalty for Their Error

The final assertion that males committing the shameless act with males are thereby "receiving in themselves the necessary penalty for their error" (Rom 1:27) remains something of a puzzle but has little bearing on our discussion. The simplest solution may be that being handed over to "dishonorable passions" as a manifestation of the wrath of God is the "penalty" for the "error" (*planēs*) of idol worship.[51] We find a similar argument in Wisdom of Solomon 12:23–24. The Canaanites "went far astray (*eplanēthēsan*) on the paths of error (*planēs*)" by taking as gods "the most dishonorable and shameful among living creatures" (my translation). God tormented them "through their own abominations (*bdelygmatōn*)," which in this case is a reference to the wasps that he sent against the Canaanites in advance of the Israelite invasion (12:8–10). The irony, from the writer's point of view, is that the Canaanites, who worshiped animals as gods, were punished by animals which had been sent by the true God (12:27). Likewise, we read in *Testament of Naphtali* that the nations "went astray [*planēthenta*] . . . and obeyed stones and trees, following spirits of error [*planēs*]" (T. Naph.

---

50. Dunn, *Romans 1–8*, 65.

51. Cf., Byrne, *Romans*, 77: "That the 'error' (*planē*) is most likely the fundamental error of refusing to 'know God' . . . is supported by the very close parallel provided by Wis 12:24 ('For they went far astray on the paths of error [*planē*], accepting as gods those animals that even their enemies despised')."

3:3, my translation). This interpretation neatly renders unnecessary both the vacuous argument that homosexuality is its own punishment and improbable proposals regarding the direct physical consequences of same-sex intercourse.[52] The inevitable penalty, the price ultimately paid for the original error of worshiping the creature rather than the creator, is the disgrace and degradation that result from committing the shameless act.

52. "Paul may suggest that the sexual perversion itself is the punishment" (Moo, *Romans*, 115). Jewett translates *aschēmosynēn* "shameful member": "males working up the shameful member with males"—and suffering soreness as a consequence (Jewett and Kotansky, *Romans*, 179). The argument, however, depends on Hippocrates's discussion of the use of friction or rubbing to "produce relaxation, constriction, increase of flesh, attenuation" (*Off.* 17), which has to do with the treatment of injuries rather than sexual stimulation.

CHAPTER 6

Back to Nature

WE NEED TO GO back to the distinction that Paul makes between "natural" and "unnatural" sexual intercourse. It raises a number of difficult questions within the frame of a biblical ethics. When we use the word "nature" today, we are usually talking about how the physical world is perceived to be *apart from the sphere of human intrusion, invention, technology, and ruination*, often as the object of scientific investigation. In Paul's context there was not the same sharp theoretical distinction between the natural order and the moral order. There is no equivalent in biblical Hebrew for the Greek word *physis*; it is not an Old Testament concept as such. The usual assumption is that the word introduces "a peculiarly Greek, especially Stoic, idea" into the analysis which presupposes a much greater overlap or interpenetration of the human and nonhuman spheres than would make sense to the modern reader.[1] So Köster: "Stoicism seeks to transcend both theoretically and practically the antitheses that had been getting steadily deeper in Gk. thought from the 5th cent., namely, necessity and contingency, nature and

---

1. Fitzmyer, *Romans*, 286; see also Brownson, *Bible*, 233–34, drawing on Engberg-Pedersen, *Paul and the Stoics*. Seneca, interestingly, berates both men and women for engaging in sexual practices that he regarded as contrary to nature. On the one hand, women have devised a "new species of invented immodesty: they actually penetrate men!"; on the other, men "exchange their clothing with women's" and prevent a boy from becoming a man "just so he can continue to take the passive role with another man" (Seneca *Ep.* 95.21; 122.7; Hubbard, *Homosexuality*, 394). Schoedel, "Same-Sex Eros," 59: "when writers of the period appeal to nature as a guide, they are referring *(a)* to the biologically and/or culturally determined character of individuals or groups . . . or *(b)* to what ought to be in the light of the universal order of things." See also the examples listed in Jewett and Kotansky, *Romans*, 175–76.

reason, natural life and human arrangement."[2] In Stoic ethics, therefore, there is a close correlation between what is natural or according to nature and what is thought to be morally right.[3]

This can be readily illustrated from the Hellenistic moralists. A general instance, first: Pisias protests at the abduction of Bacchon, known as the Handsome, by the woman Ismenadora, who has taken a fancy to him, saying that "nature is transgressed when we are ruled by women" (Plutarch *Amat.* 755C, my translation). We now mostly understand that it is not nature but human culture that decides whether or not it is good and right that women rule over men. More relevant to our theme, Dio Chrysostom condemns the sexual incontinence of a society that dishonors and corrupts "males" (*arrenōn*), transgressing the "clear and sufficient limit . . . set by nature" (*Ven.* 149).[4] In Plutarch's *Amatorius* Daphnaeus expresses the opinion that the "natural" (*tēi physei*) love between men and women is no less likely to lead to friendship than the "union contrary to nature with males" (*hē para physin homilia pros arrenas*) (*Amat.* 751C). He considers it "contrary to nature" (*para physin*) for weak and effeminate men to allow themselves to be "covered and mounted like cattle"—"a completely ill-favoured favour, indecent, an unlovely affront" to the goddess of love, Aphrodite (751E). What is natural is right, what is unnatural is wrong.

The point is made even more forcefully by Hellenistic-Jewish writers such as Josephus and Philo, in whose eyes the unnaturalness of same-sex sexual behavior is justly condemned by the Law. Philo, as we have seen, regards pederasty as the pursuit of a pleasure that is "contrary to nature" (*para physin*) and notes that the Law condemns to death the effeminate man or "man-woman" (*androgynon*) who falsifies the "coinage of nature" (*Spec. Laws* 3 38–39).[5] Hays's conclusion on this score seems unassailable: Paul "speaks out of a Hellenistic-Jewish cultural context in which homosexuality is regarded as an abomination, and he assumes that his readers will

2. Köster, "φύσις φυσικός φυσικῶς," 263.

3. See Hays, "Relations," 192–94; Vasey, *Strangers*, 131: for Paul nature is "an explicit construct of biology and culture."

4. Cf. Dio Chrysostom, *Ven.* 135–36: "Aphrodite, whose name stands for the normal intercourse (*tēs kata physin . . . synodou*) and union of the male and female."

5. See also Philo *Abraham* 133–41; Josephus, *Ag. Ap.* 2.199, 273, 275; and cf. Hays, "Relations," 192–93. Philo's distinctive contribution was to fuse the Greek concept of nature with the Jewish understanding of God and the Law: "The *nomos physeōs* is always the Torah to which even God seems subject. The law follows nature, and nature ratifies law" (DeYoung, "Meaning of 'Nature,'" 434).

share his negative judgment of it."[6] What is less certain is the further claim made by Hays that in this passage Paul equates "nature" with creation. We will get to this shortly.

NATURE IS BIG . . .

The basic observation about the moral weight of *physis* in the Hellenistic world counts against two arguments that have been made by interpreters who want to find room in Scripture for the acceptance of gay and lesbian relationships in their unobjectionable modern forms. First, the claim has sometimes been made—notably by John Boswell—that "against nature" means "against one's *personal* nature as heterosexual," as though Paul condemned only those people for whom it was *personally* unnatural to engage in same-sex activity.[7] The exegetical justification is pulled like a rabbit from the hat of the verb "exchanged": certain men and women misguidedly *exchanged* their innate heterosexual identity for a false homosexual identity. The corollary for a modern ethics would then be that it is no less *unnatural* for people with a same-sex orientation to behave as though they were heterosexual. Others have suggested, secondly, that by "natural" Paul means "socially conventional."[8] Comparison is made with the argument about head coverings in 1 Corinthians 11:2–16: it is a source of dishonor for a man to pray or prophesy with his head covered; even "nature" teaches that "if a man wears long hair it is a disgrace for him" (1 Cor 11:14). Furnish, for example, thinks that Paul's appeal here to what nature itself teaches is "nothing more than an appeal to social convention—to the practice with which he himself is familiar and that he thus regards as self-evidently 'proper.'"[9]

6. Hays, "Relations," 194.

7. Boswell, *Christianity*, 110: "For Paul, 'nature' was not a question of universal law or truth but, rather, a matter of the character of some person or group of persons, a character which was largely ethnic and entirely human." See the discussion and refutation in Hays, "Relations"; also Wright, "Homosexuality," 294–95; Soards, *Scripture*, 33–34; Brooten, *Love Between Women*, 242; Brownson, *Bible*, 228–32; and Paul, *Same-Sex Unions*, 24: "Paul is not here referring to individuals, their own experiences of sexual attraction, or their 'innate preferences,' which they have abandoned."

8. See Brownson, *Bible*, 234; and the discussion in Loader, *New Testament*, 312 and n. 73.

9. Furnish, "Bible," 30.

The main problem with these lines of interpretation, as I see it, is that they are reductionist with respect both to the wider polemical background and to the narrative sweep of Paul's argument. The argument about what is natural and unnatural in Romans 1:26–27 is made in general terms: Paul does not narrow it down to *some* women and men who take part in homosexual behavior against *their own* nature. Rather, the use of *physis* directs the first-century reader or auditor to a shared *biological-cultural* understanding of what constitutes appropriate behavior. Equally, if the prevailing idea of "nature" in the Hellenistic world was that of an ideal correspondence between the given biological order and human culture, it was bound to be expressed in practice as a spectrum of values.[10] If hairstyle belonged to the artificial end of the spectrum, we may still reasonably assume that sexual practice, which was defined both by more or less consistent and unalterable physical differences and by reproductive purpose, would have been located some distance in the opposite direction, with Pisias's opinion regarding the unnaturalness of women in leadership lying somewhere between the two. At one level, at least, Paul must have meant quite simply—and uncontroversially—that heterosexual behavior was in accordance with common sense observations about human biology whereas homosexual behavior was not.

More to the point, we need to reckon with the fact that the departure from "natural" sexual relations is put forward as a defining consequence and symptom of the exchange of "the glory of the immortal God" for man-made images. "Nature" must be at least as broad in its scope as this overarching story of the repudiation of the creator by the Greeks and their consignment to a state of uncleanness. We will have reason to question the *universal* frame of Hays's analysis, but his response to Boswell's narrow focus on the individual is correct: "The charge is a corporate indictment of pagan society, not a narrative about the 'rake's progress' of particular individuals."[11] Brooten reaches a similar conclusion: "Paul could have believed that *tribades, kinaidoi*, and other sexually unorthodox persons were born that way and yet still condemn them as unnatural and shameful,

---

10. Cf. Hays, "Relations," 196, quoting Grant: "The meaning of the term is not precisely consistent; sometimes it means something like the orderly structure of ideal reality, and other times it appears to mean . . . 'convention as understood by me.'"

11. Hays, "Relations," 200.

this all the more so since he is speaking of groups of people rather than of individuals."[12]

BUT NOT THAT BIG

The counterargument from those who wish to uphold the traditional interpretation has generally been that in Romans 1:18–31 what Paul means by "nature" is how God established things at creation: nature is "the way the world was meant to be, as created by God."[13] This would give "nature" as Paul understood it both a universal and a permanent character: for all people at all times it is unnatural and, therefore, offensive to the creator to engage in homosexual behavior. Whereas the scope of "nature" as understood by the likes of Boswell and Scroggs was too small, the conservative argument here, I think, makes it too big. As often happens, the truth is to be found somewhere between the two extremes.

The first point to make is that in Hellenistic discourse "nature" is an empirical concept. It is how the world is *perceived* to be, in its whole and in its parts; it is not in itself an appeal either to cosmological origins or to the will of God. Its value for moral discourse is that it holds out the possibility that a religious or cultural perspective might be grounded in shared self-evident observations about the world—even if the possibility sometimes proves illusory. Refusing to eat pork and food sacrificed to idols, the elderly priest Eleazar tells Antiochus Epiphanes that the Jews "do not eat defiling food, for, believing that the law is divine, we know that the Creator of the world shows us sympathy by imposing a law that is in accordance with nature (*kata physin*)" (4 Macc 5:25). The Hellenistic-Jewish apologetic grants nature primacy, at least for rhetorical purposes; the commandment is validated by its conformity to a particular perception of how the world is. The difficulty of the argument is illustrated by the fact that to the mind of the pagan tyrant nature taught quite the opposite lesson: "Why should you abhor eating the very excellent meat of this animal when nature has provided it (*tēs physeōs kecharismenēs*)?" (4 Macc 5:8). Empirical observation is barely more "objective" than divine law. How the world is perceived to be, in its whole and in its parts, is always culture-bound.

Usage elsewhere in the New Testament supports the view that "nature" refers to *how things are or how they are generally perceived to be*, not

12. Brooten, *Love Between Women*, 244.
13. Paul, *Same-Sex Unions*, 25.

specifically to their origins in creation.[14] Gentiles do "by nature" what the Law requires, they are "by nature" uncircumcised (Rom 2:14, 27); branches belong to a tree "by nature" (Rom 11:21, 24); the apostles are Jews "by nature" (Gal 2:15); the Galatians were formerly enslaved to things that were not "by nature" gods (Gal 4:8); the Ephesian believers had once been "by nature" children of wrath (Eph 2:3). Any attempt to insert reference or appeal to *how the world was created to be* in these passages would not help interpretation; indeed, it would play havoc with the distinction between Jews and Gentiles that underlies several of them. Commenting on Paul's assumption that nature teaches that it is a disgrace for a man to have long hair, Thiselton says: "Paul simply appeals to 'how things are' or 'how things are ordered' in the period and context for which he is writing."[15]

Secondly, Paul does not construct his argument in Romans 1:18-31 in such a way as to suggest that Greek homosexuality was wrong because it contradicted the creation order. He locates the source of the problem not in some infringement of the creation mandate or in the disobedience of the first couple but in a more broadly based, societal refusal to acknowledge the transcendent character of God and the decision to worship the creature rather than the creator. Some scholars maintain that the reference to "males" (*arsenes*) and "females" (*thēleiai*) in Romans 1:26–27 points back to the creation of humanity as "male and female" (*arsen kai thēlu*) in Genesis 1:27, LXX.[16] Wesley Hill, for example, draws the conclusion: "If humanity was created as 'male and female'—if in fact that was humanity's 'nature'

14. According to Köster: "φύσις is everything which by its origin or by observation of its constitution seems to be a given. To call it 'given' φύσις is already to go beyond the sphere of naive description and implies a judgment on its actual constitution or true nature" (Köster, "φύσις φυσικός φυσικῶς," 253). DeYoung also notes that *physis* may signify "origin, including birth and growth" (DeYoung, "Meaning of 'Nature,'" 430). But if in Stoic thought nature is in this regard equivalent to deity as an "originating power," the point is still that natural objects have *observable* rather than "mythological" origins. The reason the Jews did not have a comparable conception of nature, as DeYoung observes, is that they "referred all existing things to creation or to the Creator God, and the OT is primarily concerned with history, not philosophy and speculation" (DeYoung, "Meaning of 'Nature,'" 432).

15. Thiselton, *First Corinthians*, 844. Gagnon explains Paul's reference to what is natural by comparing his argument about same-sex sexual activity with the earlier statement about the self-evidence of God in the natural world (Rom 1:19–20): "visual and mental perception of the material world should lead to certain conclusions about how best to worship God" (Gagnon, "Bible and Homosexual Practice," 79).

16. See Gagnon, "Bible and Homosexual Practice," 78; Jewett and Kotansky, *Romans*, 174; Davidson, *Flame*, 637; Loader, "Homosexuality and the Bible," 39.

in the beginning—then same-sex coupling can only be judged, however common and acceptable it might have been in Paul's day, as theologically 'unnatural.'"[17] But if the appeal to "nature" makes this something of a Stoic argument, the "male"/"female" terminology arguably derives from the wider debate in the Hellenistic world—note the reference to "males" (*arrenoi*) in the quotations from Dio Chrysostom and Plutarch above.[18] Musonius Rufus scorns the sexual excess of men who "crave a variety of loves . . . not women (*thēleiōn*) alone but also men (*arrenōn*)."[19] If the language is meant to echo Scripture at all, the source is more likely to be Leviticus 18:22; 20:13, LXX than Genesis 1:27: *thēleiai* is used by Paul as the natural counterpart to *arsenos* in the explicit condemnation of male same-sex relations (cf. Lev 15:32–33 LXX).[20]

Other supposed echoes of the creation accounts are as well-explained by reference to a general biblical and Hellenistic-Jewish polemic against pagan idolatry.[21] This passage from the Greek translation of Deuteronomy shows clearly that Paul did not need to reach all the way back to Genesis

---

17. Hill, "Christ," 135. Song thinks that Paul makes reference to lesbian relations "not because he was commenting on its prevalence in Greco-Roman society, but simply because it follows from the reversal of Genesis 1.27" (Song, *Covenant and Calling*, chap. 4, Kindle loc. 1244 of 1831).

18. According to Aristophanes's myth of creation "there were three kinds of human beings, not merely the two sexes, male and female (*arren kai thēly*), as at present" (Plato *Symp.* 189E). Also Plutarch *Amat.* 23, 768E: "Now of the union of male with male (*pros arren' arrenos*) (it is, rather, not a union, 'but a lascivious assault . . .')"; "Shun adultery and disorderly bedding of the male (*arsenos*)" (*Sib. Or.* 3:764, my translation); "they not only have intercourse with men (*arsenas*) but they defile their own mothers and even their daughters" (*Let. Aris.* 152); "many lust for mingling with a male (*arsena*)" (Ps. Phoc. 214).

19. Musonius, *Discourse 12: On Sexual Indulgence* (Lutz, "Musonius Rufus," 87).

20. See Loader, *New Testament*, 314n87. Josephus's assertion that the Law "abhors the mixture of a male with a male (*pros arrenas arrenōn*); and if anyone does that, death is his punishment" (*Ag. Ap.* 2.199) is a clear reference to the Leviticus texts. Bird denies that the Hebrew text of Lev 18:22 refers to Gen 1:27–28 because it is "woman" ('*iššâ*) rather than "female" (*nĕqêbâ*) which corresponds to "male" (Bird, "Bible," 151).

21. Against DeYoung, *What Does the Bible*, 54–55. Jewett argues that the singular "lie" of Rom 1:25 refers back to "the primordial desire of humans to 'be like God'" (Gen 3:5) (Jewett, "Social Context," 227). But the context is only that of the polemic against the falseness of idolatry. The singular form ("the lie") contrasts the false worship of idols with "the truth" of God, and the definite article may only look back to the original self-deception of 1:22–23. Isaiah says of the idol-maker who looks to his idol for deliverance: "He feeds on ashes; a deluded heart has led him astray, and he cannot deliver himself or say, 'Is there not a lie in my right hand?'" (Isa 44:20; cf. Jer 10:14; Amos 2:4).

1–3 for his language in Romans 1:22–23: "Do not act lawlessly and make for yourselves an engraved likeness, any kind of icon—a likeness of male or female (*arsenikou ē thēlykou*), a likeness of any animal of those that are on the earth, a likeness of any winged bird that flies under the sky, a likeness of any reptile that creeps on the ground, a likeness of any fish that is in the waters beneath the earth" (Deut 4:16–18 LXX; cf. Wis 11:15–16). Hvalvik cites a passage from the second-century-BC Testament of the Twelve Patriarchs as evidence that in Jewish polemic "nature" was "directly connected with God's creation of the world," but the argument is less than convincing.[22] In the first place, the assertion that "God made all things good in their order" refers to the orderly arrangement of the senses and other human attributes in the body, giving the conclusion: "Thus my children you exist in accord with order for a good purpose in fear of God; do nothing in a disorderly manner, arrogantly, or at an inappropriate time" (*T. Naph.* 2:8–9). But then the argument is only that the nations went astray, abandoned the Lord, changed the order of their nature, worshiped idols, and committed the sins of Sodom (3:3–4). The appeal is not to how things were created to be, according to the terms of Genesis 1–2, but to how things are *perceived* to be: "Sun, moon, and stars do not alter their order; thus you should not alter the Law of God by the disorder of your actions" (*T. Naph.* 3:2).

To the mind of the first-century Jew or Jewish-Christian in the pagan world, confronted with idol worship at every turn, this line of thought was likely to have had greater relevance than an appeal to a creation narrative that had no express interest in the religious practices of the nations. In Paul's argument the only explicit point of contact with the creation story is the statement that the eternal power and divine nature of God "have been clearly perceived, ever since the creation of the world, in the things that have been made" (Rom 1:20). It is the specific failure to grasp this fundamental truth about God that initiates the cascading corruption of the heart and mind. Loader gets the distinction right. The "fall" operative in the passage is "a fall of the many because of idolatry, not the primeval fall of all because of Adam, and is comparable more to the topos of the 'decline-of-civilization narrative.'"[23]

22. Hvalvik, "Present Context," 149–50.

23. Sprinkle, *Two Views*, 301, citing Stowers in particular in support; and Fitzmyer: "The alleged echoes of the Adam stories in Genesis are simply nonexistent" (Fitzmyer, *Romans*, 274). Furnish argues that Rom 1:18–32 relies on the critique of pagan idolatry found in Wis 13–15, behind which lie not the Genesis creation accounts but passages

HOMOSEXUALITY AND THE GREEKS

Between the restriction of *physis* to personal orientation or social convention and the universalizing of *physis* to denote humanity's essential and immutable created being there remains the possibility that the term finds its
meaning within the frame of a *cultural or civilizational analysis*. The usual
assumption is that there are only two options available. Thomas Schmidt
writes, for example, that "Paul is describing not individual actions but the
corporate rebellion of humanity against God and the kinds of behaviour
that result."[24] Hays agrees with Scroggs that the passage gives us "Paul's real
story of the universal fall" and with Käsemann that for the apostle "history
is governed by the primal sin of rebellion against the Creator, which finds
repeated and universal expression"; and in his own words, it is "a diagno-
sis of the human condition."[25] But in Scripture there are always important
social and political categories that *fall between the individual person
and humanity as a whole*: tribes, nations, peoples, kingdoms, empires,
cultures, civilizations. These belong in the foreground of the story, not
the background. It would be fully in keeping with both the Old Testament
and Jewish thought in the Second Temple period for Paul to have had in
mind not universal humanity but the pagan civilization and cultures that
had dominated Israel's world—and had oppressed Israel—for centuries.
Of course, any particular historical culture is an expression of the general
human condition, as Paul was only too aware. This was precisely the quarrel
with the Jews that he reconstructs in this letter. The Law set them apart
culturally and religiously, but it could not save them from the existential
reality of sin. But just as the Jews as a people would soon have to come to
terms with the catastrophe of the war against Rome (AD 66–70), as Jesus
had foreseen, so too the early Jewish Christians—and a growing number
of converts from paganism—believed that the God of history was about
to overthrow the deeply offensive, idolatrous culture of the Greeks and
Romans.

---

such as Ps 115:1–8; Isa 40:18–26; 44:9–20 (Furnish, "Bible," 30).

24. Cited in Brownson, *Bible*, 230; Brownson makes the same assumption (231).
Likewise Hill: "The creational and Adamic texture of the narrative fabric Paul is weaving
means that 'nature' should probably be interpreted in light of Genesis rather than (as
some have argued) in terms of an individual's life history. In other words, Paul's canvas is
cosmic and historical rather than personal" (Hill, "Christ," 135).

25. Hays, "Relations," 190; cf. Hays, "Awaiting the Redemption," 8; Soards, *Scripture*,
20–21; and Hvalvik, "Present Context," 150: "What Paul is describing is the fall of
humanity. It is far more than a polemical denunciation of some selected gentile vices."

Evangelicals in particular may find this to be an unconventional reading of the passage, and we need to give some consideration to the exegetical grounds for reframing matters in this way. Thinking the argument through should give us a better sense of how Paul engages not with humanity in general but with *a particular historical expression of human culture*, which is precisely the challenge that faces the missional church today. I regard this as a substantial benefit of the more narrowly historical approach.

1. Paul understood his apostolic mandate to encompass the full extent of the Greek-Roman world—from Jerusalem, via Illyricum, to Spain. His task was to secure the obedience of some Gentiles from across the region in advance of the rule of Christ over the nations—as a sort of prophetic vanguard of the coming political-religious transformation (Rom 15:12, 18–19, 23–24). According to Luke, Paul told the men of Athens that he knew their "unknown god" to be the God of Israel; and he declared that this God was no longer willing to overlook the centuries of pagan ignorance and intended soon to judge this "world" or *oikoumenē* by a man whom he had appointed (Acts 17:30–31). In Luke's writings the word *oikoumenē* signifies an administered or governed territory or realm—in this context the Greek-Roman world or the world ruled by Caesar (cf. Luke 2:1; Acts 11:28; 17:6; 19:27; 24:5).[26] The "eternal gospel" that is heard in Revelation 14:6 is a call to the nations to worship the living creator God, "who made heaven and earth, the sea and the springs of water," because judgment is about to come upon the idolatrous and immoral city, "Babylon the great," Rome.[27]

2. In the opening chapters of Romans Paul consistently differentiates not between Jews and the rest of humanity but between Jews and *Greeks*. Both the Jew and the Greek face the wrath of God if they do evil (Rom 2:8–9); and the gospel is "the power of God for salvation to everyone who believes, to the Jew first and also to the Greek" (Rom 1:16). This is where the indictment of Romans 1:18–32 begins—with the revelation of the righteousness of God *to the Greek*, which is precisely the message dramatized by Luke in the Areopagus episode. From the start, it is not humanity as a whole that is in view but Greek civilization.[28] The reference

26. See Perriman, *Future of the People*, 54–56.

27. See Perriman, *Coming of the Son of Man*, 217.

28. See Perriman, *Future of the People*, 53–54. Moo suggests that Paul uses *Hellēn* ("Greek") because he has no singular of *ethnē* ("Gentiles") available to him (Moo, *Romans*, 68 and n25). But the distinction between the "Greeks" and the "barbarians" in Rom 1:14 is problematic from this point of view, and we might ask why Paul did not say "to the Jews first and also to the Gentiles/nations" in verse 16. Dunn says that "Greek"

to "their" women in verse 26 also narrows the focus to a particular group. A passage in the Jewish Sibylline Oracles book 3 (second century BC) suggests that the practice of idolatry more widely in the ancient world was blamed on the Greeks: "It is a thousand years and five hundred more since the overbearing kings of the Greeks reigned, who began the first evils for mortals, setting up many idols of dead gods. On account of them you have been taught vain thinking. But when the wrath of the great God comes upon you, then indeed you will recognize the face of the great God" (*Sib. Or.* 3:551–57). This sort of apocalyptic analysis readily accounts for Paul's language in Romans 1–2 and reinforces the point that the problem addressed had historical rather than primordial origins.

3. Paul's treatment of the theme conforms closely to a broadly Jewish "eschatology" or view of future events. We have a similar argument, for example, when Jeremiah warns Israel not to learn the ways of the nations. The Lord made the earth, set upright the *oikoumenē*, and stretched out the sky. But people were stupid, lacking knowledge; "every goldsmith was put to shame at his carved images, because they cast lies; there is no breath in them." Therefore, at "the time of their visitation," when God will pour out his anger on the nations, they will perish (Jer 10:1–15, 25, LXX). Wisdom of Solomon connects sexual immorality (*porneia*) and the "corruption of life" with the "invention of idols" (Wis 14:12). The worship of idols is "the beginning and cause and end of every evil": ritual murder of children, frenzied revels, murder, theft, deceit, corruption, unfaithfulness, tumult, perjury, turmoil for those who are good, forgetfulness of favors, defilement of souls, corruption of lineage, marital disorder, adultery, and debauchery (14:23–26). But there will be a "visitation also upon the idols of the nations," because they have become an abomination. Idols did not exist from the beginning, nor will they last forever; a "speedy end was planned for them" (14:11, 13–14). Paul's thought fits the contours of these narratives so well that it is difficult not to conclude that his interest was in the immediate Jewish controversy regarding classical idolatry and hardly at all in the absolute, universal outcomes that are assumed by Christian theology. This is the historically focused apocalyptic background against which we need, I think, to understand his condemnation of Greek-Roman homosexuality.

---

reflects "the all-pervasiveness of Greek culture," citing 2 Macc 4:36; 11:2; 3 Macc 3:8; 4 Macc 18:20; *Sib. Or.* 5:264 (Dunn, *Romans 1–8*, 40). But the texts refer precisely to the crisis of Hellenization at the time of Antiochus Epiphanes, or to the Greeks in Alexandria, or to wider Greek civilization. There is no basis for the view that a Hellenistic Jew such as Paul would use "Greek" to refer to non-Jewish humanity in general.

4. It is possible, though by no means certain, that in his letter to the saints in Rome Paul was consciously alluding to the notorious sexual depravity of the imperial household. Brownson thinks that stories about Gaius Caligula, in particular, graphically illustrate the excesses that Paul had in mind: "the movement from idolatry to insatiable lust to every form of depravity, and the violent murderous reprisal that such behavior engenders."[29] There is evidence that attitudes were becoming polarized at this time: the flagrant and outrageous practice of the Caesars, on the one hand; severe disapproval from Roman moralists, on the other. "In other words," Hubbard writes, "homosexuality in this era may have ceased to be merely another practice of personal pleasure and began to be viewed as an essential and central category of personal identity, exclusive of and antithetical to heterosexual orientation."[30] Perhaps this helps to account for the intensification of the apocalyptic rhetoric and a sense that the present form of this world was passing away (cf. 1 Cor 7:31), but it should not be taken to mean that ordinary Greeks and Romans engaging in homosexual activity were exempt from Paul's strictures.

5. To repeat the point made earlier, the appeal to "nature" and recourse to culturally freighted concepts such as "dishonor" and "shame," which are closely bound up with a particular understanding of nature, reinforce the narrative constraints of the passage. "Nature" inevitably brings into play the broad set of largely implicit assumptions that are made about what constitutes normal or right or appropriate behavior within a particular cultural or civilizational context. It reflects, in the words of Troels Engberg-Pedersen, Paul's "naive use of 'nature' in support of traditional and normative perceptions."[31]

6. Hays has argued that the "language of 'exchange' plays a central role in this passage, emphasizing the direct parallelism between the rejection of God and the rejection of created sexual roles."[32] Just as people have

---

29. Brownson, *Bible*, 157; cf. Gushee, *Changing Our Mind*, 88.

30. Hubbard, *Homosexuality*, 386; also discussed in DeYoung, *What Does the Bible*, 83–84. Elliott makes the case too strongly: "Instead of imputing to Paul a heated, irrational exaggeration as he describes general human sinfulness or an equally stereotyped Judean prejudice regarding the rampant idolatry and immorality of the non-Judean world, we can read every phrase in this passage as an accurate catalog of misdeeds of one or another recent member of the Julio-Claudian dynasty" (Elliott, *Arrogance of Nations*, 82).

31. Engberg-Pedersen, *Paul and the Stoics*, 209–10.

32. Hays, "Relations," 192. Also Dunn, *Romans 1–8*, 74: "The third appearance of the

exchanged (*metellaxan*) "the glory of the immortal God for images resembling mortal man and birds and animals and creeping things" and "the truth about God for a lie," so errant humans have exchanged (*metellaxan*) "natural relations for those that are contrary to nature" (Rom 1:22, 25, 26). We may set aside the quibble, discussed above, that Paul only says that *their females* "exchanged" natural for unnatural usage. But the observation serves equally well, if not better, the argument put forward here that he condemns same-sex relations as a preeminent feature of the idolatrous cultures of Greece and Rome. It is the Greeks who have "exchanged the truth of God for the lie and worshiped and served the creature rather than the creator." It is *their* women who have exchanged natural sexual usage for a usage that is unnatural and perhaps artificially facilitated.

COMMUNITIES OF GOD'S FUTURE

So it appears that Paul believed that there would soon be a "visitation" or judgment upon an idolatrous culture whose alienation from the living God was signaled principally by the fact that women exchanged natural use of the body for unnatural and men committed shameless acts with men. Amid the explicitly homosexual graffiti found in the ruins of Pompeii are the words "Sodom and Gomorrah," scrawled presumably by an outraged member of the local Jewish community. Hubbard notes wryly that the graffitist would have "felt his judgment confirmed by the city's ultimate fate."[33] What Paul would have made of the destruction of the city by the eruption of Vesuvius in AD 79 we can only guess, but it gives us a fair impression of the eschatological dimensions to the controversy. For Paul, in any case, judgment on this culture would be part of the coming kingdom of God, when the God of Israel would come to rule over the nations through his Son (cf. Rom 15:12).

In this eschatological narrative the churches were to be what the synagogues were failing to be—the benchmark of righteousness by which God would judge the pagan *oikoumenē*.[34] It was of critical importance,

---

word 'changed' (cf. vv. 23 and 25) seems to imply that the action described ('changing the natural use to that which is contrary to nature') is of a piece with and direct result of the basic corruption of the glory and truth of God in idolatry, a similar turning from the role of creature to what is simply a perversion of the creature's share in creating."

33. Hubbard, *Homosexuality*, 384, 422.

34. See Perriman, *Future of the People*, 60, 70–71.

therefore, that the converts from paganism in Corinth should not exhibit in their own lives the patterns of behavior outlined in Romans 1:18–32. Such activity was characteristic of pagan culture and would fundamentally compromise the eschatological purpose of communities that would inherit the kingdom of God—that new future when the idols would be cast down and Jesus confessed as Lord by the nations, to the glory of God the Father. But what are we supposed to do now that the nations of the *oikoumenē* have *abandoned* their confession of Jesus as cosmic Lord?

CHAPTER 7

The Dead End of the Traditional Story

THE CHURCH HAS COME under immense cultural and social pressure to revise or abandon its traditional opposition to same-sex relations, but the particular issue, which just happens to have been the most recent controversy, is merely symptomatic of a broad epochal transition that is under way in the Western world and perhaps globally. The question that the church faces is whether it can tell an adequate story about itself in response to this crisis—a story that must not only be rooted in Scripture, but must also register the scale of the dislocation, and imagine plausible ways forward. There are two ways in which the story may be told: either the basic shape of the narrative has been fully *determined* by the events described in the New Testament, and the story is, to all intents and purposes, *closed*; or the story of the church, which is the story of the people of God, is *undetermined*, because history is undetermined, and remains *open* to significant development. By and large, Christians who oppose moves to affirm and accept same-sex relationships will lean toward the first option. Those who want to take a more accommodating stance have had to look for ways to open up the biblical narrative to allow for a really quite startling repeal of the categorical rejection of homosexuality that we find in Leviticus and Paul. My suggestion will be that precisely our reading of Paul requires us to append to the narratives of land and kingdom the collapse of the Western Christian worldview and the triumph of secular humanism—and then to ask whether this changes anything.

HOMOSEXUALITY AND THE "GRAND NARRATIVE" OF REDEMPTION

The traditional and conservative response has been to reaffirm the face-value biblical position, which is that homosexuality is a direct consequence of rebellion against God and an expression of corrupted affections, as though nothing has fundamentally changed in the world. The 2017 Nashville Statement, for example, emphatically denies that "adopting a homosexual or transgender self-conception is consistent with God's holy purposes in creation and redemption" (Article 7) and asserts that it is "sinful to approve of homosexual immorality or transgenderism and that such approval constitutes an essential departure from Christian faithfulness and witness" (Article 10).[1]

Dogmatic formulations such as the Nashville Statement easily come across as negative and repressive, and Hill asks whether the "rules" might not be framed more sympathetically and more constructively by "the Christian story of what God did for the world in Christ." There is a compelling difference between the argument *against* same-sex relations and the argument *for* celibacy as a vocation. So as a gay Christian, Hill says that he abstains from gay sex because of the power of the biblical story and "the whole perspective on life and the world that flows from that story."[2] The "grand narrative" that he has in mind is the one about God redeeming and re-creating human beings, which determines the spiritual context for making sense of such costly obedience: 1) forgiveness of sins is promised, including forgiveness of the sin of gay sex, on the basis of Jesus's death and resurrection; 2) God "challenges, threatens, endangers, and transforms *all* of our natural desires and affections"; 3) our bodies do not belong to us but to God as members of the body of Christ; and 4) the Christian story affirms the pain of celibacy as a participation in the sufferings of Christ.[3]

I have argued, however, that this is not at all the "grand narrative" that accounts for the biblical injunctions against same-sex behavior. In the Old Testament it is the long and turbulent story about possession of the land that frames the Leviticus texts. In the New Testament it is the long and turbulent story about the rule of the God of Israel over the nations of the pagan world that gives us the overarching context for Paul's analysis in

1. https://cbmw.org/nashville-statement.
2. Hill, *Washed and Waiting*, 76.
3. Hill, *Washed and Waiting*, 76–87.

Romans 1 and for his insistence that men who lie with men as with women will not inherit the kingdom of God (1 Cor 6:9; 1 Tim 1:10). This gives us the reason both for the hostility toward same-sex relations and, as we will see in a moment, for Paul's commendation of singleness in 1 Corinthians 7. The challenge, as we go about constructing new narratives for mission after Christendom, is to find the equivalent large-scale "socio-political" storyline and to ask how that storyline shapes witness and recalibrates the redemptive subplot.

One of the things that has changed is that it is now widely accepted that same-sex orientation cannot normally be corrected or healed, whether by medical, psychotherapeutic, or faith-based methods. Homosexuality has come to be understood as an ineradicable and essentially benign anomaly in human nature rather than as the willful corruption of human nature.[4] Therefore, the behavior—engagement in intimate same-sex relations—cannot be suppressed without the risk of causing emotional and psychological harm to the person, which is why conversion therapy has become so unacceptable. But if celibacy is the only option available to LGBT people who want to be part of the covenant community, we are faced with the objection that, biblically speaking, celibacy is an *option* for people who might otherwise *choose* to marry rather than a compulsory requirement for a particular section of the population (cf. Matt 19:12; 1 Cor 7:6–9).[5] Loader makes the point: "Choosing celibacy is one thing. Obliging it by implication on all who are gay, so that they must never give natural expression to their sexuality, is another."[6] It is hard to see how an informally mandated celibacy for LGBT people would work—it's problematic enough, after all, when backed up by the traditions and disciplines that shape the practice of Roman Catholic priesthood.[7] Hays argued, before the widespread acceptance of

4. "So what I mean by normalization here is simply the recognition that homosexuality is part of the spectrum of human sexuality" (Hirsch, *Redeeming Sex*, chap. 9, Kindle loc. 2269 of 3671).

5. Hill considers the possibility that a gay Christian might marry a person of the opposite sex in order to fill the "longing to be desired, to find themselves desirable, and to desire in return" but concludes that such a marriage is likely to lead to frustration and "a kind of rupturing or handicapping of the mutual desire that ought to characterize marriage" (Hill, *Washed and Waiting*, 120–21).

6. Loader, "Homosexuality and the Bible," 19; cf. Brownson, *Bible*, 141–45.

7. Gudorf gives reasons for thinking that celibacy "is more demanding, even more destructive, in the postmodern world than in previous ages" (Gudorf, "Bible and Science," 138–39). Also McNeill, "Homosexuality," 51: "there is no reason to believe that God grants this gift to everyone who is lesbian or homosexual. On the contrary, empirical

same-sex marriage in the West, that homosexual people are no worse off than heterosexual people who cannot find a partner. They may lack the "charisma" that enables celibacy, but they are summoned, nevertheless, to "a difficult, costly obedience, while 'groaning' for the 'redemption of our bodies.'"[8] But same-sex couples do now have the option of marriage, and many will struggle to understand why they should have to submit to a mandatory celibacy. Yes, some heterosexual people never marry and have to come to terms with sexual unfulfillment, "looking to the future resurrection as the locus of bodily fulfillment," as Hays says. But this will only be a small proportion of the heterosexual community. Some of that small proportion will find that they have a "gift" for it, but many—we would expect—will live in hope of finding a sexual partner in the short and medium term and a companion in the long term. That hope may in the end be thwarted, but it is a hope that would be denied to every homosexual person from the outset, as a matter of principle. If we think that gay and lesbian Christians are otherwise normally human, we have to assume a similar distribution throughout the smaller population: many will escape singleness by finding a life partner; some will happily choose singleness; others will have singleness thrust upon them. The suggestion that they should *all* be satisfied with the hope of transformation at the resurrection begins to sound callous, unjust, and unrealistic.

PAUL AND CELIBACY

Given the importance of the celibacy option for the conservative argument, we should look more closely at what Paul actually says about refraining from sexual relations in 1 Corinthians 7:1–7. He affirms the opinion, perhaps originally expressed by the Corinthians themselves, that "it is good for a

---

studies have shown that the vast majority of gay people who have attempted a celibate lifestyle end up acting out their sexual needs in promiscuous and self-destructive ways."

8. Hays, *Moral Vision*, 402. DeYoung's argument against the "revisionist logic" with regard to celibacy is: i) it assumes that same-sex orientation doesn't change; ii) even the married man struggles with "not-to-be-fulfilled sexual desire"; iii) if "chastity is too much to ask of the person with same-sex sexual desires, then it is too much to ask of the person with heterosexual desires"; iv) it is not celibacy itself that is the "gift" in 1 Cor 7 but, quoting Thiselton, the "positive attitude which makes the most of the freedoms of celibacy" (DeYoung, *What Does the Bible*, 115). But these contentions do not address the core issue. Heterosexual people who cannot cope with chastity have the option of marriage; and "positive attitude" is a poor paraphrase for a "*charisma* from God" which is given to some but not all (1 Cor 7:7).

man not to touch a woman," meaning "not to have sexual relations with a woman." Because of sexual immorality (*porneia*), however, he concedes that each man should have his own woman and each woman her own man. They should not deny their bodies to each other, except perhaps during periods of prayer, "so that Satan may not tempt you because of your lack of self-control." He makes it clear that he would rather all people were as he is, but he recognizes that "each has his own gift (*charisma*) from God, one of one kind and one of another."

The context is important, though it is often overlooked—or over-generalized—by writers wanting to recommend celibacy for Christians and for same-sex attracted Christians in particular.[9] Paul expects the churches to face considerable distress and suffering in the transition period between the old age dominated by Greek-Roman paganism and the age to come (1 Cor 7:29–31). His principal concern is that believers should maintain their "undivided devotion to the Lord" under these difficult circumstances (1 Cor 7:35). They need to stay focused. In that regard he thinks that being unmarried is the best option, though he will argue a page or two later that he has "the right to take along a believing wife, as do the other apostles and the brothers of the Lord and Cephas" (1 Cor 9:5). The *charisma* is the ability given by God to live through the "impending distress" as a single person without being thrown off course by Satan. People who do not have that gift (they may have instead the gift of prophecy or of healing: cf. 1 Cor 12:7–10) should take the morally safer, but *more stressful*, option of marriage.

On the evidence of this passage, therefore, celibacy is not the solution to sexual immorality, marriage is. Being unmarried was Paul's somewhat pragmatic and improvised response to the problem of how to live during a period of eschatological upheaval, when believers would come under pressure to abandon their devotion to the Lord, which is the concern that dominates his practical teaching. Let your manner of life be worthy of the gospel of Christ, he says in Philippians, because "it has been granted to you that for the sake of Christ you should not only believe in him but also suffer for his sake" (Phil 1:29). It made sense under such conditions because the unmarried person had less to be anxious about (1 Cor 7:28, 33–34). It is very much to the point, here, that Paul regarded celibacy as the *easier* course. Outside the eschatological context, under normal circumstances, the opposite would be the case: marriage would be natural and relatively easy and singleness would be strained and difficult. But this freedom from

9. For example, Shaw, *Plausibility Problem*, 110–15.

care could not be had at the expense of sexual immorality. So singleness solved an eschatological problem but created a moral one.

It is difficult, therefore, to draw cogent conclusions from this text regarding celibacy as an option for people who experience same-sex attraction. For Paul, the eschatological crisis leads to a preference for the *freedom* of singleness, which leads to the problem of sexual immorality, which is solved either by a *charisma* or by marriage. According to the traditional non-affirming argument, it is the inherent immorality of same-sex relations that leads to the requirement of celibacy; but the same immorality is also the problem raised by singleness—so we are back where we started from. Not all have the *charisma* of self-control, just as not all have the gift of prophecy or of healing; and heterosexual marriage is not a viable framework to contain the burning passion of same-sex attraction.[10] At least, it is hard to avoid the conclusion that the celibacy option for gay and lesbian people *also requires a same-sex marriage option*. Would it not be consistent with Paul's moral logic, Brownson asks, "to encourage these gay and lesbian persons not called to celibacy to live lives of faithful commitment in gay or lesbian marriages or marriagelike relationships?"[11] Is it right that such people—at least, those among them who do not have the *charisma*—are left to "burn with passion" and be tempted by Satan because of their lack of self-control (1 Cor 7:5, 9)?[12] In Paul's day, of course, this would hardly have been a consideration: the *malakoi* and *arsenokoitai* who came to faith in Corinth would have been expected to clean up their act and behave like normal heterosexual people. But things are different now.

When the disciples suggest to Jesus that his ruling on divorce and adultery is so hard that it would be better not to marry, his response is that "there are eunuchs who have made themselves eunuchs for the sake of the kingdom of heaven" (Matt 19:12). This is not quite the same argument as Paul's: Jesus has in mind disciples who will be sent out, not ordinary church communities facing persecution. Some men have been involuntarily emasculated, but remaining single for the sake of the kingdom of God is tantamount to self-emasculation. Presumably, Jesus means this metaphorically, and we may suspect that he is talking about himself; but

10. Cf. Hill, *Washed and Waiting*, 120–22.

11. Brownson, *Bible*, 143.

12. Gudorf finds in Paul's argument in 1 Cor 7:9 that "it is better to marry than to be aflame with passion" biblical justification for same-sex marriage: "Because of the temptation to immorality, homosexual marriages should be recognized by the church" (Gudorf, "Bible and Science," 140).

clearly he regards being unmarried as exceptional and in a crucial sense *harmful to the person.* You take that course only when an even more demanding vocation supervenes—"for the sake of the kingdom of God." The promotion of celibacy for same-sex attracted Christians, therefore, on the grounds that it enables effective ministry appears at first sight to be a more constructive approach. Ed Shaw, for example, writes: "Many of the most significant and inspiring steps forward in world evangelization were made by single Christians."[13] But in the end the argument is self-defeating: these are precisely the *rare* few who have the *charisma* to live chaste lives for the sake of a difficult and *extra*-ordinary religious vocation. Not all who believed in Jesus were required to renounce family life in order to proclaim the kingdom of God throughout Israel and beyond. The biblical logic still requires an alternative disciplining structure for those—in all likelihood the majority—who do not "emasculate" themselves, who lack the necessary capacity for self-control, and who stay behind to get on with normal life.

The celibacy of some gay and lesbian people may well prove to be a compelling sign of future transformation, but it probably has to be part of a mixed sexual ecology. Hill seems to recognize as much when he notes that historically the option of celibacy was pursued in "intentional Christian community"—in monastic orders, for example—sustained by "the rhythms of corporate worship and the mundane tasks of providing for one another's daily needs."[14] This remains a separationist and rigorist model. It may constitute a powerful countercultural witness and provide a benchmark of uncommon obedience, but it does not offer a practical solution for most same-sex attracted Christians. It seems to me, in the end, that the candor and integrity—I'm tempted to say, quite seriously, the "saintliness"—of Hill's book make it a compelling case both *for* a limited gay Christian celibacy and *against* a general gay Christian celibacy.

A Radical Discipleship

To his credit, Hill is painfully honest about the objections and obstacles to celibacy: "The gay Christian who chooses celibacy continually, to one degree or another . . . finds himself or herself longing for something relationally that remains tragically, tantalizingly just out of reach."[15] The solution

13. Shaw, *Plausibility Problem*, 111.
14. Hill, *Washed and Waiting*, 142.
15. Hill, *Washed and Waiting*, 125.

to the profound loneliness and unfulfilled longing of the celibate person is partly the desire of, and the desire for, God, and partly the human community of the church. Hill highlights Jesus's promise to his disciples, who had given up family and community in order to follow him, that they would receive "a hundredfold now in this time, houses and brothers and sisters and mothers and children and lands, with persecutions, and in the age to come eternal life" (Mark 10:30). He takes this to mean that celibate gay Christians are "trading what seems to be the only satisfying relationships they have or could have for ones that will prove to be at once more painful (because of all the myriad effects of sin) and most life-giving."[16]

Hill admits that seeking relational intimacy in the community of the church does not always work; it "merely changes the battleground."[17] But again we have to ask whether the New Testament paradigm is appropriate in the first place. Jesus called people to a radical pattern of discipleship because leaving homes, communities, property, possessions, and jobs was an unavoidable requisite for the task to which they had been called. The mission to proclaim the coming rule of Israel's God, first to Israel, then to the nations, had already uprooted them and would expose them to intense hardship and persecution. The story of the rich man who is told to sell his possessions, give the money to the poor, and follow Jesus, which immediately precedes the assurance given to Peter, precisely illustrates the point (Mark 10:17–31). It is those who have to abandon their *legitimate* support structures—the rich man was righteous, and Jesus loved him— in order to proclaim and live out a message of imminent eschatological transformation under extremely challenging conditions, who are promised a super-abundance of community, as they go about their mission, and life in the age to come. The man's land, property, and possessions will be of no use to him when the judgment of God comes on his people in the form of the invading Roman army. He will find himself in much the same position as the complacent fellow in Jesus's parable, who builds bigger barns to store his grain and goods, and says to himself, "Soul, you have ample goods laid up for many years; relax, eat, drink, be merry" (Luke 12:19). His barns will not save him when disaster comes. So Jesus invites the rich man to leave it all behind now, take up his cross, risk persecution and death, in order to proclaim the good news of the new future that God has in store for his people.

16. Hill, *Washed and Waiting*, 132.
17. Hill, *Washed and Waiting*, 139.

It is difficult to see how this paradigm can be used in any straight-forward fashion as an argument for the *normative* celibacy of same-sex attracted Christians in the church today. Hill's personal experience may *feel* very similar in certain respects, but the situations are really quite different. Jesus called a select group of disciples *out of the normal community life of God's people* and prepared and empowered them to continue his own mission: to proclaim the good news of the coming kingdom of God and bear witness before synagogues, councils, governors and kings (cf. Mark 13:9–10). The long term expectation was that a renewed life for God's people would emerge that would *bring to an end* the eschatological mission, that would *not be like* the eschatological mission.[18] We can speak of Jesus as the exemplar of faithfulness in this particular sense. He called a relatively small number of Jewish men and women to take up their own crosses of persecution and follow him down a narrow and difficult path leading to the life of the age to come (cf. Matt 7:13–14; 16:24–28). He was portrayed in the post-resurrection context as the firstborn of many brothers and sisters who would emulate him in his suffering and be glorified with him (Rom 8:29). Paul made it his life ambition to share Christ's sufferings, "becoming like him in his death, that by any means possible I may attain the resurrection from the dead" (Phil 3:10–11). For the writer to the Hebrews Jesus was the "founder and perfecter" of the faith of those who would be subjected to the same humiliation and violence (Heb 12:1–4).

This is the New Testament narrative of mission: the emulation of the suffering of Christ, in the expectation of vindication and a share in his glory, for the sake of the eventual rule of God over the nations.[19] There is something profoundly misleading, therefore, about the InterVarsity theological statement responding to the LGBT movement when it says: "Jesus was single and serves as the perfect model of imaging God in all his interactions, and the Apostle Paul elevates singleness as a high calling for believers, that they might devote themselves to God undistracted by marriage and worldly matters."[20] The only Jesus we know of is the first-century Jewish prophet-king who inaugurated the reformation of God's

18. In context, the "end" of the mission of the disciples comes before they have gone through all the towns of Israel, with the destruction of Jerusalem and the vindication of the Son of Man (Matt 10:22–23; 24:13–14; Mark 13:13); see Perriman, *Coming of the Son of Man*, 27, 47–70.

19. I develop this theme in Perriman, *Coming of the Son of Man*, 98–129; Perriman, *Future of the People*, 117–21.

20. InterVarsity, "Responding to the LGBT Movement," 2.

people in defiance of its leadership and was killed for his trouble. The only Paul we know of is the first-century Jewish apostle who waived the right to travel with a wife, who was frequently imprisoned, who was subjected to thirty-nine lashes from the Jews on five occasions, who was beaten with rods, once stoned, three times shipwrecked, who suffered hunger and thirst, cold and exposure (cf. 2 Cor 6:4–5; 11:23–27), as he carried the name of Jesus, the Son seated at the right hand of God, "both before nations and kings and before sons of Israel" (Acts 9:15, my translation). Neither of these figures stands as a role model in any core respect for the normal churchgoing Christian, heterosexual or otherwise.

There is not a direct correlation between the suffering of those who were being conformed, through persecution, to the image of the tortured and crucified Christ and the suffering of gay and lesbian Christians who choose—or are obliged to choose—to deny themselves the physical and emotional intimacy of a marriage-like relationship. Picking up on Hays's description of discipleship as a "difficult, costly obedience," Hill writes: "I have come to realize my need to take the New Testament witness seriously and acknowledge that groaning and grief and feeling broken are legitimate ways for me to express my cross-bearing discipleship to Jesus. It's not as if groaning means I am somehow doing something wrong. Groaning is a sign of my fidelity."[21] But if Paul is not talking about the pain of repressed or sublimated desire, we have to press the critical question of whether such a testimony, for all its power, is well-founded.

After the "exodus," after the "exile," when the long journey of the mission to Israel and the nations of the pagan world was over, when the churches had been vindicated and rewarded for their faithful perseverance, everything had to settle down again, and the normal rhythms of human life were resumed under the guidance of the Spirit of the new covenant. At this point it is no longer possible, ordinarily, to prioritize the deracinated community of the church over marriage and family or to imagine that Christian fellowship compensates for the excruciating loneliness that may attend celibacy. Indeed, it is Hill's own testimony that it does not: "Admittedly, entrusting our souls to the fellowship of the church, being open about our struggles with homosexuality and our longings for love, can seem to make loneliness worse, not better."[22] He complains that "we regularly encounter a dearth of theological and pastoral reflection when

21. Hill, *Washed and Waiting*, 140.
22. Hill, *Washed and Waiting*, 134.

we seek to grapple with the practicalities and confusions of long-term sexual abstinence."[23] No doubt the church can learn to support celibate gay Christians better, and perhaps a well-developed and -supported model of "spiritual friendship" would go some way toward making up the emotional deficit.[24] But this does not alter the fact that we appear to have been designed for a peculiar sort of committed "marital" intimacy and companionship that cannot be reproduced in the wider community of the church.

SAME-SEX RELATIONSHIPS IN THE COMMUNITY OF THE RESURRECTION

Not everyone accepts that the traditional redemptive narrative must exclude same-sex relationships. The Anglican theologian and ethicist Robert Song follows the story through to the final resurrection and then comes back with a different perspective on the callings—traditionally marriage and celibacy—by which sexuality is managed in the time before the eschaton. The argument is that the biblical idea of marriage is determined 1) by the original act of creation, 2) by the analogy with the relationship between God and his people, and 3) by the prospect of the fulfillment of creation in Christ, which is "not only its repristination, but also its transformation." The transformation is indicated in Jesus's teaching that there will be no marriage in the resurrection (Matt 22:23–33; Mark 12:18–27; Luke 20:34–36), and it is this which provides the biblical springboard for the theological proposal.

There will be no marriage in the resurrection for the obvious reason that, in Jesus's words, the "sons of the resurrection . . . cannot die again" (Luke 20:35–36, my translation). "Where there is resurrection," Song writes, "there is no death; where there is no death, there is no need for birth; where there is no birth, there is no need for marriage."[25] In the first place, this is what makes Christian celibacy meaningful: "Human flourishing has been given a profound reorientation: full humanity, full participation in the imaging of God, is possible without marriage, without procreation, indeed without being sexually active. Celibacy, in other words, has become an appropriate stance for those who wish to live in the new age."[26] But given

23. Hill, *Washed and Waiting*, 190.

24. Hill, "Christ," 124–47; and see https://spiritualfriendship.org.

25. Song, *Covenant and Calling*, chap. 1, Kindle loc. 418–19 of 1831.

26. Song, *Covenant and Calling*, chap. 1, Kindle loc. 460–62 of 1831. Cf. Hill, *Washed*

the eschatological relativization of marriage, Song asks whether in the new order inaugurated by Christ other callings might not be conceivable which in their different ways would likewise bear witness to the future resurrection life. Same-sex relationships are not given in creation, but if *in Christ* procreation is no longer an ultimate good, there may be forms of intimate non-procreative same-sex relationships that also testify to an eschatological reality that transcends the cycle of birth and death.[27] Song proposes to call such relationships "covenant partnerships"—a more formal version of Hill's argument for "spiritual friendship" as a vocation for celibate people, a sort of monastic community in microcosm, though in Song's view such partnerships could be sexual in nature. They would be characterized by three goods: first, those who enter into them would be committed to faithfulness; secondly, they would embody a commitment to permanence; and thirdly, they would be fruitful in ways other than the production of children through sexual union: fostering and adoption, hospitality, mission partnering, activism, and so on.[28]

The book was published in 2014, and the proposal has rather been overtaken by events. The UK Marriage (Same-Sex Couples) Act was passed by Parliament in July 2013 and came into force in England and Wales in March 2014. The parallel act in Scotland was in force by the end of 2014. There seems now little point in adding a further marriage-like vocation for committed same-sex couples—though Vasey laments the tendency to "borrow and adapt scripts that govern the relationship of men and women in straight society" rather than write new scripts for gay and lesbian people.[29] There is something missionally compelling, nevertheless, about the methodology: the church bears a concrete, embodied, enacted, and vocal witness not only to the death and resurrection of Jesus but also, ultimately, to the prospect of new creation. Jesus's argument about marriage and the resurrection is one of the few direct insights into the nature of the

---

and Waiting, 187: "Insofar as there will be no marrying or being given in marriage in the resurrection . . . the celibate person's life now serves as a direct sign of the eschatological state."

27. Song, *Covenant and Calling*, chap. 2, Kindle loc. 625 of 1831.

28. Song, *Covenant and Calling*, chap. 2, Kindle loc. 638–44 of 1831. The idea was also proposed by Vasey (Vasey, *Strangers*, 233). It is a Christian version of Diotima's argument about male love: "men in this condition enjoy a far fuller community with each other than that which comes with children, and a far surer friendship, since the children of their union are fairer and more deathless" (Plato, *Symp.* 209D).

29. Vasey, *Strangers*, 233.

resurrection existence that we find in the Bible, so it would make sense, on the face of it, to look for ways to anticipate in the patterns of communal life the irrelevance of marriage in the future state. But there are difficulties.

First, the immediate and clear objection in Scripture to same-sex relations is not that the partnership is incapable of producing offspring but that it is unacceptable for a man to lie with a man as with a woman. The sexual act is offensive in itself, not—at least, not in any obvious way—as a departure from the order of procreation. A man who lies with a man as with a woman is still likely to have had children by lying with his wife: it is just not enough. Homosexuality in the New Testament is, for that reason, already an unequivocal and preeminent *sign*, but of the obsolescence of a Godless culture and the imminent arrival of a new régime. It seems impossible to hold that perspective in constructive tension with the idea that certain forms of non-procreativity may prefigure the final renewal of heaven and earth.

Secondly, Paul's argument for celibacy, as we have seen and as Song recognizes, is a pragmatic one, not a theological one. Jesus's singleness looks equally pragmatic in view of the itinerant and hazardous nature of his mission; and the disciples leave behind home, families, and livelihood because they have been called to follow him down this road (Matt 10:38–39; 16:24–26; 20:20–28; Mark 8:34; 10:35–45; Luke 9:23–25; 14:27). It is the specific nature of the mission, first to Israel, then to the nations of the Greek-Roman world, that compels the abandonment of settled marital and procreative life. The New Testament itself does not draw the conclusion that being unmarried anticipates the resurrected state.

Thirdly, the hope of resurrection arose out of just this insecurity and disruption. In the world of Second Temple Judaism, Wright says, resurrection had to do with both the restoration of Israel and the "newly embodied life" of all God's people. "All of this was concentrated, for many Jews, in the stories of the righteous martyrs, those who had suffered and died for YHWH and Torah. Because YHWH was the creator, and because he was the god of justice, the martyrs would be raised, and Israel as a whole would be vindicated."[30] The background to Jesus's response to the Sadducees is found in prominent traditions regarding national crisis and persecution. In the first place, there is the statement that comes as the climax to Daniel's account of the turmoil provoked by the Hellenizing king Antiochus Epiphanes, which ultimately led to the Maccabean revolt.

---

30. Wright, *Resurrection*, 205.

At a time of great trouble righteous Jews would be delivered; many of the dead would be raised, "some to everlasting life, and some to shame and everlasting contempt"; and the "wise," who resisted the severe pressure to apostatize and succeeded in turning many to righteousness, "shall shine like the brightness of the sky above . . . , like the stars forever and ever" (Dan 12:1–3). Jesus echoes this passage when he describes the outcome of the judgment of Israel at the end of the age, when "all causes of sin and all law-breakers" are removed from the kingdom: "the righteous will shine like the sun in the kingdom of their Father" (Matt 13:43).[31]

The hope of the vindication of Israel's righteous dead is also found in other Hellenistic-Jewish texts. Wisdom of Solomon extols the righteous Jew, who calls himself a "servant of the Lord," who is persecuted and killed by impious Gentiles because "he is inconvenient to us, and he opposes our actions and reproaches us for sins against the law and ascribes to us sins against our training" (Wis 2:12–20). But "the souls of the righteous are in the hand of God," the author says. They have been tested as gold in a furnace, as a sacrificial whole burnt offering, and have been found worthy. In a clear echo of Daniel 12:2–3, it is said that "in the time of their visitation they will shine out, and as sparks through the stubble, they will run about" (Wis 3:7; cf. 1 En 39:7; 104:2). When Jesus speaks of the "sons of the resurrection," who neither marry nor are given in marriage (Luke 20:36), this is the sort of narrative that he has in mind: when Israel is restored following the catastrophe of divine judgment, the righteous dead, will be raised to share in the life of the age to come. They are the martyrs who "alone are able to overcome the passions of the flesh, since they believe that they do not die to God, even as our patriarchs Abraham, Isaac and Jacob did not die to God, but live to God." They die for the sake of God but "for God now live, as do Abraham, Isaac, Jacob and all the patriarchs" (4 Macc 7:18–19; 16:25, translation modified). Jesus appears to have shared with the tradition reflected in 4 Maccabees the belief that the righteous dead, who died for the sake of God, would be raised along with the patriarchs.

The dispute with the Sadducees, therefore, is over the Pharisaical belief in a limited resurrection at the time of the restoration of righteous Israel and the defeat of its enemies. The idea, presumably, is that the resurrected dead then live in Jerusalem alongside living Jews in the age to come—an outcome that is perhaps anticipated in the peculiar account of the bodies of the "saints" coming out of the tombs after Jesus's resurrection and entering

---

31. See Hagner, *Matthew 1–13*, 394; France, *Matthew*, 537.

the holy city (Matt 27:52–53). This is a problematic eschatological scenario, and we should hesitate before drawing from it firm conclusions about non-procreative vocations in the church. It may well be the case that in the new heaven and new earth, once death has finally been destroyed, there will be no need for marriage and procreation. But the attempt to line same-sex partnership up with the singleness of Jesus and Paul and the homelessness of the disciples and make it serve as a sign of new creation disregards important narrative distinctions. Resurrection without marriage for Jesus and celibacy for Paul were corollaries not of new creation but of *eschatological transition and the renewal of the people of God.* The celibate person at Corinth was a sign of impending distress.

If we consider same-sex partnerships or same-sex marriage today in a similar light, we are likely to conclude, after a similar fashion, that they are corollaries not of new creation but of *historical adaptation.* The question, then, is whether that adaptation can be assimilated to a plausible biblical narrative trajectory. I agree that it is important to locate the ethical question (should the church affirm certain forms of same-sex relationship?) in an eschatological narrative, but I think that this can be done in a way that keeps our focus on the *historical* challenge faced by the church in the West today. As it stands, Song's narrative does not explain why it is *now*, two thousand years after the community of the resurrection was established, that we are having to devise such radically new disciplines. If we do not work the collapse of the Western Christendom worldview and the relentless rise of modernity into the narrative, the solution appears arbitrary.

CHAPTER 8

Progressive Narratives

THE PROBLEM WITH THE closed redemption-creation-fall-consummation narrative is that it leaves little room for maneuver. In particular, it affords no way of responding to the epochal moment of the collapse of the post-classical, Christianized worldview of Europe and the emergence, to put it in the simplest terms, of secular modernity. The redemptive storyline—the traditional "canonical narrative," as R. Kendall Soulen calls it—follows a fixed and minimally plotted trajectory from creation and fall, through the death of Jesus, to the final restoration of creation.[1] The vast tracts of history that stretch between these beginning, middle, and end points are of no theological significance. The momentous events that make up the *political* experience of the people of God leave no impression on the evangelical consciousness, except as prophetic foreshadowings, types of the Christian life, and occasions to rediscover the power of the unique saving intervention in Jesus. What is lost, Soulen argues, is "creative theological engagement with the hard edges of human history."[2] The assumption is that we cope with crisis and change by diligently getting on with the work of redemptive mission. History will have to look after itself.

---

1. Soulen refers to the four "key episodes" of creation, fall, incarnation and inauguration of the church, and final consummation as the traditional "canonical narrative"—a story that "permits Christians to read the multiplicity of biblical stories (and legal codes, genealogies, letters, etc.) in reasonably coherent and consistent terms" (Soulen, *God of Israel*, 15, 17, 31).

2. Gudorf makes a similar point about the rejection of natural law in favor of *sola Scriptura*: it "left Protestant theology with difficulty in dealing with historical transformations in consciousness and culture" (Gudorf, "Bible and Science," 135).

How, then, might we go about constructing an open, progressive, but still *evangelical* narrative that can frame and make sense of massive social and cultural change? The argument has sometimes been put forward that same-sex relationships may be affirmed by the church on the same hermeneutical grounds that the church now opposes slavery and affirms (though not unanimously) the full equality of women.[3] The Bible takes both slavery and patriarchy for granted; there is no agenda to overturn these "unjust" systems, nor even any unequivocal recognition that they are morally wrong; but there is perceived to be—so the argument goes—an underlying *theological or moral trajectory* that carries the church beyond these ancient cultural arrangements toward the eventual affirmation of social and gender equality in the modern era. Some maintain that homosexuality is a similar case: Paul did not campaign against slavery, he required women to be submissive to their husbands and to keep quiet in church, and by the same token he maintained the traditional Jewish position regarding same-sex relations. The church has moved with the rest of society with respect to slavery and gender equality, so why should we not do the same in the case of homosexuality, which in the eyes of most people now in the secular West is no less a matter of natural human rights than the abolition of slavery and the emancipation of women?

The thesis has been developed in different ways. Brownson, for example, attempts to explain how the underlying "moral logic" of Scripture allows for the accommodation of same-sex relationships within the purview of the biblical vision. When we seek to apply commands and prohibitions outside their original context, it is important that we "ask not only what is commanded or prohibited but why."[4] His argument is that the "moral logic" behind Paul's condemnation of same-sex eroticism in Romans 1:24–27 is not that it is a "violation of divinely intended gender complementarity"; rather, it is that in Paul's view same-sex sexual activity "reflects an expression of excessive and self-centered desire—and is thus *lustful*."[5] Behind this is a deeper logic regarding "the one-flesh kinship bond," which is formed when a person recognizes that "one's own gratification is

---

3. On the biblical and historical toleration of slavery see Davison, *Amazing Love*, 39–42: "Just as some biblical writers assumed that slavery is acceptable, so some assumed (though in far fewer instances) that sex between two women or two men is unacceptable" (42).

4. Brownson, *Bible*, 259.

5. Brownson, *Bible*, 260–61.

possible in the context of loving self-giving to the other."[6] So what the Bible fundamentally presupposes, teaches, and *projects into the future* as the basis for human sexuality, Brownson argues, is not gender complementarity but a broader notion of human flourishing and social harmony. The biblical prohibitions have in view behavior that is contrary to human flourishing and social harmony. They do not apply in the case of modern same-sex relationships marked by moderation and disciplined desire, in which intimacy "contributes to the establishment of lifelong bonds of kinship, care, and mutual concern."[7]

In similar fashion, Davison describes how Christian tradition has evolved with regard to the understanding of marriage and celibacy, birth control, and sexual difference and complementarity. He then locates the affirmation of ethical same-sex relationships in a process of unfolding revelation. The Old Testament principle of "an eye for an eye" is an improvement on "unrestrained vengeance," but Jesus explicitly taught a "more glorious (and difficult) principle, of forgiveness": no longer an eye for an eye, but turn the other cheek and go the extra mile (Matt 5:38–42). The argument is that modern science and developments in moral consciousness have brought us to the point where we can see that the radical pattern of Christian marriage may beneficially be applied also to same-sex relationships. "That isn't about selling out the Church's teaching to prevailing cultural assumptions. Rather, it opens up the possibility that we might commend God's often profoundly counter-cultural message about the truest meaning of sexual love to everyone."[8]

The denial that this is a sell-out, however, seems disingenuous. The affirmation of same-sex relationships is deeply and consistently contrary to the biblical witness. While there may be reasons to think that the Bible is "uncomfortable" with slavery and patriarchy and finds ways to mitigate or undermine these given social arrangements, not least by affirming the equality of slaves and free, women and men in Christ (cf. Gal 3:28), the same cannot be said about homosexuality. There is no redemptive thread to cling to. There is no latent moral potential waiting to be released. Homosexuality is not an "institution" like slavery or patriarchy, imposed on human society, which might one day be eradicated; it is a form of interpersonal behavior, which Paul judges to be unnatural and shameful, the

6. Brownson, *Bible*, 263.

7. Brownson, *Bible*, 277.

8. Davison, *Amazing Love*, 74.

outworking of corrupted desires. If anything, in this regard, the biblical texts are more, not less, intolerant than the surrounding culture—a point convincingly made by William Webb: "The same canons of cultural analysis, which show a liberalizing or less restrictive tendency in the slavery and women texts relative to the original culture, demonstrate a more restrictive tendency in homosexuality texts relative to the original culture."[9] At the same time, any open-ended, progressive narrative must give due weight to the constraints and pressures that modernity has placed on Christian thought. No doubt the church can claim some credit for the abolition of the slave trade, and we may just be able to discern moral trajectories in the Bible that move in the direction of emancipation and sexual equality. But it cannot be denied that these social-ethical gains owed as much (if not more) to a broad-based post-Enlightenment defiance of tradition and advancement of human rights as to inherent Christian motivations. The evangelical abolitionist Wilberforce was a man of his times.

In this respect, David Gushee's approach is more candid, even if in the end we run into the same hermeneutical road block. His argument is that the LGBT issue is a *faith/science integration issue*, of which there have been many."[10] The accounts of creation in Genesis 1–2 are based on a pre-scientific understanding of the natural world. In the modern era a broadly scientific description of the human species has led to a revision of the traditional understanding of homosexuality. It is no longer a matter of men and women behaving badly. Some people innately experience same-sex attraction and cannot find a "helper fit" for them from among members of the opposite sex. Just as the church has had to come to terms with scientific models of the cosmos and human origins at odds with the biblical narratives, so "we face the challenge of integrating contemporary scientific findings about gender and sexual orientation into our theological story of the world God made."

How are we to resolve the cognitive dissonance between the "stubborn facts" of human reality and the ancient assumptions made by the biblical

9. Webb, *Slaves*; see also Greene-McCreight, "Logic," 257–58; Gagnon, "Bible and Homosexual Practice," 44–45; and Hays, *Moral Vision*, 389: "Though only a few biblical texts speak of homoerotic activity, all that do mention it express unqualified disapproval. Thus, on this issue, there is no synthetic problem for New Testament ethics. In this respect, the issue of homosexuality differs significantly from matters such as slavery or the subordination of women, concerning which the Bible contains internal tensions and counterposed witnesses. The biblical witness against homosexual practices is univocal."

10. Gushee, *Changing Our Mind*, 91.

writers—and, indeed, by Jesus himself? Gushee's solution is simple and pragmatic: it is *normally* the case that gender identity is "clearly male or female" and corresponds to "gender assignment" and that "sexual orientation is heterosexual." But we are stuck with the fact that a small percentage of the population does not fit the majority definitions. Such people should be "accepted for who they are, and assisted, where necessary, in the ways most congruent with their overall well-being."[11] The empirical reality, Gushee argues, is transformative. He invokes the standard set of analogues. The current controversy regarding same-sex relations is like previous moral paradigm shifts that the church has had to make—the inclusion of Gentiles, the abolition of slavery, the abandonment of anti-Semitism, the full equality of women. "Some of us believe that in our time an older, destructive paradigm based on a particular way of connecting the biblical dots *has not survived the transformative encounters we are having with LGBTQ fellow Christians*, encounters in which we experience regular and astonishing reminders of God's presence."[12]

Gushee's appeal to "transformative encounters" with openly gay and lesbian Christians is powerful, but the analogy with other reforms remains debatable: in the New Testament slaves, women and Jews are explicitly *included* in the covenant community; people who engage in same-sex sexual relations are explicitly *excluded*. The social *dynamics* of the controversy may appear the same, but the reasons for it are very different. We will return to the analogy with the inclusion of Gentiles in the final chapter. The argument from science cannot be ignored—we are undoubtedly operating with a very different epistemology, a very different way of perceiving and interpreting the world. But if it is not to appear arbitrary, we need to be able to tell a convincing "theological story," not merely about "the world God made," but about the nature and purpose of the church under the particular social and intellectual conditions which have generated this controversy.

Such a narrative cannot be grounded in an *intrinsic* biblical vision of moral progress. On the one hand, the method overlooks the powerful *narrative* logic shaping Paul's analysis in Romans 1:18–32. Eschatology is reduced to ethics, the large movements of history to generalities about human flourishing. The distinction that controlled Paul's argument was not the one between bad and good sexuality but the one between an idolatrous and unclean Greek civilization, supremely characterized by the public

11. Gushee, *Changing Our Mind*, 93.
12. Gushee, *Changing Our Mind*, 109–10.

celebration of homosexuality, and a coming world in which the nations would serve the living creator God. On the other hand, the affirmation of same-sex relationships requires a dislocation of the storyline that was simply unimaginable from the perspective of the New Testament. Moral trajectories sometimes break or are sharply refracted at the boundary between worldviews, which is why the question needs to be resolved at the "eschatological" level. How do we structure the story of the people of God? How do we identify the disruptive transitions from one era to the next? How do we give prophetic outline to the place of the church in the age to come? Eschatological trajectories and moral trajectories are two quite different things.

NARRATIVE MODELS

N. T. Wright has famously proposed that the Bible is like an unfinished five act Shakespearian play. The first four acts present the story through to Jesus: 1) creation; 2) fall; 3) history of Israel; 4) life and death of Jesus. The writing of the New Testament constitutes the first scene of act five, giving hints at the same time regarding "how the play is supposed to end."[13] The task of the church is then to "live under the 'authority' of the extant story, being required to offer an improvisatory performance of the rest of the final act as it leads up to and anticipates the intended conclusion." The authority of the Bible is expressed in the creative commitment of the actors to what has gone before.

This is a good place to start. It is firmly grounded in the program of locating Jesus and Paul in the narratives of Second-Temple Judaism that has come to dominate New Testament scholarship, including evangelical scholarship, over the last thirty or forty years; and it is well-known. The explicit inclusion of the history of Israel goes some way toward addressing the shocking hermeneutical and theological deficiencies of the closed creation-fall-redemption-consummation model. But Wright's outline leaves us with a lot more history—in fact, an indefinite amount of very unpredictable history—to get through in the last few rushed scenes of the final Act.

---

13. Wright, *New Testament*, 140–42. Others have developed the trope. Bartholomew and Goheen, for example, have rewritten the plot around the kingdom theme and have taken the liberty of adding a sixth act to remove the element of uncertainty introduced by Wright and wrap the whole thing up (Bartholomew and Goheen, *Drama*, 26).

It seems to me that we have a more realistic Shakespearian analogy in the multipart histories, such as the Henry VI trilogy of plays. Part One would be the biblical story of how the God who called Abraham out of the shadow of Babel came to be worshiped by the nations of the ancient pagan world—a grandiose tragicomic history of disobedience and mercy, exile and restoration, death and resurrection, witness and persecution, faithfulness and vindication.[14] Part Two is the less well-known but no less tumultuous story of what we now call "Christendom": God's rule over the nations of the former pagan empire, which has its celebrated highlights (the ecumenical councils, the Reformation, the abolition of slavery, the global missionary movement, etc.), but is heavy-going for the average theatre-goer, and by the end we are left with the impression that the real action has shifted elsewhere.[15] We are currently, perhaps, some way into the second act of Part Three: the struggle of the church to survive and bear witness in a secular age, with plenty of drama still to come. Who knows where the reckless human journey is headed next? In this more complex model the basic hermeneutical point remains the same: we are acting out a story in faithful continuity with the biblical narrative on the vast stage of creation, confident that in the end the creator will bring the curtain down for a last time . . . and, amid rapturous cosmic applause, raise it again on a new heaven and a new earth (Rev 21:1–8). But the point is that we are not just reciting the same evangelical mantras, not just singing the same evangelical songs over and over, not just rehearsing the same personal transformations in order to fill the theological void between Jesus and the final judgment. We are trying to—having to—make sense of history for the sake of a credible future.

The difficult dramaturgical question that we face here is: how much has changed between Part Two and Part Three? I would suggest that the biblical cycle of stories effectively comes to an end with the collapse of Christendom as the concrete historical expression of the rule of God over the nations that were formerly the Greek-Roman *oikoumenē*. Perhaps this

14. In view of the preceding analysis, this could be broken down into the story about the land and the story about how God came to rule over the nations through Jesus. But the conviction regarding the defeat of empire goes back at least to the exilic period: it is territorial insecurity that drives the hope of regional hegemony—the rule of YHWH in the place of the kings of Babylon, Persia, Greece, and finally Rome.

15. I recognize that the church also spread eastward in the early period, but the focus here is on the historical unfolding of the New Testament mission, which had in view almost exclusively the *oikoumenē* governed by Rome.

should be seen as the judgment of God on an uninspired, institutionalized, moribund church, which could find no more constructive response to the turmoil of social and intellectual change in the eighteenth and nineteenth centuries than to withdraw into its heavily fortified traditions and pull up the drawbridge. There is certainly some sort of *re-formation* now under way. But again, the question is: can modernity be explained in biblical terms, or do we have to recognize that we have moved beyond the biblical horizon, that we are having to live and tell the story of the people of God in uncharted territory? An adequate account of the changes that have taken place cannot be given here, but some key aspects may be highlighted on the basis of the earlier analysis of the historical and biblical material.

1. The cultural circumstances that appear integral to Paul's critique in Romans 1:18–32 have changed. We do not—even as *evangelicals*—now regard homosexual behavior as the defining feature of a civilization given over to idolatry. On the one hand, most people who take a traditional stance on the issue are at pains to say that it is just one sin among many, and that none of us is in a position to cast the first stone. On the other, it is not obvious that the modern gay movement is the product of willful idolatry in any meaningful sense and not, in the words of Michael Vasey, "a defence of certain humane perspectives . . . that are under threat in wider society—including an expressive rather than brutalized masculinity."[16] If we look at the Western world, we may well decide that over-consumption or narcissism or sexual promiscuity generally, not same-sex relations, is the hallmark of our culture. If we cannot make the same argument about the secular humanist as Paul made about the Greek, where does that leave his censure of same-sex relationships?

2. The sense of collective identity that underpinned the biblical stories about the land and the kingdom of God and accounted for the destruction or exclusion of people who engaged in homosexual activity is much weaker in the modern era. We affirm, instead, the right of the "autonomous individual" to make her or his own lifestyle choices, provided that no harm is done to others. The sixth of Peter Berger's defining characteristics of the "autonomous individual" is that "I have the capacity to choose my life, my world and finally my own self, and I assert the right to realize this capacity."[17] That locates us in a world very different to that of the Old Testament Jew or of the first-century Christian. We can resist it up to a point in

16. Vasey, *Strangers*, 132.

17. Berger, "Western Individuality," 327.

the name of Christian community, but we think and act like moderns, not like the ancients.

3. The entrenched patriarchalism that shaped both the forms of same-sex behavior in the ancient world and the divergent reactions to it is no longer operative. In a defense of Jewish belief and custom aimed self-consciously at the Greek, Josephus explains the laws of Jewish marriage. The Law allows for no other arrangement than the "natural" one (*tēn kata physin*): "a man with his wife, and that this be used only for the procreation of children." Then he directly states that the Law "abhors the mixture of a male with a male; and if anyone do that, death is his punishment" (*Ag. Ap.* 2:199). But it is immediately clear that for Josephus the *natural* arrangement also entails the explicit dependency and inferiority of the woman: she is demanded in marriage from the father, who has the power to "dispose of her," because "a woman, they say, is inferior [*cheirōn*] to a man in all respects" (2:201, my translation). Arguably, it is the breakdown of this link between a patriarchal, homosocial culture and homosexual practice, and the emergence of a thoroughly egalitarian culture that has decisively shifted the ground, as much as any reassessment of the type of homosexual practice addressed.

4. We no longer think of nature as an unchangeable physical and moral order instituted by God and expressive of the mind of God. Charles Taylor, in *A Secular Age*, describes the transformation that has taken place. At an earlier stage of human history "the social order is seen as offering us a blueprint for how things, in the human realm, can hang together to our mutual benefit, and this is identified with the plan of Providence, what God asks us to realize."[18] In the modern era the immanent order of nature has come to be envisaged without reckoning with God, and eventually "the proper blueprint is attributed to Nature." What primarily drives this process is scientific enquiry, but this has obviously made "nature" subject to investigation and critical interpretation. We cannot now think of it as simple, immutable, and self-evident. Western societies have mostly come to the firm conclusion, over the last fifty years or so, that homosexuality is unusual but not *unnatural*. It would now seem *unnatural*, in fact, to deny gay and lesbian people the right and opportunity to form loving and intimate relationships.

The seriousness of the epistemological reorientation can be illustrated from the modern evaluation of demon possession. Most of the people

18. Taylor, *Secular Age*, 543.

classified as being under the control of unclean spirits or demons in the Gospels would today be diagnosed as having medical or psychiatric conditions and would be treated accordingly. The Bible-believing church is divided over the issue. As a generalization, Christians in traditional non-Western cultures will both interpret the Bible and experience "demon possession" on supernaturalist presuppositions: they will treat it as a *real thing*. In the West conservative evangelicals are probably in two minds, struggling to sustain a theologically motivated literalist understanding of the phenomenon within an extremely unsympathetic rationalist world view. We find it difficult to agree now that what looks like epilepsy or a personality disorder is really a manifestation of the presence of evil spirits. The point is certainly debatable, but in the long run it seems likely that the rational interpretation will prevail, and the notion of demon possession will survive only as symbolic representation. The analogy with same-sex relations becomes particularly interesting when demon possession in the Gospels is understood *apocalyptically*, as symptomatic of Israel's subjection to an unclean pagan presence or of the clash between the early church and the formidable powers that inspired the idolatrous empire (cf. Matt 12:27–28; Mark 5:9; Luke 8:30; Rev 16:13; 18:2). The casting out of demons is a sign of the coming kingdom of God; it belongs to the same narrative as the exclusion of people who exchange natural sexual usage for unnatural. The apocalyptic reframing makes excellent sense of the New Testament details, I would argue, but equally it underscores the fact that the narrative has moved on. Our understanding of "nature" has fundamentally changed.

5. The idea found occasionally among the Greeks that enduring same-sex relationships may be grounded in a fixed personal ontology has been rationalized, normalized, and thoroughly—sometimes quite forcefully—integrated into the moral fabric of society. The particular patterns of behavior may look much the same, but the large cultural matrix in which they are embedded, which is often invisible to the interpreter, has changed out of all recognition. Same-sex attraction is not to be explained speculatively—as a consequence of Promethean bungling, for example, or the splitting of primordial archetypes. It is considered to be a matter, more or less, of scientific fact. If science were to change its mind and rule out biology, then it would become a matter of human rights. The modern world simply has no rational or ethical grounds on which to oppose same-sex relationships. At its worst, same-sex behavior is no worse than heterosexual depravity; at its best, it is as good as heterosexual virtue.

6. Finally, we have to keep in mind that the Western world is moving away from Christianity, not toward it. This is not a backsliding that might be halted by revival. It seems highly unlikely—historically speaking, at least— that Western civilization will again confess that Jesus Christ is Lord, to the glory of the God of Israel. After a traumatic adolescence modernity has grown up, left home, and moved on. While its Christian parent culture is still alive, it will visit occasionally and pay its respects, at least for weddings and funerals; but the assumption is that eventually the parents will die and be buried, and modernity in turn will produce its own offspring, who will barely recall their historical origins.

So the argument here is not so much that Paul could not have imagined modern forms of same-sex relationships. It is rather that the whole epistemological and moral order of modernity is different. Paul could not have imagined the modern world. He foresaw a day when every knee would bow and every tongue would confess that Jesus was Lord, but he could not have foreseen the massive shift of allegiance to secular liberal humanism *in the age to come after the age to come.* The ancient understanding of homosexuality was governed by a conception of nature as fixed and sacred, the priority of the community over the individual, the moral authority of collective disgust, and a pervasive patriarchalism and homosocial order. Each of those considerations has been replaced in the modern era: nature is an empirical construct, subject to revision and development; private morality is decided, in principle, with reference to the intrinsic rights of the individuals involved; any public objection to same-sex relations on the grounds of "uncleanness" (*akatharsia*) or "disgust" is now intolerable; and there is everywhere a determination finally to root out the oppressive knotweed of patriarchy and to cultivate in its place a mixed and thoroughly egalitarian ecology. The *moral significance* of homosexual behavior cannot be determined by looking at either the ancient or the modern practice in isolation from the cultural matrix. The theatre of the world has undergone a massive refurbishment. The church is having to act out its age-old story on a stark modernized stage, with a very different backdrop, very different stage furniture, under severe lighting, with far more sophisticated special effects, and in front of a very different audience.

THE ESCHATOLOGICAL HORIZON OF MODERNITY

Our consideration of Paul's argument in Romans 1:18–32 has suggested that the missional community of God's people should keep in mind a clear distinction between the *final* horizon of God's renewal of creation and whatever more immediate and pressing *historical* horizon may be in view. For Paul the historical horizon was shaped by the conflict with an overarching supernatural-political pagan system, with the principalities and powers that ruled the ancient world. For us it will be determined, in some manner, by the crisis engendered on the other side of the Christendom bell curve by the rise of Western secular humanism. In some respects the current situation is the mirror image of the eschatological challenge confronting the early church, except that what lies ahead is not the triumph of Christianity across the Roman Empire but the *marginalization* of Christianity in an increasingly self-confident secular environment.

There is a *final* eschatology (the tautology is difficult to avoid) that shapes the witness of the church as it seeks to be a sign to the world that God will overcome the last enemy and make all things new. The creator, and not sin or Satan or death, will have the last word. But equally, the missional church after Christendom needs to express in its communal and public life a distinctive hope *relevant to the immediate historical challenge* of responding well to the accelerating secular-humanist overhaul of Western societies. The church, as it struggles to get its bearings after the long slow demise of Western Christendom, must keep one eye on the final vindication of the living creator God, who will make all things new. But the Bible teaches us to keep the other eye firmly focused on *the historical future of God's people*. (This is not to say that the church should not also keep an eye on the past and the present, but four eyes are too many for one metaphor.) This is apparent even in the argument about same-sex relations—indeed, it appears that this particular controversy is an excellent test case for thinking through the extension of the biblical storyline into the modern context.[19]

In the Old Testament male same-sex sexual activity was one of a number of unclean or "abominable" practices associated with the Canaanites that could get Israel vomited out of the land. The significance of the homosexual rape stories is that they are the nearest we get to concrete depictions of the sort of behavior that was condemned—the first demonstrated by the

---

19. Cf. Bird, "Bible," 163: "The status of homosexual acts and persons has emerged as perhaps the most important case for testing our understanding of Christian identity and community."

Canaanites, the second by one of the tribes of Israel. Ezekiel makes it clear that Israel would suffer the same fate as the people of Sodom: God heard the outcry of the oppressed and saw the abomination that Sodom did, and he removed the city; he has seen the greater transgressions of Israel and will remove the nation from the land (Ezek 16:48–50).[20] The prohibition against same-sex relations, therefore, was not simply a legal restriction; it was part of a long story about possession of the land that would culminate in exile.

By the time we get to the New Testament period Israel has indeed been exiled from the land; and in a sense, although the people returned from Babylon, they remained "in exile" under pagan powers—first the Persians, then the Greeks, then the Romans—through to the New Testament period.[21] So the overriding eschatological or future-oriented questions for the Jews were: When would God judge the pagan world? When would the kingdom be restored to Israel (cf. Acts 1:6)? When would they inherit the kingdom? We can agree here, up to a point, with Hays: "neither the word of judgment against homosexuality nor the hope of transformation to a new life should be read apart from the eschatological framework of Romans."[22] But for Hays this framework is oriented toward the final renewal of creation, and I have argued that this collapses the immense "political" dimensions of Paul's vision.[23] Historical narratives and eschatological narratives in the New Testament are not as remote from each other as is usually assumed. At the forefront of Paul's mind, as an apostle to the nations, was the belief that the "Greek" predilection for unnatural and shameful homosexual practices was the outstanding characteristic of a decadent pagan culture *that was coming to an end*. Churches, therefore, that had rigorously cleansed themselves of such practices would be a compelling sign that the present form of that world was passing away (1 Cor 7:31) and that a new state of affairs was soon

---

20. Jesus has similar condemnation for the cities of Israel: "And you, Capernaum, will you be exalted to heaven? You will be brought down to Hades. For if the mighty works done in you had been done in Sodom, it would have remained until this day. But I tell you that it will be more tolerable on the day of judgment for the land of Sodom than for you" (Matt 11:23–24).

21. Not all scholars have been persuaded by N. T. Wright that Jews in the first century believed themselves still to be in exile (Wright, *New Testament*, 268–71), but as a shorthand way of speaking about the continuing subjection of Israel to pagan powers it works well enough.

22. Cf. Hays, *Moral Vision*, 393.

23. See Perriman, *Future of the People*.

to emerge. Again, it was not merely a question of right or wrong behavior: God's future was at stake.

Neither of these narratives is precisely relevant for the church today. History is not cyclical. We are not simply repeating the experience of the first-century church. We are moving out of and away from a Christian culture, not toward one. The normalization of homosexuality—along with other boundary "transgressions," particularly in relation to sexuality and gender—is a leading characteristic of a post-Christian culture that is aggressively redefining what it means to be human, not according to Genesis 1–3, but according to a broad set of scientific-libertarian values and a technological-progressive narrative. It is a mark not of moral decadence but of moral reordering. If the current prominence of the controversy is an *eschatological* sign of anything, it is that the Christian world is passing away. The narrative framework is not the same. It is common these days for even quite conservative scholars to stress the narrative shape of biblical truth: in his discussion of Romans 1:18–31, for example, Hays makes the point that the "normative application of principles is fundamentally dependent *on a particular narrative framework.*"[24] But narratives move forwards, they change direction, they spring surprises. What is at stake now is not possession of the Land or the conversion of the ancient pagan world but the credibility and sustainability of the Western church's witness to the God and Father of our Lord Jesus Christ, as Christianity fights against being consigned to its own outer darkness, where there is already much wailing and gnashing of teeth.

One course of action open to the church at this point would be to attempt to turn back the clock, to revert to the premodern paradigm and maintain a dogmatic antagonism toward homosexuality. This does not seem to me to be a realistic or sustainable option. The church in the West is having to come to terms with the fact that its primary mode of existence for the foreseeable future, in real public terms, will be as a redundant priestly-prophetic community.[25] This entails a "missional" adjustment of literally (for once) biblical proportions, comparable to the exile of Israel from the land, the destruction of Jerusalem, or the overthrow of classical paganism; and it means, among other things, that we are having to reconsider how we

24. Hays, *Moral Vision*, 395, italics added.

25. Cf. Gushee's two narratives—one of "cultural, ecclesial and moral decline," one of "marginalization, resistance and equality" (Gushee, *Changing Our Mind*, 112–15, italics removed).

deal with the "problem" of same-sex relationships.[26] The straightforward biblical approach of outright condemnation and forceful exclusion seems now to be unworkable.

In his book on "mere sexuality" Todd Wilson points out that the historic Christian consensus about sexuality lasted from the fourth to the mid-twentieth century and "has only seriously been called into question within the last forty to fifty years with the liberalization of Christian sexual ethics in the foment of the 1960s sexual revolution."[27] His point is that the sexual revolution is something of a novelty and he exhorts the church to reinstate the traditional paradigm as the theological frame for addressing questions about same-sex relationships. But the narrative argument that we are pursuing here may lead us to conclude that the ethical tradition simply cannot be sustained under modern conditions. In this new age, we may be discovering that we have no choice but to reevaluate the fundamental shape of the church's relation to society. It is very unlikely that the sexual revolution is a passing fad; it would appear to be an integral and entirely *reasonable* development given the terms of the secular humanist program. Nor can the rethinking be explained and dismissed as "pervasive interpretive pluralism."[28] The internal *debate* about sexuality, which admittedly is chaotic and impulsive in many respects, is nevertheless symptomatic of the deep theological overhaul that has to take place if the church is to maintain the credibility of its biblical identity. The option to revert to paradigms that prevailed under different circumstances remains open and is not without theological appeal, but the *narrative-historical* dynamic of biblical existence suggests that the church always has to move forwards.

---

26. Seitz rejects the idea that the church is moving "toward gradual enlightenment" on the ground that "in the modern homosexual phenomenon we are confronting something truly without precedent" (Seitz, "Sexuality," 178–79). But he considers this only with regard to a purported development between the Old and New Testaments. The transition between the two parts of the canon is only one aspect of the historical development to which the Bible bears witness, and consistency within the canon with respect to this particular matter of sexual behavior does not itself preclude the possibility of substantive historical developments beyond the purview of Scripture. Moreover, the narrative-historical thesis does not require us to think that modernity is a move toward enlightenment, only that it is an epochal transformation.

27. Wilson, *Mere Sexuality*, 34.

28. Wilson, *Mere Sexuality*, 28–29.

Benchmarking Modernity

The aim here has not been to propose a comprehensive, practical response but to outline a plausibly "evangelical" space in which churches and missional groups might rethink their engagement with gay and lesbian people, whether believers or otherwise. This space has been constructed not ethically or socially but *narratively*, as part of a retelling of the biblical story that first highlights certain critical "eschatological" perspectives, and then makes those perspectives transparent to history. But if we bring history into focus in this way, we are bound to recognize that there are forces at work in our own age that are generating *new* eschatological horizons, beyond anything envisaged in Scripture. The "problem" of loving, stable, egalitarian relationships between people of the same sex has proved to be one of the most painful and disturbing signs of this development, but it seems to me that the approach pursued here offers a defensible basis for accommodating such relationships *as a sign of the presence of God in the midst of profound cultural transition.*

There may, however, be another side to the eschatological model which would give a sharper prophetic edge to the witness of the church in the secular West. For all the anxieties people may currently have about globalization, population growth, migration, terrorism, environmental degradation, climate change, and so on, the modern world remains firmly convinced that it must set its own agenda and rely on its own resources. In that respect, nothing has changed since Babel. The biblical story tells us, however, that the hubris of Babel or Babylon or "Babylon the great" is always under, and will eventually have to reckon with, the judgment of the creator God. We may think of such judgment as real or notional. We may imagine it taking the form of an ecological crisis caused by climate change, for example; or if that level of apocalyptic realism makes us nervous, we may develop the thought in more abstract and symbolic terms. But if modern civilization is in some sense to be "judged" by the God of heaven and earth—and there is every reason to think, *biblically speaking*, that it will be—it will not be on the same grounds that the idolatrous Greek-Roman world was judged. It will not be according to the narrative of Romans 1:18–32.

In the modern eschatological storyline the task of the church, I suggest, will not be to reproduce the exact moral life of the New Testament communities but to model a way of living—in humility, by grace, always in need of forgiveness—that has meaning *under the particular limiting conditions of modernity.*[29] This is unavoidable. The church must remain true to its identity as a new creation people, but *as a prophetic people* it must also aim to be the *benchmark* by which Western secular humanism might plausibly be judged. The church must embody in its corporate life—inevitably as a compromise, as a frank accommodation, as a historical adaptation—a standard of moral life to which the dominant culture might reasonably be expected to attain. What does new creation look like not in ultimate terms but in *penultimate* terms? What does ideal human flourishing look like under the radically new social and ethical conditions of the post-Christendom age? Put simply, it appears that the church must do secular humanism better than the world does it. This reflects the fact that the church cannot fully dissociate itself from secular humanist culture: we are raised in it, educated by it, work for it, share its aspirations, breathe the blustery air of its worldview, play its games, fight its wars one way or another, consume its products, add to its waste, pollute its oceans, celebrate its achievements, participate in its political processes, benefit from and contribute to its structural injustices. But the church should have the perspective, freedom, and resources to do secular humanism *better*, either concretely or symbolically—with love for others, with self-discipline and restraint, with humility, with long-term vision, with a strong moral compass, with a sense of eschatological purpose, with a bigger story to tell, with the power of the Holy Spirit, with a profound sense of security under Christ as Lord, and with knowledge of the Creator.

One of the strongest practical arguments for the legalization of marriage for same-sex couples is that it provides a social framework for the stabilization of sexual behavior. The point is made by Brownson: "it does not take much moral imagination to realize that, even if one may not fully embrace the morality of committed gay and lesbian unions, such unions may represent a substantial moral improvement over anonymous and unrestrained sexual activity."[30] The evangelical ethicist Lewis Smedes argued

---

29. Quoting the Catholic ethicist Lisa Cahill, Gushee writes: "Christian sexual ethics in the world we actually live in must help people come to 'the most morally commendable course of action concretely available' in their particular circumstances" (Gushee, *Changing Our Mind*, 97).

30. Brownson, *Bible*, 144. Pilling, *Report of the House of Bishops*, para. 209, notes that a central theme in John, *Permanent, Faithful, Stable*, is "the need for the Church to support permanent, faithful and stable relationships among bisexual and gay people, in order to counter some of the tendencies within the bisexual and gay community as a whole."

back in 1976, in his book *Sex for Christians*, that a third option for gay and lesbian people after "healing" and celibacy was "optimum homosexual morality," which meant, in effect, *de facto* same-sex monogamy.[31] It is part of Ken Wilson's argument for a "Third Way" that as a pastor he is coming across a growing number of LGBT people who are not attracted to the stereotypically decadent "homosexual lifestyle" but want to express their sexuality in loving faithful relationships. "I saw people who knew that sex wasn't just a lustful itch to be scratched; like others, they knew that sex is part of the process of forging a pair-bond, the kind of intimacy that can see a person through thick and thin for a lifetime."[32] Many will feel that it is fundamentally right and wise to affirm and support this yearning.

David Gushee differentiates between three levels of sexual ethic. First, Western society by and large affirms a *mutual consent ethic*: you can engage in sexual activity with whomever you like as long as it is mutually consensual and does not cause harm. Secondly, a significant number of secular people endeavor to restrict sexual activity to one relationship, as long as the relationship lasts. Gushee labels this a *loving relationship ethic*. Thirdly, the church has traditionally advocated a *covenantal-marital ethic*, which has required a man and woman to make a binding lifelong commitment to "remain faithful to the promises of that covenant, including fidelity and exclusivity" until death. He firmly rejects any "weakening of a covenantal-marital ethics norm," but he believes that there are LGBT Christians who "want to make a lifetime covenant with one person, and they would like some support from their congregations in doing so."[33] The church does not have a monopoly on marriage, but it does have a vested theological interest in relational faithfulness, and there is a clear opportunity here to support gay and lesbian Christians to establish a realistic benchmark against which same-sex relationships, in this very different secular age, might be measured.

Same-sex marriage, as such, is still a novelty, a venture into the unknown, and it remains to be seen whether it will work in the long run for more than a small percentage of gay and lesbian couples. According to Andrew Goddard there are supporters of gay rights, among them Christians, who think that "the pattern of homosexual desire is such that

31. Smedes, *Sex for Christians*, cited without page reference in Toulouse, "Muddling Through," 27–28.

32. Wilson, *Letter*, chap. 2, Kindle loc. 824–25 of 3155.

33. Gushee, *Changing Our Mind*, 102n53, 104.

it cannot be expected to be monogamous." He cites the view of Andrew Yip that only "a tiny number of male couples are physically faithful to each other."[34] It may turn out that it is less disapproval of same-sex relations than the insistence on lifelong faithful monogamy (assuming that the same standards are applied to heterosexual couples, which is a big assumption) that discourages the participation of gay and lesbian people in the covenant community—or perhaps encourages them to pursue the option of a life of celibacy. But while the jury is out, it seems to me better to *include* same-sex marriages as a positive statement about relational faithfulness than to allow their *exclusion* to signal the alienation of the church from its culture.

SIGNS OF THE TIMES

In the days of King Ahaz, when the kings of Syria and Ephraim threatened Jerusalem, God spoke to Ahaz and to his people through three significantly named boys: Shear-jashub, Immanuel, and Maher-shalal-hash-baz (Isa 7:3, 14–16; 8:3–4). These either were Isaiah's own sons or were born into the prophetic circle associated with him. In different ways, they were a concrete sign to Ahaz and to the people of Judah that YHWH was with his people to deliver them at this time of great political crisis. Isaiah will wait for the Lord and hope in him: "Behold, I and the children whom the LORD has given me are signs and portents in Israel from the LORD of hosts, who dwells on Mount Zion" (Isa 8:18). In a similar way, I think that we have to consider the possibility that, in this modern transitional moment, the unsought but unqualified inclusion of same-sex married couples in the life and ministry of the church is a sign and portent from the Lord, both for worse and for better. It is a sign, in the first place, of the harsh and disorienting reality of the marginalization of the church in the secular West and of the slow dawning of a new age. We may acknowledge the force of Brownson's point, for example, that the presence of a "queer" minority is a natural deconstruction of "the pervasive tendencies of majority voices to become oppressive and exclusionary."[35] But more positively, the visible inclusion of same-sex celibate and married people may be interpreted by prophetic voices as a concrete and incontestable sign of the church's commitment to gay and lesbian people generally; as a sign of its continuing commitment to marriage under radically altered social conditions; as a sign of its awareness of

34. Goddard, "James V. Brownson," 43.
35. Brownson, *Bible*, 253.

alternative, non-stereotypical visions of what it means to be masculine and feminine;[36] as a sign that the church is determined not to withdraw into a deepening sectarian isolationism but to maintain its priestly commitment to secular society; and as a sign of the continuing relevance of the biblical vision of the living creator God, who is always a God of the future, as the world reconstructs its anthropology.

36. Cf. Vasey, *Strangers*, 233: "On this view, the men who emerge as gay, although perceived as aberrant, are involved in the recovery of a more affectionate and intimate masculinity and a consequent reconciliation with the feminine. While the way this works for individuals may be problematic and is certainly contested, the emergence of a gay identity is both a symptom of gender stress in the culture and one of the ways by which this stress is being addressed."

CHAPTER 9

The Art of Evangelical Storytelling

THE SOCIAL LEGITIMACY OF long-term same-sex relationships or marriages is now, by and large, a given in the West. Not everyone approves, and not every subculture approves, but it has become an unassailable premise of public morality that homosexual relationships are no different from heterosexual relationships. It is not something that the evangelical church has chosen, but we have to deal with the reality of enduring, principled gay and lesbian marriages, often with dependent children, both in society at large and amongst believers. We are no longer addressing the biblical and theological questions in order to make a decision. The decision has been made for us. What a biblical-theological method now needs to do is frame this new reality and find a way forward.

My argument, which I have presented deliberately as an *evangelical* argument, has been that this frame is provided by the prophetic assimilation of momentous and unprecedented historical changes into the story of the people of God. We learn not least from the texts dealing with same-sex sexual behavior in Scripture that the controlling narrative is not the theologically reductionist one about creation, fall, redemption, and consummation, but the much-more complex and contested one about the experience of the people of God in history, from age to age. The prophetic mind of the apostolic church, tutored by the Jewish scriptures, could imagine that its faithful witness to the risen Jesus would culminate in the overthrow of a pagan civilization characterized by its tolerance of homosexuality and the inauguration of a new religious and moral order. But it could not foresee the next once-in-an-epoch earthquake, fifteen hundred years or more after that. If Scripture teaches us to tell the story of the people of God *in history*, with creation and new creation as prologue and epilogue, we should not be surprised that history has now taken us beyond the limited historical outlook of the New Testament. History has become a powerful generative force in the construction of the church's relation to post-Christian society. It is not the backdrop to the story; it *is* the story.

Clearly, though, we are left with some profound tensions. On the one hand, nothing in this line of argument makes the unequivocal biblical opposition to same-sex sexual activity go away. On the other, the presence of believing same-sex single and married people generates acute pastoral strains. In many contexts they are likely to feel that they are misunderstood, regarded with distrust, and kept at a distance. In some contexts it will be made very clear to them that they are not welcome. In this final chapter I want to outline three ways in which the biblical narrative may help us begin to learn how to address these tensions: first, a general proposal regarding the *wisdom* required to manage the accommodation; secondly, an argument for the practice of honest storytelling as the most appropriate form of witness; and thirdly, a reconsideration of the controversial analogy with the inclusion of Gentile believers in the early Jewish-Christian movement and with the deliberations of the apostles at the Jerusalem council in Acts 15. The idea is simply to demonstrate that although we have traveled a long way beyond the *historical* horizons of Scripture, we can nevertheless find good methodologies in the biblical narratives that will facilitate the writing and performance of new scripts.

THE CREATIVE WISDOM OF GOD

There may be grounds, in the first place, for an appeal to the biblical category of wisdom as a mode of pragmatic intellectual adjustment to culture, distinct from Law and "doctrine." In the Old Testament the exercise of wisdom draws on wider sapiential traditions—Mesopotamian and Egyptian—in order to explain Israel's experience of the world and offer practical guidance for life in the here and now. Hebrew wisdom (*hokĕmāh*), Fohrer says, "is largely defined by a corresponding world of thought common to the ancient Orient, so that the terms, and the OT Wisdom books in which they mostly occur, belong to the circle of a Wisdom literature which in essentials is the same throughout the region."[1] Moses "was instructed in all the wisdom of the Egyptians, and he was mighty in his words and deeds"

1. Fohrer, "σοφία, σοφός," 477.

(Acts 7:22). It operates within, and to some extent cooperates with, the overarching covenantal storyline. Those who give heed to wisdom "will walk in the way of the good and keep to the paths of the righteous. For the upright will inhabit the land, and those with integrity will remain in it, but the wicked will be cut off from the land, and the treacherous will be rooted out of it" (Prov 2:20–22). But it also on occasion challenges the dominant narrative. The book of Job, notably, tests the fundamental connection between righteousness and well-being almost to breaking point.

Wisdom brings observation and reflection to bear on human living. Lawrence Boadt explains how ancient Jewish sages endeavored to hold together the theoretical and the practical, analysis and ethics: "On the one hand, they saw wisdom as a serious intellectual pursuit of knowledge about the world and its rules of order and the dynamics behind its mysterious operations; on the other, they sought the proper human response to all dimensions of this world, especially in terms of understanding themselves in relation to their human nature and to God the Creator."[2] God gave Solomon wisdom and understanding, breadth of mind like the sand on the seashore, and Solomon "spoke of trees, from the cedar that is in Lebanon to the hyssop that grows out of the wall. He spoke also of beasts, and of birds, and of reptiles, and of fish" (1 Kgs 4:33). The second-century-BC work Wisdom of Solomon develops the theme:

> For he himself gave me an unerring knowledge of the things that exist, to know the constitution of the world and the activity of the elements, the beginning and end and middle of times, the alterations of the solstices and the changes of the seasons, the cycles of the year and the constellations of the stars, the natures of animals and the tempers of wild animals, the violent forces of spirits and the thoughts of human beings, the varieties of plants and the powers of roots, and all things, both what is secret and what is manifest, I learned, for she that is the fashioner of all things taught me, namely wisdom. (Wis 7:17–22)

But such wisdom can hardly be exercised today without assimilating— not uncritically—the input of scientific enquiry and the perspectives that it generates, and for this reason Dan Via has suggested that "some findings of science may be recontextualized and made theologically and ethically useful."[3] How we understand ourselves *in relation to our human nature*

2. Boadt, "Wisdom," 1380.

3. Via, "Bible," 17–18; also Bird, who argues that we find in the wisdom tradition

is precisely a wisdom question, though one that must take us beyond the purview of the ancient Jewish tradition. The "accommodation" of couples in committed same-sex relationships may be accounted for in terms of an open, prophetic narrative, congruent with historical experience, that moves from land to kingdom to Christendom to the post-Christendom marginalization of the church, but it is *interpreted ethically and managed pastorally* as part of a dynamic—and indeed reinvigorated—wisdom tradition.

The thought might be pushed in a more controversial direction, toward the renewal of a central theological paradigm. Wisdom is closely associated with the creative activity of God: she is the "fashioner of all things" (Wis 7:22; cf. Prov 8:22–31; Sir 1:1–10); and part, at least, of what is happening in the prologue to John's Gospel is that the creative power of God, as Word and Wisdom, becomes flesh with subversive, disruptive and recreative effect (John 1:14). The wisdom-like Word, which was with God and was God at the beginning, took up residence in Israel (cf. Sir 24:8–12; 1 En 42:1–2) in the person of Jesus in order to bring about something new. Whether John intended it or not, this audacious but deeply Jewish narrative subsequently provided the platform for an accommodation of the creative Word of God to the *logos* of Hellenistic thought.[4] But if the Platonist rationalism of the ancient Greek world has now been superseded, we have to ask whether a further adaptation needs to be made. We should tread carefully, but in a sense we are asking only how we might *best speak about* a process of intellectual and cultural transformation that has been under way for some time. At this slow boundary between two ages, is there a valid rhetorical move to make that would find in the renewal of the church's missional engagement with Western culture a manifestation of the subversive, disruptive and recreative wisdom of God?

"biblical authorization for the appeal to science to inform our understanding and judgment of homosexual orientation and practice" (Bird, "Bible," 168). But against this see Davidson, *Flame*, 167–69.

4. See, for example, Karamanolis, *Philosophy*, 47–48: the Christian theory of *Logos* allowed "a subtle link between Hellenic philosophy and Christianity, such that both of them qualify as offshoots of *Logos* and both enjoy the status of a rational enquiry for the truth." But since the Christian theory equated the *Logos* with the God who had revealed himself in the Word-made-flesh, "Christianity emerges as the completion of that tradition of the unfolding of *Logos*."

LONG AGO AND FAR AWAY

There are good examples of missional groups that have succeeded in demonstrating a credible love and commitment to the LGBT community while holding to a traditional view on same-sex relations. In her book *Redeeming Sex* Deb Hirsch describes two ways of being church. A "bounded set" model prioritizes *belief* and *behavior* before *belonging*, with tightly controlled borders. Under such conditions mission means people on the inside going out to persuade people on the outside to change their beliefs and behavior so that they can come in and belong to the community. But gay people, she says, "like all people, just want to be recognized and accepted for who they experience themselves to be, despite the degree of choice or not involved in their lifestyles. It is a profoundly *human* issue, and followers of the incarnate God ought to be very sensitive to this."[5] This acceptance needs to be expressed not just by missionaries going out of the church but *by the community itself*. This is almost impossible under the bounded set arrangement, so she proposes an alternative "centered-set" model for missional church that "has a 'hard,' well-articulated and vibrant theological center, but tends to be 'soft' at the edges."[6] What this means in practice is a core group that is committed explicitly to the traditional understanding of marriage between a man and a woman as the only good context for sexual behavior but is generously and transparently open to the embrace and love of LGBT people. Rosaria Butterfield's recommendation of "radically ordinary hospitality" is an application of the model at the domestic level.[7] It is a powerful way of including gay and lesbian seekers or "God-fearers" in and around authentic and disciplined Christian community.

We may wonder, though, to what extent such a model is replicable or sustainable in the long run. It introduces a tension at the heart of community life that would require a high level of pastoral management and perhaps a rare charisma, and may in the end prove unworkable other than in a few outstanding cases. There is the problem of how to "convert" and incorporate *into the heart of the community* people who are already in stable same-sex marriages and perhaps have children. More fundamentally, the formal segregation of heterosexual and homosexual believers is problematic ecclesiologically. The New Testament insists that all who confess Jesus

---

5. Hirsch, *Redeeming Sex*, chap. 6, Kindle loc. 1610 of 3671.

6. Hirsch, *Redeeming Sex*, chap. 11, Kindle loc. 2750 of 3671.

7. See Butterfield, *Gospel*; and Carlson, "Rosaria Butterfield."

as Lord participate in the life and ministry of the church through the gifting of the Holy Spirit. The qualifications for being an elder or overseer that we find in the Pastoral Letters include being a "man of one woman" (1 Tim 3:2; Tit 1:6, my translation). Exactly what this meant is unclear, but it appears to allow for the exclusion of some men from this leadership role on what are essentially social grounds (they have more than one wife? they have remarried?).[8] There is perhaps precedent here for excluding from eldership someone who is the "man of a husband" or the "woman of a wife." But the restriction seems arbitrary and at best a provisional measure.

There are other ways to preserve the symbolic distinction between the New Testament ideal and the modern accommodation. Stephen Holmes argues for a reaffirmation and restatement of the historic Christian view of heterosexual marriage as the place for procreation and as a powerful image of God's love for Israel and of Christ's for the church. "The otherness of the two spouses and the possibility of procreation are intrinsic to marriage on this understanding. Outside of marriage, sexual activity cannot be licit, and so celibacy is the only ethical option."[9] But he accepts, albeit hesitantly, the modern idea that some people have a fixed same-sex orientation and recognizes that "the pressure to extend marriage to gay and lesbian people" is enormous and "perhaps unavoidable." "There is a huge, and theologically appropriate, pressure to find a way of making space for same-sex marriage in the Western church at present." His solution is "pastoral accommodation." Churches opposed to same-sex partnerships might nevertheless "find space within their life for people living in such partnerships out of pastoral concern." Pastoral accommodation means "making space for imperfect patterns of life whilst maintaining a clear witness to perfection."[10]

The question is how do we maintain that clear witness to "perfection." Holmes makes the point with respect to the toleration of polygamy in some missionary contexts that pastoral accommodation "does not mean pretending ethical standards do not exist."[11] It may become necessary,

8. See the discussion in Mounce, *Pastoral Epistles*, 172.

9. Holmes, "Listening," 183; see also Gushee, *Changing Our Mind*, 40–41.

10. Holmes, "Listening," 190–91. See also Pilling, *Report of the House of Bishops*, para. 274, quoting O'Donovan: "A pastoral accommodation is a response to some urgent presenting needs, without ultimate dogmatic implications."

11. Holmes, "Listening," 191. The difference is that the missionaries were moving *toward* monogamy; accommodation was a temporary concession. That would not be the case with the accommodation of same-sex marriage: we would be moving *away from* the heterosexual norm.

however, to express and maintain the standard through means other than the ostensible "purity" of the community. We do as much, after all, in the case of heterosexual marriage: we tolerate divorce and turn a blind eye to cohabitation and sex outside of marriage, while maintaining in principle— through preaching and teaching, through the language and symbolism of the marriage service—the biblical ideal of lifelong covenantal marriage as the only legitimate context for sexual activity.[12] So rather than make a statement about heterosexual marriage as the creational norm by excluding faithful gay and lesbian people from leadership or specific ministries, or from membership of the covenant community, we have to find other ways to carry *creation order signifiers*.

Our reading of Paul's argument in Romans 1:18–32, however, has suggested that any creation order signifiers are accessed, in the first place, through the biblical story as a prophetic engagement with history. The obvious mode of witness to the original "doctrine," therefore, if we do not want to be regarded as "liberal despisers of the tradition," in Luke Timothy Johnson's phrase, is *the honest remembering and telling of this story*.[13] The early church affirmed the inclusion of Gentiles in the covenant but preserved—with remarkable candor—a long counternarrative of Jewish exceptionalism right through to Jesus's curt and begrudging response to the Canaanite woman, who had to be satisfied with scraps from the children's table (Matt 15:21–28), and Peter's craven withdrawal from fellowship with the uncircumcised (Gal 2:11–14). The church in the West has repudiated slavery and patriarchy; many are loath to endorse judicial and political violence no matter how "just" the cause; the conquest stories in Joshua leave a bad taste in the mouth; we are horrified by the curse pronounced on the Babylonian infants (Ps 137:9); and the stormy debate over the morality of penal substitutionary atonement blows unabated. But those parts of the Bible that appear to celebrate or condone these problematic details have not been expurgated—not formally, at least. The hermeneutical pressure to quarantine, allegorize, theologize, turn a blind eye to, or otherwise mitigate

---

12. Cf. Toulouse, "Muddling Through," 34: conservatives have found "muddled rationalizations" to accommodate other practices (divorce and remarriage, women speaking in church) that are condemned in the Bible. Also Wilson, *Letter*, chap. 2, Kindle loc. 671–73 of 3155: "I couldn't shake the thought that if we applied the same pastoral consideration to the LGBT community that we give to the divorced and remarried, we'd come up with something much different than the categorical exclusions from church and ministry that we have practiced."

13. Johnson, "Homosexuality and the Church."

the texts of violence and injustice has been considerable, but in the end the evangelical church is best served by the acknowledgment that this is what was said, this is how things were. The texts are part of our story and cannot be erased. They can probably be better understood.

So if the modern church chooses to affirm the inclusion of people in committed homosexual relationships, the difficult, uncompromising counternarratives about safeguarding the cleanness of the land and the integrity of the churches as witnesses to the coming wrath of God against the Greek should not be forgotten. The prominence given to "unnatural" same-sex relations is not incidental to the New Testament story; it provides us, I have argued, with an invaluable key for understanding the scope and purpose of Paul's eschatology. But *remembrance* also frees us from the need to register the contradiction by barring faithful gay and lesbian people from participation in some area or other of church life and ministry. It frees us from the need to make them second-class citizens. This brings us, finally, to the much-disputed question of the theological and practical legitimacy of the analogy with the inclusion of Gentiles in the early church.

THE ANALOGY WITH THE JERUSALEM COUNCIL

Scholars looking for biblical support for the full inclusion of openly gay and lesbian people in the life and ministry of the church have sometimes made appeal to the debate over the status of believing Gentiles at the Jerusalem council in Acts 15. Jeffrey Siker, for example, asks whether there is any biblical precedent for the modern development. He rejects the comparison with the inclusion of ethnic minorities and women on the grounds that such groups were not regarded as sinful. But the analogy with the initial resistance of the leadership of the Jerusalem church to the accommodation of Gentiles seems more appropriate and more fruitful. "While I can understand the sense of moral revulsion that many heterosexual Christians today may have when they contemplate homosexual relationships, is it in essence much different from the moral revulsion that early Jewish Christians apparently felt when contemplating association with impure and unclean Gentile Christians?"[14]

The council is convened in Jerusalem to address the question of whether converted pagans should be "circumcised according to the custom

14. Siker, "Homosexual Christians," 188; see also Johnson, "Homosexuality and the Church"; Runcorn, "Evangelicals."

of Moses." Paul and Barnabas bring reports of what God is doing among the Gentiles, but some believers from the party of the Pharisees demand that they be circumcised and keep the Law (Acts 15:3–5). There is extensive and no doubt heated debate, but eventually Peter argues, on the basis of his own experience, that the hearts of Gentile believers have been made clean by their belief that God raised his Son from the dead, that God has given them the Holy Spirit for that reason, and that there is, therefore, *already* no distinction between Jewish and Gentile believers. He asks the Pharisees: "why are you putting God to the test by placing a yoke on the neck of the disciples that neither our fathers nor we have been able to bear?" The Jews will not be saved by works of the Law; they are in the same position as the Gentiles: they *will* be saved (note the future tense: this is an eschatological argument with future transformations in view; it's not just about personal salvation) through the grace of the Lord Jesus (15:10–11).

The assembly gives Paul and Barnabas a hearing, and James pronounces his verdict on the matter. He states his view that this remarkable development is consistent with the prophetic expectation that God will "shake the house of Israel among all the nations as one shakes with a sieve," resulting in the destruction of "all the sinners of my people"—he has in mind the "crooked generation" of Acts 2:40. God will then rebuild the ruined temple (either literally or symbolically) and restore the nation, and "all the Gentiles who are called by my name" will seek the Lord (Acts 15:15–17; cf. Amos 9:9–12, LXX; Jer 12:14–17). Since James has gone to the trouble of invoking the eschatological narrative, he presumably thinks of these first Gentile converts as a sign of the *coming* judgment of God on his people, as firstfruits of a *future* turning of the nations to seek the God of Israel. There is certainly more to this than the simple "evangelical" program of universal salvation through faith in Jesus. The vision in Amos is not so much that membership of Israel will be opened to Gentiles apart from the Law as that the chastened nations will make pilgrimage to the glorious new Jerusalem to learn the ways of Israel's God.[15]

James then proposes that they should not trouble "Gentiles who turn to God" but should write to them with a minimal set of requirements—to

15. Cf. Stuart, *Hosea-Jonah*, 398: "Thus in the restoration, God's people will 'possess' . . . i.e., have control over those nations once their enemies, in fulfillment of the restoration blessing of power over enemies." Andersen and Freedman translate: "Those over whom my name is pronounced [i.e., my people Israel] will possess the remnant of Edom and all the nations" (Andersen and Freedman, *Amos*, 891). James exploits the divergent Septuagint reading, but the basic eschatological narrative remains the same.

abstain from the things polluted by idols, from sexual immorality, from eating what has been strangled, and from blood (Acts 15:19–20). The purpose is to enable Jewish Christians and Gentile believers to coexist in their local communities. The arrangement presupposes the Jewish-Christian point of view. As Fitzmyer says: "James thus appeals for a sympathetic understanding of Jewish Christian sensitivities."[16] The underlying idea is that Gentile believers are in the same position vis-à-vis Jewish believers as foreigners were in the land of Israel. They are, in effect, "sojourners"; they are not yet regarded as fully qualified members of the commonwealth of Israel. The restrictions derive not from the so-called Noachic regulations, as commonly supposed, but from the Holiness Code of Leviticus 17–18.[17] Leviticus prohibits sacrificing to demons (Lev 17:7–9). The relevance to non-Israelites is made explicit in connection with the second requirement: "If any one of the house of Israel or of the strangers who sojourn among them eats any blood, I will set my face against that person who eats blood and will cut him off from among his people" (17:10). The blood should be drained from an animal before it is consumed, for "the life of every creature is its blood" (17:13–14). The command to abstain from "sexual immorality" has in view the prohibitions of Leviticus 18:6–18, excluding the miscellaneous prohibitions of 18:19–23. The prohibition against *porneia* (the word is not found in the Greek translation of the Holiness Code) has here been extended to include specifically "marriage within degrees of blood relationship or affinity."[18]

So we can summarize the main stages of the debate as follows. 1) Gentiles are coming in increasing numbers to believe that the God of Israel has raised his Son from the dead and made him Lord. 2) This remarkable development is interpreted in terms of an eschatological narrative about the impending judgment and restoration of Israel and the eventual turning of the nations to worship the living God. 3) Pharisaic believers in Jesus understandably are of the view that Gentile converts should be circumcised and should observe the Law of Moses if they are to be part of the covenant people and have a share in the future kingdom of God. 4) Paul, Barnabas, and Peter argue that Gentiles are *already* demonstrably part of this Jesus movement, since they have received the Holy Spirit, and should not be required to keep the Law. 5) James proposes a *pragmatic* solution—an

16. Fitzmyer, *Acts*, 556.

17. Cf. Fitzmyer, *Acts*, 566.

18. Bruce, *Acts*, 299.

accommodation—that allows Jews to be Jews and Gentiles to be Gentiles, and for the two groups to live and worship together in the cities of the Greek-Roman world.

Can we now tell a similar story—not the *same* story—about the current division between heterosexual believers and same-sex believers? Objections to the analogy have been raised. Kathryn Greene-McCreight, for example, protests: "To suggest that there is an analogy between Jew/Gentile and hetero/homosexual is a major category error; it is to compare apples and paper clips. The argument takes one biblical image, the inclusion of the Gentiles, and pulls it out of its canonical context to serve as the primary if not sole biblical touch point to support the weight of the revisionist position."[19] In a rather constructive analysis Goddard argues that the question which the analogy may help us to resolve must be quite narrowly defined: "It is whether or not those who are homosexual can become Christians and full members of the body of Christ as homosexuals."[20] I do not think that the analogy can answer that question. I do not think that it can be made to support the weight of the revisionist position. But there is an undoubted congruence between the two narratives, and if we conclude on other grounds that we have to live with this new state of affairs despite the contradiction, the analogy may provide a *model* that will help us to think wisely about *coexistence*.[21] The argument might run something like this.

1. There are gay and lesbian people, some of them celibate, some of them not, who believe that Jesus is the Son of the living creator God, who worship and pray in his name, who manifest in their lives the presence and power of the Holy Spirit. Modern social anthropology recognizes homosexuality not as a *perversion* of normal heterosexual behavior, not as morally degenerate, but as a valid minority expression of human sexual identity. Gay and lesbian people are so by nature, just as Gentiles are Gentiles "by nature" (cf. Gal 2:15; Rom 2:14).[22] If we accept these premises,

---

19. Greene-McCreight, "Logic," 256.

20. Goddard, *God, Gentiles*, 16.

21. See the objections presented in Gagnon, "Bible and Homosexual Practice," 43–44.

22. Cf. Goddard, *God, Gentiles*, 14: "Gentiles are such by nature [*physis*, Gal 2.15; Rom 2.14] and, although the causes of homosexual attraction remain mysterious and controversial, there is growing evidence that at least some experience of homosexual attraction may have a significant 'natural' or biological component. Even if this proves not to be the case it is clear that, as with heterosexual attraction, few if any gay people consciously choose to experience homo-erotic feelings."

then the "cleanness" of same-sex people *by faith* is a new phenomenon in the modern era, much as the "cleanness" of Gentiles *by faith* was a new phenomenon in the first century, and similarly disruptive.

2. We have no Jewish scriptural precedent for the crisis of modernity, no prophetic narrative that we can appeal to in order to account for the inclusion of same-sex believers. This is where we are most sharply confronted with the limitations of the analogy.[23] However, I have suggested that the demand for the evangelical church to acknowledge the legitimacy of committed same-sex relationships—indeed, the legitimacy of being a gay or lesbian person—is proving to be a defining moment in the church's own "eschatological" crisis, as we come to terms with living in the modern world. For Peter the faith of uncircumcised Gentiles highlighted the fact that the Jews had long failed to keep the Law, and were now facing the wrath of God (Acts 15:10; cf. 2:37–41). In the same way, we may think that the pouring out of the Spirit on gay and lesbian people, both celibate and married, may remind us that the evangelical church, for all its proud possession of a biblical ethics, has often found that yoke too heavy to bear.

3. Traditionalists do not necessarily question the faith of gay and lesbian people, but because Scripture prohibits same-sex relations, they insist that they must abstain from same-sex activity. They must take on the yoke of the morality of the heterosexual tradition, just as the Jewish traditionalists expected Gentile believers to take on the yoke of the Law of Moses.

4. Others argue, however, in defense of same-sex believers, on the one hand, that same-sex marriage *in the context of a scientific and egalitarian culture* is not what is condemned in Scripture, but more importantly that their faith and the work of the Holy Spirit in their lives are evidence that God has *already* accepted them. If God has demonstrably given his Spirit to people engaged in same-sex sexual relationships, then it would appear that what was previously considered *unclean* has now been declared *clean*. Reading Acts 10 proved to be a turning point in Vicky Beeching's journey toward wholeness: "God was letting me in on a new perspective, one of

---

23. Goddard highlights two other differences, but they seem inconsequential (Goddard, *God, Gentiles*, 15–16). First, he argues that the condition of being Gentile is directly bound up with the election of Israel, but this is just as true for the homosexual person who must be excluded from, or refused entry into, the people of God. Secondly, it is incorrect to say that "Gentile identity was constructed by Jews and was not the Gentiles' own identity." The Gentiles are simply "the nations" (*ta ethnē*). What was determined by the Jews was that the nations were unclean. Arguably, gay and lesbian *identity* has been chosen by gay and lesbian people somewhat as an act of self-defense, but in any case the point is that the church has traditionally regarded them as "unclean."

radical acceptance and inclusion. 'Do not call unclean what I have made clean' echoed around my head and heart. The person I'd always been—a gay person—was not something to be ashamed of. God accepted me and loved me, and my orientation was part of his grand design."[24] There is, therefore, so the argument goes, no difference in Christ between non-gay and gay. Just as at the end of the age of Second-Temple Judaism Gentiles were joined to Christ without ceasing to be Gentiles, without becoming Jews, so, at the end of the Christendom era, homosexual people are being joined to Christ without ceasing to be homosexual, without becoming heterosexual.

5. We then need a James figure, who allows both sides of the argument to stand, who recommends not troubling same-sex believers, but who proposes a contextually appropriate *modus vivendi*, a way of coexisting, a minimal set of requirements to be imposed on the "new" group of believers *for a specific reason*—that they might live well amongst or alongside the established community, insofar as this is problematic.[25]

A Letter to Same-Sex Attracted Believers?

What might the requirements be in this case? What disciplines of lifestyle and behavior would facilitate good relations between traditionalists and gay and lesbian believers? Here are some initial suggestions to illustrate the point, at least; and we may think, though this is straying outside the scope of the analogy, that the heterosexual Christian community should be invited to submit to a comparable set of disciplines.

1. Same-sex believers might be required to abstain and dissociate themselves from those aspects of same-sex culture that could be regarded, at least in a popular sense, as "idolatrous" and immoral, as ideologically and blatantly opposed to the biblical account of faith in the one, true, living creator God. I have argued that there is a controlling eschatological context for the causal link between homosexuality and idolatry that we find in Romans 1, which may not apply today. But because all forms of homosexuality have until fairly recently been tarred with the same

24. Beeching, *Undivided*, chap. 20, Kindle loc. 2396–99 of 3980.

25. Siker noted the potential for such a pastoral development of the analogy but did not pursue the idea (Siker, "Homosexual Christians," 194n16). Beeching rather suggests that LGBT+ Christians would be accepted "without extra legalism that would prevent us from having the blessings enjoyed by straight Christians" (Beeching, *Undivided*, chap. 21, Kindle loc. 2496–97 of 3980), but this misses the point: Gentiles are required to compromise.

brush of moral turpitude by the heterosexual mainstream, there is still a lingering association with a corrupt, promiscuous, and Godless sexual culture. If heterosexual and homosexual marriages are now regarded as parallel arrangements, there is more clearly a homosexual *porneia* to be shunned. "If *porneia* among heterosexuals includes promiscuity, violence, and exploitation," Johnson writes, "then the church must condemn similar forms of homosexual activity. If the church condemns the bath-house style of gay life, it must also condemn the playboy style of straight life."[26]

2. Married same-sex believers should be encouraged to tell the same biblical story—one which starts with the creation of humanity as male and female, and which includes strict prohibitions against same-sex relations. Whatever the cultural and pastoral demands of the present, and whatever embarrassment we may feel about the past, we do not help ourselves by rewriting our history. To my mind, this is the most constructive way of accommodating what is an inescapable tension.

3. Same-sex couples should be required, our modern James might argue, to do "marriage" more or less on the same terms that other-sex couples do marriage. The legalization of marriage in the West has given the church some grounds on which to hold same-sex couples accountable, whether or not they regard themselves as Christian, to the same standards of love and faithfulness as other-sex couples. Same-sex weddings in churches will presumably follow a traditional script, with the obvious adjustments.

4. The final requirement would no doubt be controversial. It appears that two issues lie at the heart of the Jewish critique of male same-sex behavior: the degrading penetration of the male, and effeminacy. It may be unworkable, it may be considered intrusive and an infringement of basic human rights, but for the sake of argument our fair-minded apostle might ask gay men to abstain from anal sex as being "degrading" and from conspicuous or flagrant effeminacy, if only *out of respect for the "sensitivities" of the non-affirming Christian community*.[27] There probably needs to be a contextual dimension to such "rules" of sexual behavior. In an age of globalization and migration it has to be recognized that some traditional communities have much stronger "sensitivities" than others.

26. Johnson, "Homosexuality and the Church."

27. Loader suggests that some gay men "find it highly offensive when others assume that they are obsessed with sexual orgasm or are constantly engaging in anal sex. For many, the latter plays no part" (Loader, "Homosexuality and the Bible," 48). A 2011 study has suggested that gay and bisexual men have a more diverse "sexual repertoire" than is perhaps typically appreciated: see "New Study Finds Gay and Bisexual Men."

Overt expressions of same-sex affection, for example, will be more tolerable in some settings than others. There is an obvious parallel in Paul's appeal for respect and compromise in the case of disputes between the "strong" (Gentile believers?) and the "weak" (Jewish believers?) about food sacrificed to idols and the observance of holy days (Rom 14; 1 Cor 8:7–13), which is the basis for Ken Wilson's "Third Way" proposal for managing the inclusion of same-sex believers as a "disputable matter."[28]

The force of the analogy should not be overstated. The modern narrative is driven in the first place by social developments and not simply by the proclamation of the gospel in a new context. Sexual orientation is like ethnicity in certain respects but not in others. It was clear enough from the Jewish perspective what a Gentile was, but the modern definitions of same-sex identity are in a state of flux. There is no individual or organization with the authority of James today to devise and promote the compromise, and no direct scriptural vision for a modern James to appeal to.[29] But the pragmatic thrust of the argument may recommend it; and when the tide of cultural change is flowing firmly in the direction of liberalization, there is perhaps something to be said for explicitly requiring concessions from same-sex believers for the sake of the unity of God's people. It allows the core theological question to remain somewhat unresolved, and it shifts the focus toward dealing with the internal relational problem generated by the modern normalization of LGBT identities. As it turned out, the "sojourner" paradigm broke down and the apostolic letter became obsolete as the church established itself across the Greek-Roman *oikoumenē* as a fully Gentile entity. A similarly managed coexistence between heterosexual and homosexual believers may also be only provisional while we wait to see where history takes us next.

---

28. Wilson, *Letter*, chap. 4.

29. Goddard thinks that the lack of a James figure is precisely the problem: "If 'traditionalists' seem to be lacking in 'Peter' figures, 'revisionists' are in desperate need of someone like 'James.' Although many have sought to address the traditional prohibitionist texts of Scripture and explain why they believe they are not relevant to the current debate, there has been no serious attempt to find any textual warrant in Scripture for changing the church's teaching on homosexuality" (Goddard, *God, Gentiles*, 12).

Bibliography

Andersen, Francis I., and David Noel Freedman. *Amos*. The Anchor Yale Bible. New Haven: Yale University Press, 1974.

Anderson, Arnold A. *2 Samuel*. WBC. Grand Rapids: Zondervan, 1989.

Aune, David E. *Revelation 17–22*. WBC. Grand Rapids: Zondervan, 1998.

Bailey, Sarah Pulliam. "Poll Shows a Dramatic Generational Divide in White Evangelical Attitudes on Gay Marriage." *The Washington Post*, 2017. https://www.washingtonpost.com/news/acts-of-faith/wp/2017/06/27/there-is-now-a-dramatic-generational-divide-over-white-evangelical-attitudes-on-gay-marriage/.

Balch, David L. "Concluding Observations by the Editor, Including a Comparison of Christian with Jewish Biblical Interpretation." In *Homosexuality, Science, and the "Plain Sense" of Scripture*, edited by David L. Balch, 278–304. Grand Rapids: Eerdmans, 2000.

Bartholomew, Craig G., and Michael W. Goheen. *The Drama of Scripture: Finding Our Place in the Biblical Story*. Grand Rapids: Baker Academic, 2004.

Bauckham, Richard J. *Jude, 2 Peter*. WBC. Grand Rapids: Zondervan, 1983.

Beeching, Vicky. *Undivided: Coming Out, Becoming Whole, and Living Free From Shame*. London: William Collins, 2018.

Berger, Peter. "Western Individuality: Liberation and Loneliness." *Partisan Review* 52.4 (1985) 323–36.

Bergner, Mario. *Setting Love in Order: Hope and Healing for the Homosexual*. Grand Rapids: Baker, 1993.

Bird, Phyllis A. "The Bible in Christian Ethical Deliberation Concerning Homosexuality: Old Testament Contributions." In *Homosexuality, Science, and the "Plain Sense" of Scripture*, edited by David L. Balch, 142–76. Grand Rapids: Eerdmans, 2000.

Block, Daniel I. *The Book of Ezekiel, Chapters 1–24*. NICOT. Grand Rapids: Eerdmans, 1997.

Boadt, Lawrence. "Wisdom, Wisdom Literature." In *Eerdmans Dictionary of the Bible*, edited by David Noel Freedman, 1380–82. Grand Rapids: Eerdmans, 2000.

Boswell, John. *Christianity, Social Tolerance, and Homosexuality: Gay People in Western Europe from the Beginning of the Christian Era to the Fourteenth Century*. Chicago: University of Chicago Press, 1980.

Brooten, Bernadette J. *Love Between Women: Early Christian Responses to Female Homoeroticism*. Chicago: University of Chicago Press, 1996.

Browning, Frank. *The Fate of Gender: Nature, Nurture, and the Human Future*. New York: Bloomsbury, 2017.

Brownson, James V. *Bible, Gender, Sexuality: Reframing the Church's Debate on Same-Sex Relationships*. Grand Rapids: Eerdmans, 2013.

Bruce, F. F. *The Book of Acts*. NICNT. Grand Rapids: Eerdmans, 1988.

Burridge, Richard. *Imitating Jesus: An Inclusive Approach to New Testament Ethics*. Grand Rapids: Eerdmans, 2007.

Butterfield, Rosaria. *The Gospel Comes with a House Key: Practicing Radically Ordinary Hospitality in Our Post-Christian World*. Wheaton, IL: Crossway, 2018.

———. *The Secret Thoughts of an Unlikely Convert: An English Professor's Journey into Christian Faith*. Pittsburgh: Crown & Covenant, 2012.

Byrne, Brendan. *Romans*. Sacra Pagina. Collegeville, PA: Liturgical, 1996.

Carlson, Lindsey. "Rosaria Butterfield: Christian Hospitality Is Radically Different from 'Southern Hospitality.'" *Christianity Today*, April 24, 2018. https://www.christianitytoday.com/ct/2018/april-web-only/rosaria-butterfield-gospel-comes-house-key.html.

Chalke, Steve. "The Bible and Homosexuality: Part One." *Premier Christianity*, 2013. https://www.premierchristianity.com/Featured-Topics/Homosexuality/The-Bible-and-Homosexuality-Part-One.

Dallas, Joe. "Another Option: Christianity and Ego-Dystonic Homosexuality." In *Homosexuality in the Church: Both Sides of the Debate*, edited by Jeffrey S. Siker, 137–44. Louisville: Westminster John Knox, 1994.

Davidson, Richard M. *Flame of Yahweh: Sexuality in the Old Testament*. Peabody: Hendrickson, 2007.

Davison, Andrew. *Amazing Love: Theology for Understanding Discipleship, Sexuality and Mission*. London: Darton, Longman & Todd, 2016.

DeFranza, Megan K. "Journeying From the Bible to Christian Ethics in Search of Common Ground." In *Two Views on Homosexuality, the Bible and the Church*, edited by Preston Sprinkle, 69–101. Grand Rapids: Zondervan, 2016.

DeYoung, James B. "The Meaning of 'Nature' in Romans 1 and Its Implications for Biblical Proscriptions of Homosexual Behavior." *JETS* 31.4 (1988) 429–41.

DeYoung, Kevin. *What Does the Bible Really Teach About Homosexuality?* Nottingham: InterVarsity, 2015.

Diamond, Lisa. *Sexual Fluidity: Understanding Women's Love and Desire*. Cambridge: Harvard University Press, 2008.

Dover, Kenneth James. *Greek Homosexuality*. Cambridge: Harvard University Press, 1989.

Dreher, Rod. *The Benedict Option: A Strategy for Christians in a Post-Christian Nation*. New York: Sentinel, 2017.

Dunn, J. D. G. *Romans 1–8*. WBC. Dallas: Word, 1998.

Elliott, Neil. *The Arrogance of Nations: Reading Romans in the Shadow of Empire*. Minneapolis: Fortress, 2008.

Engberg-Pedersen, Troels. *Paul and the Stoics*. Louisville: Westminster John Knox, 2000.

Fetsch, Emily. "Are Millennials Leaving Religion Over LGBT Issues?" *Public Religion Research Institute*, March 13, 2014. https://www.prri.org/spotlight/leaving-religion-lgbt-issues/.

Fitzmyer, Joseph. *The Acts of the Apostles*. The Anchor Yale Bible. New Haven: Yale University Press, 1974.

———. *Romans*. London: Chapman, 1993.

Fohrer, G. "σοφία, σοφός." *TDNT* 7:477.

France, R. T. *The Gospel of Matthew*. NICNT. Grand Rapids: Eerdmans, 2007.

Fredrickson, David, E. "Natural and Unnatural Use in Romans 1:24–27: Paul and the Philosophic Critique of Eros." In *Homosexuality, Science, and the "Plain Sense" of Scripture*, edited by David L. Balch, 197–222. Grand Rapids: Eerdmans, 2000.

Furnish, Victor Paul. "The Bible and Homosexuality: Reading the Texts in Context." In *Homosexuality in the Church: Both Sides of the Debate*, edited by Jeffrey S. Siker, 18–35. Louisville: Westminster John Knox, 1994.

Gaffney, John. "Anti-Hollande Sentiments Have Fuelled the Popularity of France's Manif Pour Tous Movement." *The London School of Economics and Political Science*, 2013. https://blogs.lse.ac.uk/europpblog/2013/06/03/manif-pour-tous/.

Gagnon, Robert A. J. "The Bible and Homosexual Practice: Key Issues." In *Homosexuality and the Bible: Two Views*, by Dan O. Via and Robert A. J. Gagnon, 40–92. Minneapolis: Augsburg, 2003.

———. *The Bible and Homosexual Practice: Texts and Hermeneutics*. Nashville: Abingdon, 2010.

———. "A Book Not to Be Embraced: A Critical Review Essay on Stacy Johnson's *a Time to Embrace*." *Scottish Journal of Theology* 62.1 (2009) 61–80.

———. "The Old Testament and Homosexuality: A Critical Review of the Case Made By Phyllis Bird." *Zeitschrift für die Alttestamentliche Wissenschaft* 117.3 (2005) 367–94.

Goddard, Andrew. *God, Gentiles and Gay Christians: Acts 15 and Change in the Church*. Cambridge: Grove, 2001.

———. "James V. Brownson: *Bible, Gender, Sexuality*: A Critical Engagement." Kirby Laing Institute for Christian Ethics, 2014. https://pdfs.semanticscholar.org/026e/f3e5b3f42d35d62c1d7ee00db65b7d4b95b3.pdf.

Greene-McCreight, Kathryn. "The Logic of the Interpretation of Scripture and the Church's Debate." In *Homosexuality, Science, and the "Plain Sense" of Scripture*, edited by David L. Balch, 242–60. Grand Rapids: Eerdmans, 2000.

Grenz, Stanley J. *The Social God and the Relational Self: A Trinitarian Theology of the Imago Dei*. Louisville: Westminster John Knox, 2001.

Grossman, Lisa. "Sexuality Is Fluid—It's Time to Get Past 'Born This Way.'" *New Scientist* July 22, 2015. https://www.newscientist.com/article/mg22730310-100-sexuality-is-fluid-its-time-to-get-past-born-this-way/.

Gudorf, Christine E. "The Bible and Science on Sexuality." In *Homosexuality, Science, and the "Plain Sense" of Scripture*, edited by David L. Balch, 121–41. Grand Rapids: Eerdmans, 2000.

Gushee, David P. *Changing Our Mind: Definitive Edition of the Landmark Call for Inclusion of LGBTQ Christians with Response to Critics*. 3rd ed. Canton: Read the Spirit, 2017.

Hagner, Donald A. *Matthew 1–13*. WBC. Dallas: Word, 1993.

———. *Matthew 14–28*. WBC. Dallas: Word, 1995.

Hailes, Sam. "How Evangelicals Took Over the Church of England." *Premier Christianity*, November, 2017. https://www.premierchristianity.com/Past-Issues/2017/November-2017/How-evangelicals-took-over-the-Church-of-England.

Hallett, Martin. *Still Learning to Love: A Personal Journey to Wholeness in Christ*. N.p.: HOW Publications, 2004.

Hallock, Emily. "A Man of Honor: What Same-Sex-attracted Christians Can Give the Church." *Plough Quarterly*, n.d. https://www.plough.com/en/topics/community/church-community/a-man-of-honor.

Halperin, David M. *One Hundred Years of Homosexuality: And Other Essays on Greek Love*. New York: Routledge, 1990.

Hamilton, Victor P. *The Book of Genesis, Chapters 1–17*. NICOT. Grand Rapids: Eerdmans, 1990.

Harrison, Glynn. "A Better Story: Re-Imagining the Biblical Vision for Sex and Marriage." *Evangelical Focus*, September 28, 2016. http://evangelicalfocus.com/blogs/1954/glynn_harrisson_A_Better_Story_Re_imagining_the_Biblical_Vision_for_Sex_and_Marriage.

Hartley, John E. *Leviticus*. WBC. Grand Rapids: Zondervan, 1992.

Hays, Richard B. "Awaiting the Redemption of Our Bodies: The Witness of Scripture Concerning Homosexuality." In *Homosexuality in the Church: Both Sides of the Debate*, edited by Jeffrey S. Siker, 3–17. Louisville: Westminster John Knox, 1994.

———. *The Moral Vision of the New Testament: A Contemporary Introduction to New Testament Ethics*. New York: HarperCollins, 1996. EPub ed., 2013.

———. "Relations Natural and Unnatural: A Response to John Boswell's Exegesis of Romans 1." *Journal of Religious Ethics* 14.1 (1986) 184–215.

Hill, Wesley. "Christ, Scripture and Spiritual Friendship." In *Two Views on Homosexuality, the Bible and the Church*, edited by Preston Sprinkle, 124–47. Grand Rapids: Zondervan, 2016.

———. *Washed and Waiting: Reflections on Christian Faithfulness and Homosexuality*. Kindle ed. Grand Rapids: Zondervan, 2016.

Hirsch, Debra. *Redeeming Sex: Naked Conversations About Sexuality and Spirituality*. Kindle ed. Downers Grove, IL: InterVarsity, 2015.

Holmes, Stephen R. "Listening to the Past and Reflecting on the Present." In *Two Views on Homosexuality, the Bible and the Church*, edited by Preston Sprinkle, 166–93. Grand Rapids: Zondervan, 2016.

Horrocks, Don. "Changing Views on Homosexuality." *Evangelical Alliance*, June 13, 2014. https://www.eauk.org/current-affairs/politics/changing-views-on-homosexuality.cfm.

Hubbard, Thomas K. *Homosexuality in Greece and Rome: A Sourcebook of Basic Documents*. Berkeley: University of California Press, 2003.

Huss, Bernard. "The Dancing Sokrates and the Laughing Xenophon, or the Other 'Symposium.'" *The American Journal of Philology* 120.3 (1999) 381–409.

Hvalvik, Reidar. "The Present Context in the Light of the New Testament and Its Background: The Case of Homosexuality." *European Journal of Theology* 24.2 (2015) 146–59.

InterVarsity Christian Fellowship/USA. "Responding to the LGBT Movement: A Theological Statement." https://www.fresnoamh.org/wp-content/uploads/2018/02/LGBT_Theological_Statement_03-29-12_rev.13272-0.pdf.

Jewett, Robert. "The Social Context and Implications of Homoerotic References in Romans 1:24–27." In *Homosexuality, Science, and the "Plain Sense" of Scripture*, edited by David L. Balch, 223–41. Grand Rapids: Eerdmans, 2000.

Jewett, Robert, and Roy D. Kotansky. *Romans*. Hermeneia. Minneapolis: Fortress, 2007.

John, Jeffrey. *Permanent, Faithful, Stable*. London: Darton, Longman & Todd, 2013.

Johnson, Luke Timothy. "Homosexuality and the Church." *Commonweal*, June 11, 2007. https://www.commonwealmagazine.org/homosexuality-church-0.

Jones, Stanton L., and Don E. Workman. "Homosexuality: The Behavioural Sciences and the Church." In *Homosexuality in the Church: Both Sides of the Debate*, edited by Jeffrey S. Siker, 93–115. Louisville: Westminster John Knox, 1994.

Jones, Stanton L., and Mark A. Yarhouse. "The Use, Misuse, and Abuse of Science in the Ecclesiastical Homosexuality Debates." In *Homosexuality, Science, and the "Plain Sense" of Scripture*, edited by David L. Balch, 73–120. Grand Rapids: Eerdmans, 2000.

Kaoma, Kapya. "The U.S. Christian Right and the Attack on Gays in Africa." *HuffPost*, March 18, 2011. https://www.huffingtonpost.com/rev-kapya-kaoma/the-us-christian-right-an_b_387642.html.

Karamanolis, George. *The Philosophy of Early Christianity*. Durham: Acumen, 2013.

Käsemann, Ernst. *Commentary on Romans*. London: SCM, 1980.

Köster, H. "φύσις φυσικός φυσικῶς." In *TDNT* 9:263.

Kuruvilla, Carol. "Former Megachurch Pastor Rob Bell: A Church That Doesn't Support Gay Marriage Is 'Irrelevant.'" *HuffPost*, February 20, 2015. https://www.huffingtonpost.co.uk/2015/02/20/rob-bell-oprah-gay-marriage_n_6723840.html.

Loader, William. "Homosexuality and the Bible." In *Two Views on Homosexuality, the Bible and the Church*, edited by Preston Sprinkle, 17–48. Grand Rapids: Zondervan, 2016.

———. *The New Testament on Sexuality*. Grand Rapids: Eerdmans, 2012.

Lutz, Cora E. *Musonius Rufus "The Roman Socrates."* New Haven: Yale University Press, 1947.

Marin, Andrew. *Love Is an Orientation: Elevating the Conversation With the Gay Community*. Downers Grove, IL: InterVarsity, 2009. Kindle ed.

Martin, Dale B. "*Arsenokoitēs* and *Malakos*: Meanings and Consequences." In *Biblical Ethics & Homosexuality: Listening to Scripture*, edited by Robert Lawson Brawley, 117–36. Louisville: Westminster John Knox, 1996.

Mayer, Lawrence S., and Paul R. McHugh. "Sexuality and Gender Findings From the Biological, Psychological, and Social Sciences." *The New Atlantis* 50 (2016). https://www.thenewatlantis.com/docLib/20160819_TNA50SexualityandGender.pdf.

McCarter, P. Kyle, Jr. *II Samuel*. The Anchor Yale Bible. New Haven: Yale University Press, 1974.

McDowell, Sean, and John Stonestreet. *Same-Sex Marriage: A Thoughtful Approach to God's Design for Marriage*. Grand Rapids: Baker, 2014. Kindle ed.

McNeill, John J. "Homosexuality: Challenging the Church to Grow." In *Homosexuality in the Church: Both Sides of the Debate*, edited by Jeffrey S. Siker, 49–58. Louisville: Westminster John Knox, 1994.

Milgrom, Jacob. *Leviticus 17–22*. The Anchor Yale Bible. New Haven: Yale University Press, 2000.

Miller, Ed L. "More Pauline References to Homosexuality?" *Evangelical Quarterly* 77.2 (2005) 129–34.

Moo, Douglas J. *The Epistle to the Romans*. NICNT. Grand Rapids: Eerdmans, 1996.

Mounce, William D. *Pastoral Epistles*. WBC. Nashville: Nelson, 2000.

Murphy-O'Connor, Jerome. "Sex and Logic in 1 Corinthians 11:2–16." *Catholic Biblical Quarterly* 42.4 (1980) 482–500.

"New Study Finds Gay and Bisexual Men Have Varied Sexual Repertoires." *Indiana University News Room*, October 18, 2011. http://newsinfo.iu.edu/news/page/normal/19977.html.

Ould, Peter. "It's Easy to Talk About Banning Gay Conversion Therapy. But How to Do It—and Where's the Evidence?" *Christian Today*, June 23, 2017. https://www.christiantoday.com/article/its-easy-to-talk-about-banning-gay-conversion-therapy-but-how-to-do-it-and-wheres-the-evidence/110164.htm.

Ozanne, Jayne. *Just Love: A Journey of Self-Acceptance*. London: Darton, Longman and Todd, 2018.

Paris, Jenelle Williams. *The End of Sexual Identity: Why Sex Is Too Important to Define Who We Are*. Downers Grove, IL: InterVarsity, 2011.

Paul, Darel E. *From Tolerance to Equality: How Elites Brought America to Same-Sex Marriage*. Waco: Baylor University Press, 2018.

Paul, Ian. *Same-Sex Unions: The Key Biblical Texts*. Cambridge: Grove, 2014.

Perriman, Andrew. *The Coming of the Son of Man: New Testament Eschatology for an Emerging Church*. Milton Keynes: Paternoster, 2005.

———. *The Future of the People of God: Reading Romans Before and After Western Christendom*. Eugene, OR: Cascade, 2010.

———. *Speaking of Women: Interpreting Paul*. Leicester: Apollos, 1998.

Perry, Jackie Hill. *Gay Girl, Good God: The Story of Who I Was, and Who God Has Always Been*. Nashville: B&H, 2018.

Pilling, Joe. *Report of the House of Bishops Working Group on Human Sexuality*. London: Church House, 2013.

Riddell, Peter. "Australia: Same-Sex Marriage and Religious Adherence." *Evangelicals Now*, January 2018. https://www.e-n.org.uk/2018/01/world-news/australia-same-sex-marriage-and-religious-adherence/.

Riess, Jana. "Same-Sex Marriage Has Support Among Most American Religious Groups, Study Shows." *National Catholic Reporter*, May 1, 2018. https://www.ncronline.org/news/opinion/same-sex-marriage-has-support-among-most-american-religious-groups-study-shows.

Roberts, Alastair. "Bill Nye, Progressive Science, and the Threat of Nature." *Alastair's Adversaria*, April 26, 2017. https://alastairadversaria.com/2017/04/26/bill-nye-progressive-science-and-the-threat-of-nature.

———. "Why American Elites Support Same-Sex Marriage." *The Gospel Coalition*, July 25, 2018. https://www.thegospelcoalition.org/reviews/from-tolerance-equality/.

Royal College of Psychiatrists. "Royal College of Psychiatrists' Statement on Sexual Orientation." April 2014. https://www.rcpsych.ac.uk/pdf/PS02_2014.pdf.

Ruden, Sarah. *Paul Among the People: The Apostle Reinterpreted and Reimagined in His Own Time*. New York: Image, 2010.

Runcorn, David. "Evangelicals, Scripture and Same Sex Relationships—an 'Including Evangelical' Perspective (Appendix 4)." In *Report of the House of Bishops Working Group on Human Sexuality*, edited by Joseph Pilling (Chair). London: Church House, 2013.

———. "Same Sex Marriage & Scripture: An Affirming Evangelical Response (Part 3)." *ViaMedia*, October 18, 2018. https://viamedia.news/2018/10/18/same-sex-marriage-scripture-an-affirming-evangelical-response-part-3/.

Schoedel, William R. "Same-Sex Eros: Paul and the Greco-Roman Tradition." In *Homosexuality, Science, and the "Plain Sense" of Scripture*, edited by David L. Balch, 43–72. Grand Rapids: Eerdmans, 2000.

Schuh, Steve. "Challenging Conventional Wisdom: How a Conservative Reading of the Biblical References to Homosexuality Fails to Support Their Traditional Interpretation." *Courage*, 2007. http://www.courage.org.uk/articles/Challenging.shtml.

Scroggs, Robin. *The New Testament and Homosexuality: Contextual Background for Contemporary Debate*. Philadelphia: Fortress, 1983.

Seitz, Christopher. "Sexuality and Scripture's Plain Sense: The Christian Community and the Law of God." In *Homosexuality, Science, and the "Plain Sense" of Scripture*, edited by David L. Balch, 177–96. Grand Rapids: Eerdmans, 2000.

Selmys, Melinda. *Sexual Authenticity: An Intimate Reflection on Homosexuality and Catholicism*. Huntington: One Sunday Visitor, 2009.

———. *Sexual Authenticity: More Reflections*. N.p.: Vulgata, 2013.

Sharmon, Jon, and Ian Jones. "Half of Anglicans Say There Is Nothing Wrong with Same-Sex Relationships." *The Independent*, February 15, 2017. https://www.independent.co.uk/news/uk/home-news/half-anglicans-nothing-wrong-same-sex-relationships-church-of-england-synod-a7580561.html.

Shaw, Ed. *The Plausibility Problem: The Church and Same-Sex Attraction*. Nottingham: InterVarsity, 2015.

Shellnutt, Kate. "Actually, Eugene Peterson Does Not Support Same-Sex Marriage." *Christianity Today*, July 13, 2017. https://www.christianitytoday.com/news/2017/july/eugene-peterson-actually-does-not-support-gay-marriage.html.

———. "Lifeway Prepared to Stop Selling the Message Over Eugene Peterson's LGBT Comments." *Christianity Today*, July 12, 2017. https://www.christianitytoday.com/news/2017/july/lifeway-prepared-to-stop-selling-message-over-eugene-peters.html.

Shermer, Michael. "Beware Bogus Theories of Sexual Orientation." *Scientific American*, December 1, 2016. https://www.scientificamerican.com/article/beware-bogus-theories-of-sexual-orientation/.

Siker, Jeffrey S. "Homosexual Christians, the Bible, and Gentile Inclusion: Confessions of a Repenting Heterosexist." In *Homosexuality in the Church: Both Sides of the Debate*, edited by Jeffrey S. Siker, 178–94. Louisville: Westminster John Knox, 1994.

Smedes, Lewis B. *Sex for Christians: The Limits and Liberties of Sexual Living*. Grand Rapids: Eerdmans, 1976.

Smith, Mark D. "Ancient Bisexuality and the Interpretation of Romans 1:26–27." *Journal of the American Academy of Religion* 64.2 (1996) 223–56.

Soards, Marion L. *Scripture & Homosexuality: Biblical Authority and the Church Today*. Louisville: Westminster John Knox, 1995.

Song, Robert. *Covenant and Calling: Towards a Theology of Same-Sex Relationships*. London: SCM, 2014.

Soulen, R. Kendall. *The God of Israel and Christian Theology*. Minneapolis: Augsburg Fortress, 1996.

Speiser, E. A. *Genesis*. The Anchor Yale Bible. New Haven: Yale University Press, 1974.

Sprinkle, Preston, ed. *Two Views on Homosexuality, the Bible and the Church*. Grand Rapids: Zondervan, 2016.

Steele, Jeremy. "United Methodists Vote to Keep Traditional Marriage Stance." *Christianity Today*, February 26, 2019. https://www.christianitytoday.com/news/2019/february/united-methodist-lgbt-vote-conference-plan.html.

Stetzer, Ed. "Evangelicals Across the Spectrum Are Clarifying Marriage as a Core Belief." *Christianity Today*, November 1, 2016. https://www.christianitytoday.com/edstetzer/2016/october/evangelicals-all-over-spectrum-are-clarifying-marriage-as-c.html.

Stone, Ken. "Gender and Homosexuality in Judges 19: Subject-Honor, Object-Shame?" *JSOT* 67 (1995) 87–107.

Stuart, Douglas. *Hosea–Jonah*. WBC. Grand Rapids: Zondervan, 1987.

Taylor, Charles. *A Secular Age.* Cambridge: The Belknap Press of Harvard University Press, 2007.

Thiselton, Anthony C. *The First Epistle to the Corinthians: A Commentary on the Greek Text.* Grand Rapids: Eerdmans, 2000.

Thornton, Bruce S. *Eros: The Myth of Ancient Greek Sexuality.* New York: Routledge, 1997.

Toulouse, Mark G. "Muddling Through: The Church and Sexuality/Homosexuality." In *Homosexuality, Science, and the "Plain Sense" of Scripture,* edited by David L. Balch, 6–42. Grand Rapids: Eerdmans, 2000.

Trimmer, Michael. "Steve Chalke's Oasis Trust Removed From the Evangelical Alliance." *Christian Today,* May 2, 2014. https://www.christiantoday.com/article/steve-chalkes-oasis-trust-removed-from-the-evangelical-alliance/37171.htm.

Tushnet, Eve. *Gay and Catholic: Accepting My Sexuality, Finding Community, Living My Faith.* Notre Dame: Ave Maria, 2014.

Vasey, Michael. *Strangers and Friends: A New Exploration of Homosexuality and the Bible.* London: Hodder & Stoughton, 1995.

Veyne, Paul. "La Famille Et L'Amour Sous Le Haut-Empire Romain." *Annales. Économies, Sociétés, Civilisations* 33.1 (1978) 35–63. https://www.persee.fr/doc/ahess_0395-2649_1978_num_33_1_293904.

Via, Dan O. "The Bible, the Church, and Homosexuality." In *Homosexuality and the Bible: Two Views,* by Dan O. Via and Robert A. J. Gagnon, 1–39. Minneapolis: Augsburg, 2003.

Vines, Matthew. *God and the Gay Christian: The Biblical Case in Support of Same-Sex Relationships.* New York: Convergent, 2014.

Ward, Roy Bowen. "Why Unnatural? The Tradition Behind Romans 1:26–27." *Harvard Theological Review* 90.3 (1997) 263–84.

Wax, Trevin. "What's Really Going On with Evangelicals and Same-Sex Marriage." *The Gospel Coalition,* November 2, 2016. https://www.thegospelcoalition.org/blogs/trevin-wax/whats-really-going-on-with-evangelicals-and-same-sex-marriage/.

Webb, William J. *Slaves, Women & Homosexuals: Exploring the Hermeneutics of Cultural Analysis.* Downers Grove, IL: InterVarsity, 2001.

Weerakoon, Patricia, and Kamal Weerakoon. "The Biology of Sex and Gender." In *The Gender Conversation: Evangelical Perspectives on Gender, Scripture, and the Christian Life,* edited by Edwina Murphy and David Starling, 317–30. Macquarie Park: Morling, 2016.

Wenham, Gordon J. *Genesis 1–15.* WBC. Grand Rapids: Zondervan, 1987.

Williams, Craig A. "Greek Love at Rome." *Classical Quarterly* 45.2 (1995) 517–39.

———. *Roman Homosexuality.* 2nd ed. Oxford: Oxford University Press, 2010.

Wilson, Ken. *Letter to My Congregation, Second Edition: An Evangelical Pastor's Path to Embracing People Who Are Gay, Lesbian, Bisexual and Transgender Into the Company of Jesus.* Kindle ed. Canton: Read the Spirit, 2016.

Wilson, Todd. *Mere Sexuality: Rediscovering the Christian Vision of Sexuality.* Grand Rapids: Zondervan, 2017.

Wright, David F. "Homosexuality: The Relevance of the Bible." *Evangelical Quarterly* 61.4 (1989) 291–300.

Wright, N. T. *The Letter to the Romans.* Nashville: Abingdon, 2002.

———. *The New Testament and the People of God.* London: SPCK, 1992.

———. *The Resurrection of the Son of God.* London: SPCK, 2003.

Yarhouse, Mark A. *Homosexuality and the Christian: A Guide for Parents, Pastors, and Friends*. Kindle ed. Bloomington: Bethany, 2010.

Yenor, Scott. "How the New Corporate Elite Sold Same-Sex Marriage to the American Public." *Public Discourse*, April 22, 2018. https://www.thepublicdiscourse.com/2018/04/21309/.

Zylstra, Sarah Eekhof. "Major Ministry Kicked Out of Evangelical Alliance UK Over Homosexuality Stance." *Christianity Today*, May 5, 2014. https://www.christianitytoday.com/news/2014/may/major-ministry-kicked-out-evangelical-alliance-chalke-oasis.html.

Modern Names Index

Ancient Documents Index

∽

NEW TESTAMENT

Printed in Great Britain
by Amazon

33157215R00113